AFTER THE FIFTH SUN

AFTER THE FIFTH SUN
Class and Race in North America

JAMES W. RUSSELL

PRENTICE HALL, Englewood Cliffs, New Jersey 07632

Library of Congress Cataloging-in-Publication Data

Russell, James W.
    After the fifth sun : class and race in North America / by James
W. Russell.
        p.   cm.
    Includes bibliographical references and index.
    ISBN 0–13–036237–9
        1. North America—Race relations.   2. Social classes—North
America.   I. Title.   II. Title: After the 5th sun.
    E49.R87   1994
    305.8'0097— dc20   93–38544
                                                                              CIP

Cover credit: Diego Rivera, *Marriage of the Artistic Expression of the North and South on This Continent.* Fresco mural, 22' × 75' (detail). San Francisco City College.

Acquisitions editor: Nancy Roberts
Editorial/production supervision and interior design: Joan Powers
Cover design: Maureen Eide
Production coordinator: Mary Ann Gloriande

© 1994 by James W. Russell
Published by Prentice-Hall, Inc.
A Paramount Communications Company
Englewood Cliffs, New Jersey 07632

Printed in the United States of America
10   9   8   7   6   5   4   3   2   1

ISBN 0-13-036237-9

Prentice-Hall International (UK) Limited, *London*
Prentice-Hall of Australia Pty. Limited, *Sydney*
Prentice-Hall Canada Inc., *Toronto*
Prentice-Hall Hispanoamericana, S.A., *Mexico*
Prentice-Hall of India Private Limited, *New Delhi*
Prentice-Hall of Japan, Inc., *Tokyo*
Simon & Schuster Asia Pte. Ltd., *Singapore*
Editora Prentice-Hall do Brasil, Ltda., *Rio de Janeiro*

Contents

Preface

On August 13, 1521, the largest and most developed of North America's societies, the Aztec empire, fell to Spanish invaders. The conquest was a prophecy come true, for the Aztecs had believed that their era, which they called that of the Fifth Sun, was fated to end catastrophically, as it did. After the destruction of Aztec society—after the Fifth Sun—the Spanish and later European colonizers built new societies in which they occupied the dominant class positions and forced Indians, imported African slaves, and Asians into subordinate positions. It was after the Fifth Sun that race became an issue in the class structuring of North America's societies, and it has been an issue ever since. Class and racial relations thus developed in patterned ways in all parts of North America, but the patterns have had significant differences as well as similarities in the areas that became the United States, Mexico, and Canada. These class and racial patterns as they have developed over nearly a half millennium of North American history since that fateful day in 1521 are the subjects of this book.

This project began in the spring of 1990 when a Fulbright award afforded me the opportunity to take up residence as a visiting researcher at the Universidad Nacional Autónoma de México (UNAM) in Mexico City. At about the same time, the Mexican government announced that it was reversing its traditional economic policies and seeking dramatically closer economic ties with the colossus to its north. Specifically, it wished to follow the example of Canada, which two years earlier had signed a free trade agreement with the United States. It appeared to me that the trilateral Canada–United States–Mexico free trade agreement, which quickly came to be known as the North American Free Trade Agreement (NAFTA), was a proposal of overwhelming historical importance. It further appeared to me that politicians and economists would be primarily involved in analyzing and commenting upon the advantages and disadvantages of NAFTA. Proponents of NAFTA would argue that integration of North America's economies would bring about rationalization and efficiency, and that this would be a logical development in the context of economic globalization. The United States, Mexico, and Canada would form a bloc to compete with European and Asian blocs. Critics of NAFTA would argue that integrating the first world economies of the United States and Canada with the third world economy of Mexico would only be to the advantage of capital and not labor.

While these were obviously key issues, it appeared to me that there were other issues that did not quite fall within the strict considerations of politicians and economists. In particular, if NAFTA were to come about, it would come about in societies that had different forms of social relations and would therefore force changes in at least some of those relations. That concern with the social impact of NAFTA prompted me to embark on a study of the forms of social inequality in NAFTA's three member countries. Whatever the political fortunes of NAFTA, I concluded, it would be valuable to have a comparative study of social inequality in the United States, Mexico, and Canada, if for no other reasons than to sharpen understanding of each country through comparisons and to demonstrate the options in social thinking and policies that exist.

I have tried both to describe the separate inequalities comparatively and to account for how they developed. In doing so, I constantly found myself, when writing about one country, writing with the citizens of the other countries in mind. For example, a number of points that I have included about inequality in the United States will seem painfully obvious to people who have grown up there. But Canadians or Mexicans are less likely to be as familiar with the points. People in the United States generally know that not all whites are literally Anglos, as they are often referred to in Mexico. But that fact is not as apparent south of the border. The same general approach was followed in deciding what to include about Mexico and Canada. People in Mexico are well aware of the country's Indian background and character. Many people in the United States, however, do not know that 80 percent of North America's Indians live in Mexico. Canadians know that they are culturally different from people in the United States. But Mexicans are less likely to appreciate those differences, and people in the United States are less likely to have thought about them. I have, therefore, written this book with an eye toward the curious in all three countries and have attempted to cover what is interesting as well as significant about the separate logics of social inequality.

This project could not have been undertaken without the support of the Fulbright Commission, which funded my two-year stay in Mexico. I am deeply grateful for that support and feel honored to have been able to serve in the program. Mr. Clint Wright, the chief administrator of the Fulbright program in Mexico during 1990 and 1991, carried out his office in an exceptionally professional, diplomatic, and affable manner, helping me and other grantees in numerous ways. He also provided critical support in obtaining the second year of funding for my stay, which enabled the project to be completed.

My hosts at the Centro de Investigaciones sobre América del Norte of the Universidad Nacional Autónoma de México provided support, encouragement, and an exceptionally cordial atmosphere in which to work. They and other former colleagues at UNAM critically listened to or read my ideas about social inequality in Mexico, steering me to sources of additional information and, in a number of cases, away from misconceptions. I am especially grateful to Mónica Verea Campos, the director of the center, Barbara Driscoll de Alvarado, an authority on Asian-Mexican history, Adolfo Aguilar Zínser, Alfredo Alvárez, Fernando Barrios, Rosa Cusminsky Mogilner, Mónica C. Gambril, Remedios Gómez Arnau, Sylvia Gorodezky M., Richard Griswold del Castillo, María Teresa Gutiérrez Haces, Ana Maria de L. Aguado Molina, Elaine Levine, Heriberto López Ortiz, Paz Consuelo Márquez Padilla, Alejandro Mercado Celis, Silvia Nuñez García, César Pérez Espinosa, Eduardo Ramírez García, Antonio Rivera Flores, Ana Luz Ruelas Monjardín, Carlos Salas, Rosío Vargas Suárez, and Silvia Velez. Among those who offered additional useful advice on the manuscript at various stages of its completion were Thomas Anderson, Jerry Lembcke, James Cobbledick, Arthur MacEwan, and Leon Sarin. I would also like to acknowledge the reviewers, including Brad Hertel, Virginia Polytechnical Institute, Blacksburg; Charlotte Wolf, Memphis State University; Leslie Laczko, University of Ottawa; and Steven Nock, University of Virginia, Charlottesville. Nancy Roberts, senior editor at Prentice Hall, saw the project through from conception to completion, always offering encouraging advice at critical junctures.

About the Author

James W. Russell is Professor of Sociology at Eastern Connecticut State University. From 1990 to 1992 he was visiting Fulbright Professor of Sociology at the Universidad Nacional Autónoma de México in Mexico City. His other books include *Introduction to Macrosociology* (Prentice Hall, 1992), *Modes of Production in World History* (Routledge, 1989), and *Clase y Sociedad en los Estados Unidos,* coauthored with Silvia Nuñez García (Editorial Universidad Nacional Autónoma de México, 1994).

NORTH AMERICA

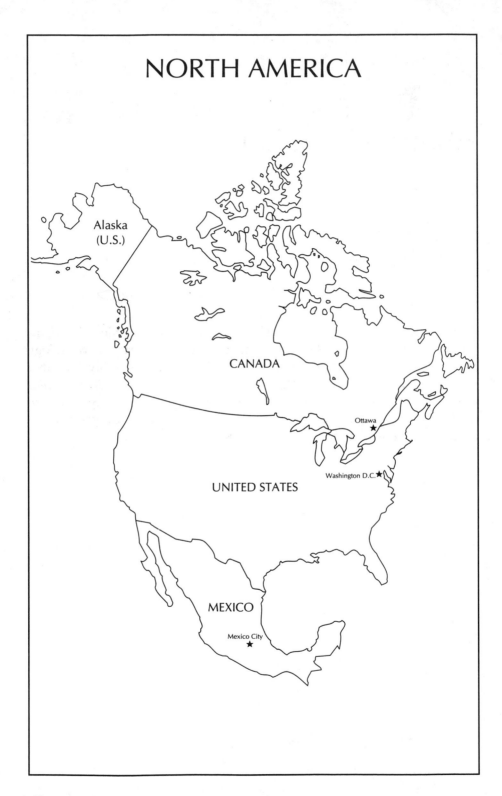

Alaska
(U.S.)

CANADA

Ottawa ★

Washington D.C. ★

UNITED STATES

MEXICO

Mexico City
★

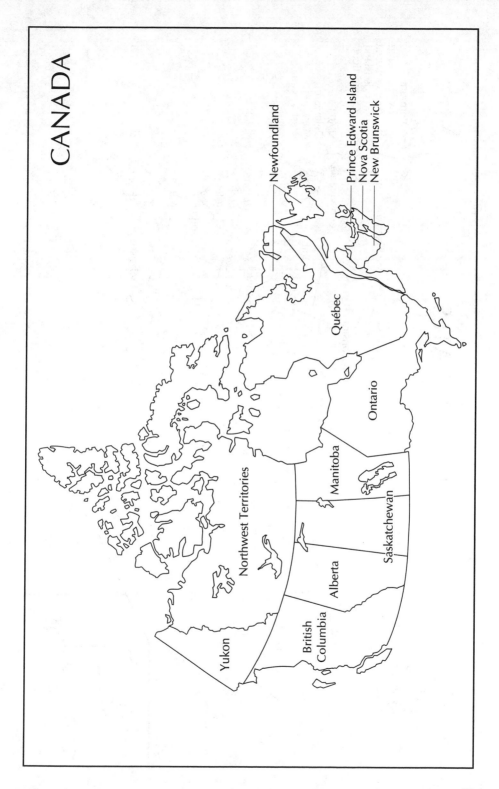

CANADA

Newfoundland

Prince Edward Island
Nova Scotia
New Brunswick

Québec

Ontario

Manitoba

Saskatchewan

Northwest Territories

Alberta

British
Columbia

Yukon

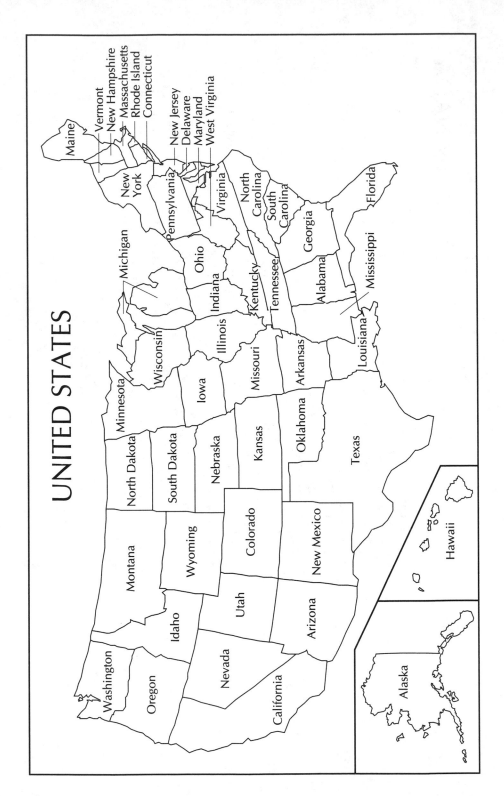

UNITED STATES

Maine

Vermont
New Hampshire
Massachusetts
Rhode Island
Connecticut

New Jersey
Delaware
Maryland
West Virginia

New York

Pennsylvania

Virginia

North Carolina

South Carolina

Florida

Michigan

Ohio

Georgia

Indiana

Kentucky

Tennessee

Alabama

Mississippi

Illinois

Wisconsin

Louisiana

Minnesota

Iowa

Missouri

Arkansas

North Dakota

South Dakota

Nebraska

Kansas

Oklahoma

Texas

Montana

Wyoming

Colorado

New Mexico

Idaho

Utah

Arizona

Washington

Oregon

Nevada

California

Hawaii

Alaska

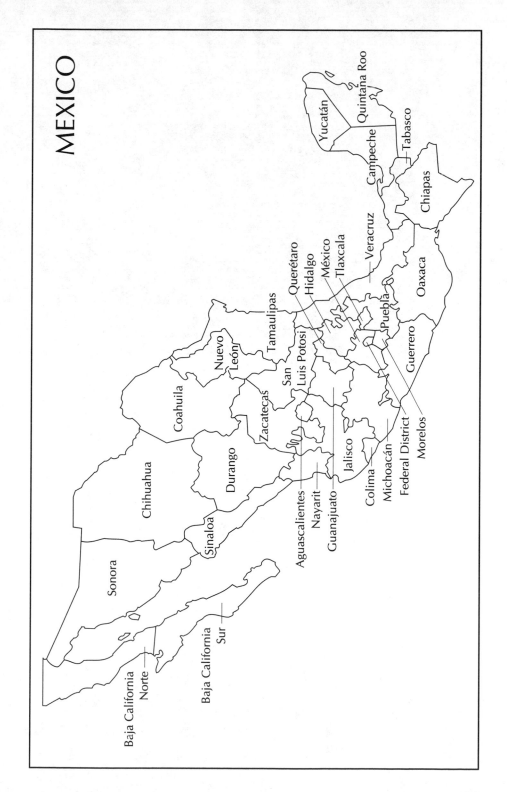

MEXICO

Baja California Norte

Baja California Sur

Sonora

Chihuahua

Sinaloa

Coahuila

Durango

Nuevo León

Zacatecas

Tamaulipas

Aguascalientes

Nayarit

Guanajuato

San Luis Potosí

Jalisco

Colima

Michoacán

Federal District

Morelos

Querétaro

Hidalgo

México

Tlaxcala

Puebla

Guerrero

Veracruz

Oaxaca

Chiapas

Tabasco

Campeche

Quintana Roo

Yucatán

✳ CHAPTER 1

Introduction

The visual evidence of social inequality between and within North American societies is glaring. Anyone who has traveled the length of North America knows that there is a vast gulf that divides the average standards of living of the United States and Canada from that of Mexico. The United States and Canada have all of the opulence of first world countries, while Mexico has all of the extensive poverty and misery of a third world country. That Mexico and the United States share a common 1,945-mile border—a border that culturally separates Latin from Anglo America, as well as the two countries—makes the contrast all the more striking. Unlike other areas of the world, where there is a continuum of gradual economic changes between bordering countries, between Mexico and the United States there are more discrete, jarring differences. The Rio Grande, as it is known on the United States side, or the Rio Bravo, as it is known on the Mexican side, is the world's only river that separates first and third world societies. In all other parts of the world the distances between first and third world areas are much greater. But while tempting, it is misleading to see the first and third world regions of North America as being entirely separated by that border, for Mexico contains first-world-appearing neighborhoods, shopping malls, and workplaces while the United States and Canada contain third-world-appearing pockets of poverty. North America's first and third worlds, while centered on opposite sides of the Rio Grande, interpenetrate each other.

The visual evidence of social inequality within each of North America's societies is everywhere. In the United States, homeless people wander downtown streets as private guards patrol the neighborhoods of the rich. In between, there are neighborhoods of modest working-class and more comfortable middle-class houses. Overlapping and cross cutting the urban geography

1

of class is the geography of racial divisions. White and minority areas are immediately distinguishable, often divided by a clear physical barrier such as railroad tracks or a freeway. People in the United States prefer to keep at a distance as much as possible those whom they perceive to be social inferiors or whom they fear. A tour through most large Mexican cities reveals other types of extremes. The poor live nearly everywhere, but there are also neat middle-class houses, and there are mansions, the occupants of which are rich by anyone's standards. Unlike U.S. cities, where class and racial inequalities are compartmentalized or "rationalized" according to neighborhood and area, most large Mexican cities are more like helter-skelter mosaics of rich, poor, and in-between types of housing. Mexico City's rich move about between islands of privilege—mansions, expensive restaurants, clubs, exclusive stores—in what is otherwise a sea of poverty. They develop subjective blinders that allow them to see but not see the poor, to look through them as it were.

Monterrey, Mexico's third largest city and home to a substantial part of its business elite, is a bit different. There, the city's upper and middle classes, like their U.S. counterparts, have physically separated themselves from the poor into an area that architecturally looks like Phoenix and other climatically similar U.S. desert cities. Coming over a hill from the main part of Monterrey, one encounters U.S.-style lawns and suburban houses that sprout parabolic antennas from their roofs to capture U.S. television. Monterrey, though, is an exception. In most Mexican cities the upper and middle classes cannot put as much distance between their living quarters and those of the poor. Instead, they surround their houses with fortified walls, topped in many cases with barbed wire or jagged glass to discourage intruders. Railroad tracks and freeways separate classes and races in the United States, but outside walls separate them in most parts of Mexico.

STRUCTURES AND CULTURES OF NORTH AMERICA

The obvious visual evidence of gross continental inequalities is the immediate catalyst of this study. Social differences within North America are as severe as anywhere in the world. In order to study these differences, a comparative approach seems the most appropriate. Its advantage is that it allows determination of what is distinct and often taken for granted about each society through contrasting examinations of alternative patterns in other societies.

Comparative studies of societies can be divided between those that examine primarily structural conditions, such as technological levels, economies, or class systems, and those that examine cultural conditions, such as values, religions, beliefs in general, and music. It is somewhat pointless to try to determine which is more important or which came first—structure or culture—since all societies have both structures and cultures. Both are complementary aspects of all societies, neither one of which can be neglected. In this study the main focus will be on the structural features of economies, labor forces, class, and racial positions, with attention also being devoted where necessary to cultural features that include religions, values, and social perceptions.

The necessity of examining both structural and cultural features in societies was nowhere more brilliantly demonstrated than in the work of the great classical German sociologist Max Weber. He also pioneered the comparative method when he examined the relationship between culture and economic development in China, India, Europe, and North America, attempting to demonstrate that capitalism first developed in Europe because the Protestant Reformation produced favorable cultural conditions. Weber concluded that China and India had contained many of the conditions necessary for capitalist development, but that the sum of those conditions had not been sufficient to actually produce that development. Each of the non-European countries or areas had lacked a common necessary condition—a generalized set of cultural values that would have enabled profit making and accumulation of capital to move into first place as societal goals, as they had in sixteenth- and seventeenth-century Europe. In both Chinese and Indian culture, religious attainment was more important than economic attainment.

The great innovation of Protestantism was that it developed a way of culturally seeing the world in which economic and religious attainment did not contradict each other. One could be a successful capitalist without feeling religiously negligent. Weber found in this respect that capitalist development had proceeded much more rapidly in the Protestant than the Catholic regions of Europe.

Weber's studies are relevant for this study not only because of their comparative nature but also because late-twentieth-century North America also contains both extremes of economic development and parallel cultural differences—between, for example, Catholic Mexico and the mostly Protestant United States and Canada or between Indians in rural Oaxaca and multinational corporation managers in Mexico City as well as New York City.

The United States, Mexico, and Canada share, in addition to the North American continent, the same type of economic structure. All three are essentially capitalist societies in which there is significant private ownership of businesses and production and distribution of goods according to market principles. Since each national class structure is based on essentially market relations of production, it follows that to some degree the same types of economic classes exist in all three countries—owners of large businesses, employed managers and professionals, workers, and owners of small businesses.

TABLE 1–1   The North American Societies: Structural Features

	UNITED STATES	MEXICO	CANADA
Economy	Market	Market	Market
Technology	Postindustrial	Agricultural	Postindustrial
Politics	Two party	One party	Three party
World income class*	Upper	Lower middle	Upper
Development	First world	Third world	First world

*As defined by the World Bank, *World Development Report* (New York: Oxford University Press, 1990).

At the same time as each national economy obeys capitalistic principles, the economies themselves are continentally interrelated according to mainly capitalistic principles. Trade, investments, labor migration, and financial relations significantly interrelate the economic and class structures of Mexico, the United States, and, to a much smaller extent, Canada. Mexican and U.S. owners of capital invest in each other's societies, and thousands of undocumented Mexican workers cross over to the other side in search of work. To a much smaller extent, there are Canadian investments in Mexico and undocumented Mexican workers in Canada.

Geographic location greatly influences the directions and volumes of these flows of capital and labor. The United States, as the country geographically in the middle, has considerable economic relations with its southern and northern neighbors, while the relations between those neighbors themselves are, for obvious reasons of physical distance, not as close. Canada and Mexico, while contiguous to and strongly influenced by economic relationships with their common neighbor, the United States, have many fewer direct relations with each other. This relative weakness of relations between Canada and Mexico exists despite the fact that it takes longer to fly from Vancouver to Ottawa than to fly from either city over the United States to Mexico City.

Though a capitalist economic structure exists in all three countries, there is no question that overall Mexico is a significantly poorer country than either the United States or Canada and, in some ways, a structurally different country. These structural differences between the Latin and Anglo areas of North America have been variously defined and classified. Many simply see them as differences between essentially first and third world countries. Others define the differences vertically in terms of average levels of production and income within the world economy. The World Bank ranks the United States and Canada as upper-income countries and Mexico as a lower-middle-income country.[1] By world standards Mexico is an average-income country. Looking southward toward Guatemala and other Central American countries, its situation is enviable. But looking northward indicates a different reality. Still others describe one country as, variously, either an underdeveloped or developing country, and the others as developed countries. Developmentally, the United States and Canada are postindustrial societies in the sense that the largest fractions of their labor forces are no longer engaged in production of primary agricultural or secondary industrial goods. Mexico, however, is still at the agricultural stage of technological development because the largest fraction of its labor force is still engaged in farming activities.

Politically, there are structural contrasts between the three North American societies. The United States is essentially a two-party society. Republicans and Democrats almost completely monopolize electoral competitions and governmental offices with ideologies that range from conservative to liberal. In Mexico, one party, the Partido Revolucionario Institucional (PRI), has held the presidency uninterruptedly for more than sixty years and continues to hold a virtual monopoly on all governmental offices. Over the years the PRI has been an umbrella for and espoused ideological currents ranging from conservatism to social democracy. Of the three countries, Canada has the most open politics, since there are three significant political parties—Progressive Conservatives, Liberals, and the social democratic New Democratic Party—representing clearly defined and consistent ideological options.

The economic and social contrast between Mexico and its continental neighbors to the north has been statistically measured in a number of different ways. The gross national product per capita of Canada in 1988 was $16,960, and for the United States $19,840. These were from nine to eleven times as high as Mexico's $1,760,[2] and for the last decade the gap has been growing. The infant mortality rate—the number of children who die before their first birthdays per 1,000 live births—of the United States was 10 and of Canada 7, while that of Mexico was 46, from 4 to 6 times as high.[3] Put differently, every day 295 children under 1 year old die in Mexico, 231 more than if Mexico had the same infant mortality rate as the United States and 250 more than if it had the same rate as Canada.[4]

In overall cultural terms, there are clear differences between the three countries, though, once again, the cultures of Canada and the United States appear more similar than either country's does with that of Mexico. People in the United States see themselves as culturally different from Mexicans but rarely think much about their cultural differences from Canadians. Canadian intellectuals are obsessed with demonstrating that they really do have a different cultural identity than people in the United States; they generally do not think too much about their relationship to Mexico. Mexicans find it difficult to culturally distinguish the Anglos of the United States from those of Canada. In the same sense, most people in the United States and Canada would have

TABLE 1–2   The North American Societies: Basic Indicators, 1988

	UNITED STATES	MEXICO	CANADA
Population[a]	246.3	83.7	26.0
Area[b]	9,373	1,958	9,976
GNP per capita	$19,840	$1,760	$16,960
Infant mortality[c]	10	46	7
Life expectancy	76	69	77

[a]In millions.
[b]Thousands of square kilometers.
[c]Deaths in the first year per thousand live births.
Source: World Bank, *World Development Report* (New York: Oxford University Press, 1990), pp. 178, 233.

difficulty distinguishing the cultures of Mexico and other Latin American countries.

The cultural differences between Mexico and the two countries to its north are obvious, but those between the United States and Canada, while less obvious, are also significant. The United States, as Seymour Martin Lipset has convincingly shown, is the society of revolutionary origins—as is Mexico— and rugged individualism, while Canada is a society of counterrevolutionary origins and order.[5] The national identity of the United States begins with the 1776 revolutionary Declaration of Independence; the national identity of Canada, if not originating, was importantly influenced by the decision of its provinces not to go along with the War of Independence. Much of the original European settler population of Ontario, New Brunswick, and Nova Scotia was made up of the 50,000 or so Tory loyalists who moved north—voluntarily or involuntarily—after the War of Independence. Mexican visitors to Canada, who like those from the United States are steeped in heritage of their war of independence, find it odd that Canadians tend to praise the colonial relationship that they had with Great Britain.

People in the United States tend to view Canada as a slightly calmer, perhaps more civilized, society. Canadians view the United States as overly competitive and disorderly. Lipset cites the observation of Richard Lipsey as indicative: "I have stood on a street corner in Toronto with a single other pedestrian, and with not a car in sight, waiting for the light to turn green—behavior unimaginable in most U.S. cities."[6] The difference in Mexico City is that not only pedestrians but also motorists ignore street lights when they do not see any need to obey. In Mexico City I have often observed cars quickly crossing over two lanes of traffic to make turns. Such traffic behavior would evoke a riot of horn blowing in the United States and, perhaps, stunned incomprehension in Canada. But in Mexico it rarely evokes anger or horns because other motorists are used to it. One travel writer recommended that U.S. tourists in Mexico City not rent cars unless their doctors have recommended that they need *more* stress. Traffic patterns may reflect larger cultural patterns. Samuel Ramos, one of Mexico's most influential and provocative twentieth-century philosophers, could have been thinking about traffic when he went so far as to conclude that "Mexican society, without discipline or organization, is a chaos in which individuals fly about according to chance like disperse atoms."[7] But, if traffic and society in general appear disorderly in Mexico, there is a cultural order within the disorder. While motorists in the United States and Canada drive like they play baseball—in straight lines—motorists in Mexico drive like they play soccer, darting for open spaces and opportunities regardless of nominal traffic rules.

ON THE LANGUAGE OF THE INVESTIGATION

Before we proceed much further, some clarifications of terms are in order. A comparative study that involves three countries and two major angles of analysis (class and race) presents a number of difficulties in geographical and social terminology. Mexico is variously considered to be a part of North or Central America. It is clearly on the North American continent, along with the United States and Canada. But, most Mexicans do not consider themselves to be *Norteamericanos*, reserving that term for citizens of the United States. Mexico is a part of Latin America and shares many common cultural identities with its southern Central American neighbors. Mexicans, however, would be as little likely to refer to themselves as *Centroamericanos* as they would be to refer to themselves as *Norteamericanos*. For our purposes, though, we will go with the geographical convention of considering Mexico to be a part of North America.

A comparative study of the countries of North America also presents terminological difficulties in how to name the people of the United States. There is no acceptable term comparable to "Mexicans" or "Canadians". The country term "United States" does not lend itself to suffixes (as in United States*ians*). People in the United States call themselves Americans. Many Mexicans and Canadians also refer to people in the United States as Americans. But that is an imperialistic appropriation of a term that logically applies to all of the peoples of the Americas, not just those of the United States. Mexicans often call people in the United States *Norteamericanos*. But that convention overlooks the Canadian claim to the label. It also is inconsistent with the reality that Mexicans are also in continental terms North Americans. The dilemma is more easily solved in Spanish than English, where it is grammatically proper to speak of *mexicanos*, *canadienses*, and *estadounidenses*. In the text that follows I will refer to people in the United States in a variety of admittedly somewhat awkward ways, such as U.S. citizens, U.S. nationals, or people in the United States. But this approach seems preferable to reproducing the national arrogance of exclusive appropriation of the terms "American" or "North American."

There is no complete consensus regarding the naming of people from non-European backgrounds within each of the North American countries. The most widely used term for the vast majority, but not all, indigenous peoples is "Indian." The obvious problem with the term is that it is a misnomer—the indigenous peoples of the Americas are not from India, as was thought by the early explorers. In the 1970s, as a result of the movements among the indigenous peoples in the United States, the term "Native American" developed. Canadians distinguish Inuits or Eskimos from indigenous peoples to their south, whom they refer to as Amerindians. There is no one term that has won universal endorsement. But, also, none of the terms appears to be considered universally as offensive. For that reason, in the text Indian, Native American, indigenous, and Amerindian will generally be used interchangeably when writing in general terms. Indians, though, do not have a common monolithic identity. Depending on the context, it will therefore be necessary to employ more particular tribal labels such as Sioux, Cree, and Yaqui.

In the case of African-origin people in North America, there has been a clear evolution in the use of naming terms. Up until the early 1960s, the terms "Negro" (from the Spanish for "black"), "colored people," and, to a lesser extent, "brown" were customarily used in the United States. The Black Power movement swept those terms away as offensive. It only took a couple of years, during the height of the black urban rebellions in the United States, for whites to abandon use of the terms "Negro" and "colored." The terms "black," "Afro-American," and "African," in order of acceptance, took their places. In the early 1990s, Jesse Jackson proposed that "African-American" was the most desirable term. It paralleled the use of other hyphenated immigrant identities, such as Chinese-American, Polish-American, and Irish-American. Jackson's proposal appears to have initially gained acceptance. It remains to be seen how long it will prevail. For this text, the terms "black," "African-American," and "Afro–North American" will be used.

The naming of Latin American-origin people is a problem in the United States and Canada. There are a wide number of terms in use, some of which are considered objectionable, but by different people. The label "Hispanic" is the most widely used on the East Coast of the United States. It is also employed by the U.S. Census Bureau. Many people, though, object to it on two counts. First, it implies a complete Spanish background when the majority of

Spanish-speaking people in the United States and Canada also have Indian and African ancestors. Second, it implies a unitary cultural identity to the Spanish-speaking peoples when there are significant economic, social, political, and cultural differences between Mexicans, Puerto Ricans, Cubans, and Central Americans in the United States. The term "Hispanic" exists only in the United States. It is not used south of the Rio Grande. It is only when Latin Americans come to the United States that they find themselves referred to as Hispanics rather than their particular national identities—Mexicans, Puerto Ricans, Salvadorans, and so on. On the West Coast, "Latino" is used more than "Hispanic." It, as a term, implies Latin American origin. But, like the name "Hispanic," it implies a common cultural identity when significant national differences exist. For this study, we will use "Latino" when speaking of all Latin American–origin people in the United States, and the various national terms (Mexican, Puerto Rican, etc.) when speaking of the particular national communities. In a parallel sense, the Asian communities will be described in general terms as Asian-Americans and in particular terms according to nationality—Chinese, Japanese, Filipino, and so on.

The label "minority" itself is not without problems. Mexicans find that they become labeled as minority members when they enter the United States. Whites from the United States, however, rarely see themselves as a minority when they go to Mexico. Their domination, it seems, is portable, whereas that of Mexicans is not.

The very labeling of a group as a minority creates its own sui generis social realities. A group may accept its labeling as a minority but be very sensitive to the context in which it is used. In the course of the research for this book I encountered a revealing incident of the linguistic politics of the label "minority." I had just finished writing a review for a Mexico City newspaper of a book that dealt with minorities in Canada. I usually have other people review what I write for content, and since my written Spanish is far from perfect, I have it edited by native writers for grammar and style as well.

The first person who looked my review over was Mexican. Though she had grown up in Mexico, she had spent a substantial part of her life in the United States, where a large part of her political consciousness had been formed through participation in the Chicano movement. She objected to my sentence "*Canada y sus minorías*" ("Canada and its minorities"), changing it to "*Canada y las minorías*" ("Canada and the minorities"). *Sus* as an article assumed that the minorities were objects belonging to Canada's white majority. The distinction that she made grew out of the political consciousness of the Chicano movement.

The second person who looked over the review was also Mexican. But she had both grown up and had her political consciousness formed in Mexico. She changed *las* back to *sus* because it worked better stylistically. Having been a Mexican in Mexico all her life, she had never had the consciousness of being a minority imposed upon her and consequently never had to consider the political implications of *las* versus *sus*.

Related to the problem of how to name the peoples of North America is the problem of the meanings of the terms that will be used to analyze them—class and race, and, to some degree, nationality and ethnicity. The first issue to be resolved is the causal priority of the analytical concepts class and race. In this study, class is considered to be causally prior to race, although many other studies imply the opposite position. The origins of this dispute, at least in the United States, go back to the political debates between nationalists and Marxists—both activists and academics—that developed in the 1970s, as the most active phase of the civil rights movement was waning. Both sides agreed that minorities suffered from both racism and class exploitation, but they differed on which was causally more significant. The nationalist position held that blacks, Indians, and Latinos suffered discrimination and oppression in the United States mostly because the dominant group in the country was white and fundamentally racist. Nationalists further held that minority workers both experienced and felt more oppression because of the colors of their skin than because of their positions in the workplace. The Marxist position countered that racial minorites suffered discrimination and oppression mostly because the capitalist system of the country had relegated them to an inferior class position.

Part of the debate became mired in a confusion between levels of analysis. In terms of perception, at least in the 1960s and 1970s, there was more of a racial than a class struggle in the United States. The civil rights movement activated blacks and other minorities as racial groups struggling to reform the country so that there would be equality of opportunity among races. In this sense, the civil rights movement achieved its primary objective with the passage of the 1964 Civil Rights Act, which removed legal barriers to equality of opportunity for racial minorities. However, the civil rights movement had set in motion large numbers of activists who knew very well that the passage of the Civil Rights Act would not in itself produce substantive racial equality. In addition, once a reform movement has been historically set in motion, it often, at least for some of its members, moves beyond original issues to take up more general social issues such as the elimination of poverty. By the late 1960s in the United States, those who had been activated by the early 1960s civil rights movement were debating how to end a war in Southeast Asia and how to interpret spontaneous riots and rebellions that had ignited the country's largest black ghettos from Harlem, Newark, and the nation's capital on the East Coast through Chicago and Detroit in the interior to Watts on the West

Coast. In one week in 1968 more than 50,000 United States troops were deployed in black ghettos, a larger number than were deployed in Vietnam at the
time. It was clear that the country was experiencing more racial than class-
based struggle and violence.

It is also clear that during determinant historical periods the bases of societal conflicts shift. In the 1930s most societal conflict in the United States
concerned clear class questions. That was the period during which workers
fought to establish unions in the nation's largest factories. During the 1960s
the most salient societal conflict concerned racial inequality. But by the end
of the 1970s, as black and other minority movement mass activism declined,
a number of writers began to argue that class was now a more salient issue
than race per se for minorities in the United States.[8]

If we step back from the heat of given social movements and look at the
intersections of class and race structurally, a different sense of causal priority
emerges—one that does not shift according to historical periods or subjective
perceptions. Indians and blacks were first subjected to inequality on the North
American continent, as described in the coming pages, when they were enslaved. That is, social inequality for Indians and blacks did not exist as an a
priori racial condition. Rather, it was imposed upon them because the European conquerors and colonizers of North America established a type of colonial class structure that contained an inferior position into which they were
forcefully placed. There would not be and would not have been racial inequality in North America if there had not been a class structure that contained
by definition unequal class positions. For that reason, on a theoretical and
structural level, class is causally prior to race. That observation is not the same
as arguing that racial inequality completely reduces to a question of class. For
sure, a black or other minority worker who has the same type of job and receives the same income as a white worker suffers additional types of oppression. Rather, it is to argue that in a study such as this of social inequality, the
first thing to be established is the economic and class structures of the countries involved and from there to determine how racial minorities have been
placed within inferior positions within them. For that reason, the theoretical
premise of this study is that class inequality is causally prior to—but not an
exclusive determinant of—racial inequality.

But despite the fact that the concept of class is central to social science,
there is no consensus among social scientists as to what it means or how to use
it. There is no one *correct* use of the concept. The best that can be hoped for is
that each investigator who employs the concept explains what she or he means
by it. In this study I mean by classes groupings of people who share a common
economic or social position within society. I then find it necessary to analyze
economic and social class positions separately. The former are shared roles

within the work or labor forces of countries. In each of the contemporary North American countries, the following shared roles or economic classes exist: capitalists who are owners of large businesses, small business owners, the new middle class of professional and managerial employees, and wage and salary workers. In Mexico there is an additional class of peasants, small farmers who produce more for their own subsistence needs than for market sale. The past of all three countries also contained slavery and the slave class. By social classes are meant families and individuals who share common standards of living. The rich and the poor mark the polar upper and lower social class positions. In between exist working and middle social class positions.[9]

Employment of the concept of race is fraught with controversies and the pitfall of being potentially offensive. The concept arose in the seventeenth century from the belief that the human species was divided into distinct physical variations.[10] Since then, there have been a number of attempts to determine the exact number of distinct human races. These attempts, however, produced no consensus. Estimates of the number of races have ranged from three to as many as two hundred.[11] Not only was the issue of determining the number of races a problem, but so too was the criterion for distinguishing one race from another. Use of phenotype or skin color, for example, as the primary criterion presented problems because there are continuous rather than discrete differences in skin color shades from the darkest to the lightest, and there is no way to determine fixed racial boundaries. Because of these and other problems, by the middle of the twentieth century most physical anthropologists had abandoned use of race as a valid scientific concept for categorizing human beings. However, despite the decline of the scientific use of the concept of race, the popular and social uses of the term—as well as the beliefs and practices of racism—continue in vigor. It is in these latter senses that the concept is employed here.

What are socially perceived to be distinct races in North America are the descendants of Europeans, Africans, Asians, and the indigenous peoples of the Americas. These races, in the social meaning of that term, were the trunk lines from which the North American people have developed since the 1500s. Interrelations among them have produced a fifth, synthesis race of individuals who combine ancestry from two or more of the originating races. The members of this fifth, synthesis race make up the majority in one of the countries—Mexico—and in overall continental terms constitute the largest racial minority. In everyday experience and social perception, racial interaction in North America is, for the most part, between whites, blacks, Indians, Asians, and combined-race individuals, making those our main categories of analysis.

There are also linguistic, ethnic, nationality, and other differences within the North American populations. Poles, Italians, and Irish, while all of white

European descent, have felt the stings of discrimination and rejection from other whites in the United States and Canada. U.S. newspapers in the 1890s even referred to English-descent native-born citizens and Italian immigrants as separate races. English and French Canada are far from homogeneous. Tarahumara and Xochimilca Indians in Mexico belong to distinct cultures. These types of differences will enter into our discussion when necessary, but the main focus of investigation will be social differences that are perceived to be class and racially based.

There is no necessary relationship between race and culture, national, or ethnic identity. I have observed a number of curious cases on university campuses where racial appearance was deceptive. Immigrant Latina students at the university where I teach in Connecticut puzzled over the identity of a secretary because she appeared but did not act Latina. During a brief teaching assignment in Monterrey, Mexico, I encountered students who appeared identical to the students I encounter in Connecticut. In both cases racially identical persons belonged to separate nations and hence cultures. The secretary had a mestizo French and Indian background which produces the same range of physical appearances as mestizo Mexicans with Spanish and Indian backgrounds. Monterrey is in the north of Mexico, where the proportion of people of full European descent is the highest; people with names like Hernández and Gutiérrez appear in physical terms to be identical to the Connecticut students with names like Conrad and Jones. When Caribbean blacks migrate or travel to the United States, they enter into a world in which their blackness becomes much more of a badge of identity than it was at home. A black college student from Puerto Rico states, "I am Puerto Rican, not black. I don't relate to blacks here. I relate to Latinos." For her, shared culture is the most important determinant of her self-identity and being. Whites and blacks in the United States, though, perceive her primarily as black and secondarily as Latina. Race and culture may overlap, as with domestic blacks in the United States, but they do not necessarily do so, as these examples have indicated.

Finally, I have chosen not to make gender inequality a major focus of the investigation. This decision arose not out of any belief that gender was somehow not as important as class or race, but rather because I did not have the resources to treat it properly.

The rest of this book is organized along the following lines: Chapters 2 through 4 trace the origins and general development of mainly class and racial inequality in North America, with chapters on the conquest, colonial period, and uneven development of the three countries. Chapter 5 is devoted to contemporary class structures, with comparative analyses of labor forces, economic classes, and social classes. Chapters 6 through 11 are devoted to racial relations and groupings, with chapters focusing comparatively on the positions, including those of class, of whites, Indians, blacks, Asians, and mixed-race individuals in the three countries. Chapter 12 concludes the study by taking up the class consequences of new developments in the continental division of labor, including the growth of *maquiladoras* in the U.S.-Mexico border zone and free trade relations.

CHAPTER 2

The Ending of the Fifth Sun

The modern history of class and race in North America begins with violent impositions of European colonial rule over the preexisting indigenous societies. Never before, and perhaps not even after, has world history witnessed human devastation of this scale. Across all of the Americas as many as 150 million of the indigenous people would succumb within a century to the guns, forced labor, or diseases of their conquerors. During the same period, millions of Africans would be kidnapped and brought to the Americas to work as slaves. It is impossible to understand the contemporary class inequality of Indians and African-Americans without first examining these historical antecedents.

It is further no accident that racism—the ideological belief that there are superior and inferior races—developed during the period of the conquest and colonization of the Americas. Prior to that period, Europe had had only small-scale trading relationships with non-Europeans from Africa and Asia. It was only with the colonization of the Americas that Europeans would enter into extensive contacts and exploitative class relationships with Africans and indigenous Americans. The colonization of the Americas represents the first time in world history that different races were combined in class structures on a large scale. It is in this context that Europeans developed the modern ideology of racism as a pseudoscientific attempt to rationalize and justify the social fact that they were forcing nonwhites into the lowest economic and class positions.

Racist ideologists first questioned the degree to which Indians were human beings at all. In the decades following the conquest of the Aztec empire there were actual debates in Europe over the question of whether Indians were fully human beings or beings lower on the scale of development. If they were lower beings, then Christian moral principles would not apply to them. Pope Paul III resolved the dispute in 1537, at least for the church, when he issued a bull proclaiming Indians to be fully human beings. That decree, however, did not end white racist attitudes toward Indians. The next targets of racist ideology would be black slaves. Racists could justify their enslavement on the grounds that they were inferior creatures to be treated not much differently than farm animals. New World slave masters would agree with the Roman distinction that an animal was an *instrumentum mutum* while the slave was an *instrumentum semi-vocale*.

The modern history of North American class and racial inequality thus begins with European conquest and colonization. The full history of North America, though, begins with the peoples who had inhabited the continent for at least 25,000 years prior to European arrival.

INDIGENOUS SOCIETIES ON THE EVE OF THE CONQUEST

What types of societies were these that existed in pre-Columbian North America before the arrival of European colonizers? In order to answer that question, we will first have to make a brief excursus into the ways that social scientists classify societies in world history.

Anthropologists classify North America's pre-Columbian indigenous societies according to their cultures as peoples, tribes, and nations. Each successive concept is indicative of a more encompassing unit based upon shared languages, religious views, types of music, and other cultural characteristics. Several different peoples can belong to a tribe, and several tribes can belong to a single nation.

Linguists classify the North American indigenous societies according to the languages spoken, with languages being grouped on three different levels—families, languages, and dialects. Language families contain languages that have common linguistic roots but that are not necessarily mutually intelligible. English and German, for example, belong to the same language family. Dialects are offshoots of particular languages that are mutually intelligible. Across North America there were a large number of different indigenous language families. In order of numbers of speakers today, the top nine languages are spoken in Mexico, where more than five million people continue to speak indigenous languages. The 1990 Mexican census counted thirty-seven major languages. Nahuatl, with 1.2 million speakers, is the most used of the indigenous languages. In addition to the thirty-seven major languages, there are a number of minor languages, which have fewer than eight thousand speakers each.[1] These languages can be heard on the streets of almost any city. In what became the Southwest of the United States, there were at least six different language families, some of which encompassed Mesoamerica to the south and what would become Canada to the north as well.[2] The largest indigenous language in the United States—the tenth largest in North America—is Navajo, which has 149,000 speakers over the age of five. Today, a motorist driving across New Mexico and Arizona can hear it on the car radio. Of the indigenous peoples inhabiting the area of present-day Canada, there were eleven different language families. More than fifty different indigenous languages continue to be spoken.[3] Linguistic analysis reveals that there is a qualitative difference between the language family of the Inuits (Eskimos) and those of indigenous peoples to the south. The latter languages are more similar to each other than any one of them is to the Inuit languages, indicating that the two types of peoples are not ethnically related. Inuits share ethnic characteristics more closely with peoples of northeastern Siberia than with the indigenous peoples to their south. It is most likely, therefore, that the migrations of the latter were earlier and proceeded from different Asian regions than Inuit migrations. It makes sense to consider the original indigenous peoples of North America as belonging to two overall different ethnic families: Eskimos in the arctic and subarctic regions and Indians in all areas further south.

More useful, though, to our purposes than cultural and linguistic classification is to identify and classify the pre-Columbian societies according to their levels of technological development and types of economic structure. In terms of levels of technological development, overall world history has moved from societies based primarily on hunting and gathering technologies to those based on progressively more sophisticated horticultural, agricultural, and finally industrial technologies. Hunting and gathering involves obtaining food supplies by, as the name indicates, hunting animals and gathering wild fruits and vegetables. There is no actual production of food beyond its preparation and cooking. Horticulture-based societies marked a qualitative advance over hunting and gathering–based societies because they produced—as distinct from hunting or gathering—food through the planting of seeds, cultivation of the soil, and harvesting. The technological cell of a horticulture-based society is a peasant who uses a hoe to work a small plot of land. In agriculture-based societies, peasants incorporate the energy of animals in the production process by using them to draw plows. The extra energy allows the peasants to cultivate larger areas. While horticulturalists cultivate gardens, agriculturalists cultivate fields. Finally, industrial societies represent the incorporation of non-animal-based sources of energy (fossil fuels, steam, electricity), which are used to drive machines. Horticulturalists and agriculturalists use simple tools—hoes and plows—but industrialists use complex machines. From this technological angle of analysis, the preconquest indigenous societies of North America varied between hunting and gathering in the most primitive regions and horticulture in the most advanced. Nowhere had they reached the stage of agriculture—there was no plow in use before the Conquest.

In terms of types of economic structures, world history has witnessed the general movement from the earliest communally based economies to progressively more complex state, slave, feudal, and capitalistically organized economies. Communal societies were made up of small bands of mainly nomadic hunting and gathering peoples. What was of defining importance for them was the equality that existed between their members. Everyone shared equally in the same subsistence standard of living. Not only were these preclass societies, but they were also prestate societies, since there was no separate group that devoted itself full time to governance, policing, or military affairs. As horticulture developed, small village communities formed that represented intervals between the egalitarian dawn of world history and the rise of larger scale, more complex, class societies. In these communities the first separations of standards of living and social classes began to emerge as some households controlled more land than others. In time, conquerors gathered these villages into wider nets of authority, establishing themselves as rulers. These state societies represented the first full development of class societies in world history and existed in Asia, Africa, and the Americas.[4] Greco-Roman slavery represented the next form of economic structure, a structure that was partially reproduced as New World slavery after the conquest. After the collapse of Rome, Europe descended into nearly a millennium of feudalism in which local landlords dominated their dependent peasants. Capitalism, as an economic structure and later as a world system, began to consolidate itself in the sixteenth century. It is no accident that capitalist development and the conquest occurred during the same period. The European explorers, while being most immediately attracted by the lure of gold, were ultimately searching for trade routes for capitalist expansion. What they found in North America were three types of precapitalist economic structures: communally organized bands of hunters and gatherers, state-organized empires, and an intermediate formation of village communities.

Communal Societies

The communal societies of North America were for the most part made up of nomadic hunters and gatherers. They were geographically spread throughout the North American continent, the only exceptions being the territories occupied by state societies and village communities. Among the most important communally organized peoples on the eve of the conquest were the Chichimecas in northern Mesoamerica and the Apaches, Navajo, Plains Indians, Sioux, and Cree to the north. These societies lived and moved together in small bands that rarely exceeded fifty persons. Among members of these groups, there was an essential economic and social equality. There was no sense of ownership of land or any other type of means of production. There could be possession of tents and other articles. But because all possessions had to be moved from place to place as hunting territories shifted, these possessed articles were, of necessity, simple, and the opportunity to accumulate personal wealth was limited. Such social differentiation as there was, was restricted to nonclass status or prestige bases. The leader of a band enjoyed more prestige than the others but did not possess significantly more material wealth. These were also stateless societies in the sense that there was no regular group of officials who lived by taxing the rest. Political decision making certainly existed as adults within the bands met to deliberate over common problems such as when to move or how to confront enemies. But, because of the small populations of the bands, it was possible and desirable for all members to participate. In this sense, communal societies were essentially democratic, not out of ideological conviction but because their small population bases made any other form of decision making unworkable.

Village Communities

Throughout Mesoamerica and in some regions to the north there existed groupings of indigenous peoples who had achieved technological mastery of horticulture. They lived within sedentary villages; cultivated the soil as their means of achieving food, with supplements coming from hunting, fishing, and gathering; and showed evidence of social class differentiation.

Village communities developed earlier in world and North American history than state societies. They were the first locations of class differentiation. Typically, as land became valuable as a means of production, households and families sought to obtain control over greater quantities of land and the most fertile parcels. This process led to both the origins of private property and social class differentiation within village communities. Land-rich families enjoyed greater levels of consumption and social-class standards of living than land-poor families. Land-rich families though, at first, relied on their own labor. Only later would they be able to monopolize possession of enough lands such that other members became landless and were forced into the subordinate *economic* class positions of being either renters or laborers. In this sense, social class differentiation preceded economic class differentiation in both world and North American history.

Most of the village communities within Mesoamerica were contained within larger state empires. But north of Mesoamerica, there were two important examples of independent village communities: the Pueblos, centered mostly in present-day New Mexico, and the Iroquois who straddled what to-day is the border between New York and eastern Canada. The term "Pueblo" was originally applied by the Spanish to describe all of the Indians in their northern territories who lived within village communities. As such, the Pueblos should not be understood as a culturally unified single tribe or nation, but rather as a heterogeneous grouping of village communities within the northern territories of New Spain. For our purposes the term is useful because it is indicative of the highest level of technological and social organization achieved in what is today the Southwest of the United States. At the time of Spanish contact, there were between 130,000 and 248,000 Indians living within approximately a hundred Pueblo village communities.[5] They practiced horticulture, and there is evidence of elementary social class differentiation, with an elite having privileged access to consumption items.

The Iroquois, who lived across parts of what today is eastern Canada and the United States, were the most developed. They practiced horticulture, from which as much as 80 percent of their food supplies came, the balance coming from hunting, fishing, and gathering.[6] Several families lived together within longhouses, and a number of longhouses were grouped together within village communities. If there were class differences, they were slight. At the end of the fifteenth century, well before permanent European settlement, five of the Iroquois tribes or nations, including the Mohawk, joined together in the Iroquois Confederation, the most complex Amerindian political formation north of Mexico. The basic purposes of the confederation were to suppress internal warfare and be able to join forces for an effective military alliance against other tribes.

State Societies

State empires, which grouped together large numbers of village communities, were the largest in scale and most complex societies of pre-Columbian North America. A number of these, of which the Aztec and Mayan are only the most well known, existed for some two thousand years prior to the conquest in the three main zones of what archaeologists call Mesoamerica: the altiplano or central highlands spreading outward from the Valley of Mexico, where Mexico City is located today; the Gulf Coast, where the Mexican states of Veracruz and Tabasco are today; and the area that today contains the Mexican Yucatán peninsula, Belize, and Guatemala. The first state society of which there is evidence was the Olmecas, centered in Veracruz beginning approximately in 1500 B.C. The classic period of the Mayas was A.D. 300–900. In the central highlands the Aztec empire (1350–1522) was preceded by Tula (856–1168) and Teotihuacán (200–650).

The state empires were class-based societies in which the dominant class exercised its domination by virtue of controlling the state, which in turn, financed itself by collecting exploitative tribute payments from the villages and other communities that it dominated. Roger Bartra, who systematically studied Aztec documents and generalized his findings to other similar types of pre-Columbian empires, concluded that "the exploitation took the form of a tribute imposed on the communities (paid in kind, work, or primitive forms of money) that was in reality a rent paid to the sovereign for the use of the land of which, because of divine grace, he was the absolute owner."[7]

The Aztec empire was by far the largest and most developed of the state societies. The Aztec empire encompassed a territory the size of Italy and contained as many as 25 million people.[8] Its capital city, Tenochtitlán, where Mexico City lies today, had a population of between 250,000 and 500,000, making it one of the world's largest cities of its day—as Mexico City is today. A fused ruling class of military, political, and religious leaders sat at the top. The economic role of this ruling class was to accumulate and direct the investment of tribute payments in products and labor. The leaders had their own tribute-collecting bureaucracy. Once collected, tributes were invested in—aside from consumption needs of the ruling class—military and infrastructure (roads, aqueducts, etc.) maintenance and expansion. The Aztec ruling class directly controlled the Aztec state, which was the source of its economic as well as political power. At the base of Aztec society were peasants living in largely self-sufficient households and village communities. Most household food supplies came from horticulture, with supplements coming from hunting and gathering, fishing, and pastoralism. Surpluses—what was produced beyond household consumption needs—were destined for tribute payments and trade. Village communities generally had at least sporadic market days when peasants would gather to exchange their surpluses. These gave rise to an economic class of merchants and craft workers who serviced the markets. The merchants specialized in buying and selling for a profit, and the craft workers sold their products and services. In addition to the economic classes of the ruling class, merchants, and peasants, there was also a small slave class drawn mainly from war captives, debtors, and criminals. Unlike the slavery of ancient Greece and Rome or the slavery that would later come in the New World, this slavery was limited. The condition of slavery itself did not pass on to the children of slaves, and slave labor and products were not essential bases of the Aztec economy. In terms of consumption levels, that is, social classes, Aztec society spread from the lower classes of poor peasants and slaves to the rich upper class, which was made up of the members of ruling-class households. In between there existed a small middle class made up mainly of prosperous merchants in Tenochtitlán.

To this economic and social portrait of Aztec society must be added an account of the Aztec worldview and profound religiosity, which both played important institutional roles in daily life and would be key factors that would influence the course of the conquest. The Aztecs deeply believed that they lived within a divine order that governed every aspect of their lives—from the positioning of the stars to their personal destinies. That was what made sense to them and what gave purpose to their lives. Within this order their supreme god, the sun, continually had to fight against the forces of darkness and death. The sun had to emerge victorious, or all life would be extinguished. Each darkening, or eclipse, marked the beginning of the sun's battle with the forces of darkness, and each dawn indicated that the sun had emerged victorious and life would go on. According to Aztec belief, the purpose of all activities— making war, harvesting, and sacrificing victims—was to maintain this divine order. Any failure could disrupt its functioning. If a drought came, that was a sign as well as punishment, indicating that the Aztecs had not complied enough with their divine obligations. Sacrifices of their own blood would be called upon to put themselves back in place in the divine order. This was a fatalistic worldview, which indicates why the Aztecs went to the extreme of carrying out human sacrifices. They deeply believed both that it was true and that they were powerless to do anything but comply; otherwise, the whole cosmological order would collapse. That was their obligation if both they, not as individuals but as a people, and the whole divine order were to survive. The Aztecs also believed that their cosmological world—that of the Fifth Sun— had been preceded by four previous worlds, each one of which had ended in calamity. Their world also was destined to end apocalyptically—as it did.

EUROPE ON THE EVE OF THE CONQUESTS

Europe at the time of the conquests was at distinctly different levels of technological and social development than the societies of North America. In contrast to North America, where horticulture—use of hoes to cultivate gardens—was the highest level of technology achieved, Europe for more than a millennium had known more sophisticated and productive agricultural technologies that employed animal-drawn plows to cultivate fields. The Europeans would bring the animal-drawn plow with them and introduce it to the Americas. In terms of social development, unlike North America where the Aztec state society was the highest level of complexity achieved, Europe in the sixteenth century was passing from feudalism to capitalism.

European feudalism, as described most completely by Marc Bloch, was composed of essentially precommodity natural and autarkic manorial economies in which landlords dominated peasants.[9] The landlords controlled the usufruct of the land, which they rented out to peasants. Peasants for the most part produced products for their own household consumption. Their surplus products were divided between those that were used for rent payments and those that were marketed.

The development of capitalism required a radical transformation of feudalism, necessitating the development of free markets in labor, the means of production (capital), and products. Peasant labor would have to be divorced from the land, as it was, in order to be available for hire. Land—the principal feudal means of production—would have to become available for sale. Labor products would have to be sold in markets rather than consumed directly by their producers. All three types of markets were already at various stages of development in Europe at the time of the conquest such that it was possible to speak of the emergence of actual market-organized capitalist societies. But capitalist development proceeded unevenly in Europe. Some regions and whole countries advanced faster than others. City markets and workshops were the original centers of capitalistic activities, while the countrysides remained mired in feudal relationships and manorial economies. England and Holland transformed themselves at faster rates than did Spain or Portugal. The uneven development of European capitalism would be reflected in the different ways that the conquerors of North America would construct their colonial societies.

THE CONQUESTS

In North America the Spanish, English, French, and Dutch took control of different areas and the indigenous peoples within them. For the first time in North America class and race would become correlates, with Indians being forced into the lower rungs of the colonial class systems. In colonial North America, Indians became slaves, peasants, peons, and, certainly, poor. There is a clear relationship between the conquest and forced class subjugation of the indigenous populations and the continuing reality that today in the United States, Mexico, and Canada, Indians are the racial and ethnic groups that suffer the most unequal standards of living.

The largest scale and most spectacular of the conquests took place, logically, in what today is Mexico, where the indigenous population was the most numerous and developed. One of the great mysteries that has puzzled generations of historians was how it was possible for Hernán Cortés with just five hundred soldiers to overthrow a warrior empire that controlled experienced armies with hundreds of thousands of men. The puzzle has generally been answered in three ways, all of which have validity. We can see these as contributing factors rather than attempting to determine orders of importance.

First, the Aztec empire did not offer unified resistance to the invaders. The Aztecs had enemies on their borders and fifth columns within. As they continually sought to expand their boundaries and tributary areas, they met the resistance of smaller state societies, such as Tlaxcala. Within the areas that they had conquered, there was resentment and discontent among many of the village communities and subject peoples. Cortés was able to skillfully take advantage of these fissures and enlist the Aztecs' enemies in his own armies. In other cases, he defeated smaller indigenous armies on the periphery of the Aztec empire and then added their ranks to his own. In part they combined with the conquistador cause. (In military history armies that have been thoroughly routed on the battlefield by overwhelming forces have often joined their conquerors. The United States, for example, had little trouble in reorienting the loyalties of defeated Granadian and Panamanian soldiers after its invasions in 1983 and 1989, respectively.) In part Cortés obliged them to join his armies as a term of surrender. By the time Cortés made his final assault on Tenochtitlán his five hundred soldiers were backed up by more than 100,000 indigenous soldiers.

There is a certain racial mythology surrounding these events. Because Cortés had substantial numbers of Indian allies, it is misleading to see the initial conquest as entirely a battle between Spanish and Indians. Cortés marched into a situation in which the indigenous peoples were not united. They belonged to different, and often warring, state empires (such as the Aztecs and Tlaxcalans); they were simple oppressed subjects of one or another empire; or they lived outside of the control of empires and only had localized identities. To believe that the indigenous peoples could have developed a unity that overrode all of these divisions when the Spanish arrived is to believe that common racial identity is (or should be) the moving force of history.

In this respect, Mexican nationalism and national identity have been largely formed out of a particular interpretation of the conquest. According to it, Mexican national identity begins long before the arrival of the Spanish with the indigenous peoples. The Spanish conquest tragically ended their civilizations. The official interpretation views Cortés as an invader of Mexico. For that reason there are no more than a handful of obscure statues of him today in Mexico. Even more disdained in Mexican history is Cortés's Indian interpreter and lover, Malintzin or *doña* Marina, as the Spanish called her, whose skillful advice significantly aided his victories. Referred to as *la Malinche,* a variation of her Indian name, she is seen as the great betrayer of pre-hispanic Mexico. Today, the term *malinchista* is applied to Mexicans who identify more with foreigners than with their own country. The interpretation of the role of Malinche is also related to the cultural complex of *machista* ideas in which men see and fear all women as potential betrayers. The problem, as Roger Bartra has pointed out, is that there was no pre-Hispanic Mexican homeland to be betrayed. Mexico as a nation developed after, not before, the Conquest.[10] To see the indigenous peoples as having been a nation not only ignores the realities of their divisions; it is also, once again, to reduce national identity to primarily racial identity, that is, Indianness.

The second factor instrumental in the defeat of the Aztecs was disease. When the Spanish arrived in the Americas, they unwittingly brought with them the germs of diseases that had spread earlier through Europe. The Spanish themselves over generations had built up relative resistances to these diseases, but the Americas had had no biological experience with the diseases. Hence, when the contact was made, the diseases spread like wildfire through the indigenous populations. Crosby, among others, has concluded that one of the reasons why the Aztecs could not put up stronger resistance to the conquistadores was that many of them were very sick or dying from European diseases during decisive battles.[11]

The third influencing factor was the Aztec worldview or belief system. As mentioned, the Aztecs deeply believed that sooner or later their world would end apocalyptically. It was within this context that the Aztec ruler Montezuma and most of his advisers initially believed that the Spanish conquistadores were gods and harbingers of a divinely ordered destruction of their world, against which there was nothing that could be done except to accept it fatalistically. This was a subjective factor that weakened the Aztec defenses and allowed the conquistadores a relatively easy conquest. Even if the Aztecs were not completely sure that their doom had already been divinely ordained, there was enough of a generalized doubt throughout the ranks of their armies to vitiate resistance. The Aztecs had never seen guns or horses before. The deafening sounds and deadly fire spit out by the guns as well as the beasts that carried their bearers were terrifying. In addition, disfiguring diseases descended upon them. All these unsettling events confirmed the belief that the apocalyptic end was indeed near. Once conquered, the Aztec population was fatalistically predisposed, because of its deeply rooted belief system, to accept that the world of the Fifth Sun was no more and that a new world with a new god would take its place.

Following conquest of the Aztec empire, Spanish military forces moved northward over the next decades, attempting to extend their control. The Aztec empire that the Spanish conquered had stretched only as far north as the contemporary Mexican state of Hidalgo. Beyond it lived the seminomadic Chichimeca peoples, who depended mainly on hunting and gathering from the arid lands of the present-day northern states of Mexico for survival. The Chichimeca peoples merged into the Apaches, who were also nomadic hunters and gatherers who ranged over what today is Arizona, New Mexico, and Texas in the United States, and Sonora and Chihuahua in Mexico. Soon after conquering Tenochtitlán, the Spanish began their military push northward, provoking a series of wars with the fiercely independent Chichimeca peoples. Farther north, in the areas that would become the Southwest of the United States, the Spanish encountered further resistance, especially from the Apaches. At first, they made peace with the Pueblo villages. But then in 1680 the Pueblos revolted and expelled the Spanish from New Mexico. Later the Spanish were able to return and coexist with the Pueblos. But they never were able to completely subdue the Apaches and other nomadic Indians, especially in western New Mexico, which is today Arizona.[12] The final submission of all of the indigenous bands would only be accomplished by the U.S. military after the Mexican-American War (1846–48).

The other conquests that took place on the North American continent were less epic than those that took place in Mexico but were as consequential for the indigenous peoples. The first permanent English settlements on the east coast of what would become the United States, the Jamestown and Plymouth colonies, were not established for nearly a century after the Spanish conquest of Tenochtitlán. Unlike the Spanish, who confronted densely populated areas, the English encountered relatively sparse populations. Unlike the Spanish, who sought to take advantage of abundant Indian labor to construct their colonial cities and later farm their lands, the English arrived with an enclave mentality. They built their cities like fortresses, always seeking to keep the Indians beyond the limits of where they lived. Unlike the Spanish, who lived with, and who with increasing frequency interbred with, indigenous people, the English strictly segregated themselves.

As more settlers arrived seeking choice land for planting, the colonies expanded their borders at the expense of the Indians. In time, expansion provoked resistance and wars broke out. Around Plymouth in 1675, King Phillip's War, named after the English name for the Indian chief, broke out. After defeating and capturing the Indians, the settlers executed the Indian chief and placed his head on a stake in Plymouth, where it remained for twenty years. His wife and children were shipped to the West Indies and sold into slavery. The first permanent European settlers of the New York area were the Dutch, who founded New Netherlands. They too expanded their holdings violently at the expense of the Indians. In 1641, Dutch soldiers massacred all the occupants of two Indian villages on Staten Island, a part of present-day New York City, while they slept. They then burned the villages to the ground. As in Mexico, European diseases took a heavy toll among the indigenous people. In the area of the Jamestown settlement, the original eight thousand Powhattan Indians were reduced to one thousand within two generations.

French settlers founded Canada's first permanent European colony at Quebec in 1608, approximately the same time as the founding of the Jamestown colony. The French settlers pursued a different policy with the Indians than had either the Plymouth or Jamestown settlers. For the most part, instead of segregating themselves from the Indians, they formed alliances with different Indian groups in the internecine Indian wars. The largest in scale of these was between Algonquians and Iroquois in which the French sided with the Algonquians, beginning in 1609, for a half century of fighting over control of the fur trade in the lower Great Lakes and St. Lawrence areas. What sugar was to the Caribbean, fur was to New France. The French generally obtained furs, for which there was a growing world market subject to the dictates of fashion, from Indians, who often obtained them from other Indians further inland or collected them themselves. The French were thus the traders and the Indians the collectors of furs. Fur played the role of export product, as sugar did in the Caribbean. The difference was that it could not be produced under plantation conditions where a subjugated slave labor force could be concentrated. It had to be trapped over wide wooded areas. In 1649 the French decided to trap the furs themselves and dispense with the Indian middlemen, who were essentially "fur-collecting mercenary warriors."[13]

In most cases, thus, the French attempted to work with Indian allies to defeat other Indians for the interests of France. The confrontations did not have the stark European-versus-Indian character that they took in the areas that were to become the United States. The French simply entered into and took sides in preexisting internecine Indian hostilities to pursue their own interests. The general policy of entering into alliances with one or another side of warring Indian tribes was not without exceptions, though. The first contact between the Beothuk people on Newfoundland and French fishers ended in confrontation, with the French attempting to hunt down and annihilate the entire Beothuk population.[14] As in all areas of North America, European diseases also took a heavy toll among the Canadian Amerindians. In 1639 a smallpox epidemic killed two-thirds of the thirty thousand members of the Huron confederacy.[15]

CONCLUSIONS

The Indian societies of North America on the eve of the European conquests ranged, in developmental terms, from hunting and gathering bands of nomads to horticultural village communities to the state empires of Mesoamerica. Europe, by contrast, at that time was composed of agricultural societies in varying degrees of transformation from feudalism to capitalism. The conquest of North America started first in its most highly developed area, the Aztec empire, and then over the next three centuries spread to remoter regions of the continent. Because both Europe and North America at the beginning of this period of conquest and colonization were unevenly developed technologically and economically, the economic and social, as well as cultural, natures of the societies that would be constructed after the conquest would necessarily vary.

The origins of the correlations of class and race in North America go back to the sixteenth- and seventeenth-century consequences of these conquests. The colonial reconstruction of North America, to which we next turn, would add enslaved Africans to defeated Indians as subjugated races. The contemporary social inequalities suffered by Indians and blacks cannot be understood without references to their roots in these historical developments. They are the legacies of conquests and slavery. Racism, as the ideology of superior and inferior races, developed during this period as an attempt to justify and rationalize the European role in these events.

✳ CHAPTER 3

Class, Race, and Colonial Reconstruction

European explorers and colonizers planted the first seeds of capitalism in North America in the sixteenth century, but it grew and developed unevenly across the continent, as is obvious from its contemporary features in the United States, Mexico, and Canada. In large part it developed unevenly because the Spanish and English, as well as Dutch and French, colonizers implanted different varieties of capitalism and did so under different conditions.

Capitalism as such had developed unevenly across Europe as it displaced feudalism. Markets and workshops located in cities were the original centers of capitalist activities, while the countryside remained mired in traditional feudal relationships. The economies of whole countries, such as England and Holland, became proportionately more capitalistic and less feudalistic at faster rates than other countries, such as Spain and Portugal. Hence the main colonizers of the areas of North America that would become the United States, Mexico, and Canada came from countries that represented significantly different hybrids of feudal and capitalist economic features. In Spain, feudal features were proportionately more present than in England. Thus, what the Spanish institutionally implanted was proportionately more feudalistic than what the English implanted. In addition, the Spanish grafted their economic relationships onto already-existing Indian societies, whereas the English largely had a blank slate upon which to write. It followed that capitalism would develop much more rapidly in the English than in the Spanish areas.

The Spanish confronted large and complexly organized indigenous societies. They found it useful and relatively easy to absorb many of the indigenous peoples' state institutions into their own semifeudal forms of organization. The Aztec tribute payment, for example, could be easily continued as a payment to the new Spanish authorities. This blending of two types of social organizations was possible because in many respects state and feudal societies are similar. In both, the ruling classes receive payments of surplus products from subject classes, as tribute payments in the case of state societies and as rent payments in the case of feudal societies. The main difference between the two is that the rule was centralized in state societies and decentralized in feudal societies. But the form of domination, if not the source, was very similar.[1] Neither state nor feudal societies were compatible with capitalistic development. Hence the noncapitalist aspects of Aztec and Spanish social and economic organization tended to reinforce each other and act as a brake on capitalist development in New Spain.

In contrast, in the British areas of North America, the indigenous peoples were from the beginning pushed away from the areas of colonization. Their forms of social and economic organization played no part in the social and economic organization of the colonies. In a double sense the conditions for capitalist development were much more favorable in the British than in the Spanish areas of North America. The British were more inclined to be capitalistic in the first place because their home country was experiencing rapid capitalist development. Second, North America represented a kind of institutional tabula rasa for them. They had a free hand to form the kinds of social and economic institutions that they wanted. They were not forced to absorb a whole population and take into account the preexisting institutions, as were the Spanish colonizers.

To all of this must be added the different roles and consequences of religious institutions in the Spanish and British colonies. As Max Weber powerfully argued, the medieval Catholic Church's attitudes toward economic life and work acted as a brake on capitalist development.[2] Catholic theology held that the community had to devote a considerable amount of its labor and time to directly religious pursuits such as prayer and the construction of churches and viewed with suspicion labor that was directed at producing worldly wealth. Protestant theology, on the other hand, found that success in worldly pursuits was also a positive sign also of religious success, and it minimized the church's demand on labor, time, and resources. The Protestant work ethic produced generations of overproducers and underconsumers. Business owners reinvested their profits rather than spending them on luxury consumption items. Protestant workers were the answer to the capitalist dream: they worked hard without demanding high wages. Both classes of Protestants, according to Weber, significantly accelerated the accumulation of capital. If the ornately constructed Catholic Church was the symbol of colonial culture in New Spain, the no-nonsense, simple New England church was the symbol of Puritan culture.

It followed that though the Spanish and British areas would both primarily develop in a capitalistic direction, they would develop unevenly at different speeds and with different features. Mexico would inherit the institutional features of large haciendas, communal landholdings, significant natural economies, and a church that drained economic resources, while the United States and Canada would inherit an economic ethic more in tune with capitalist needs and an almost wide-open territory within which capitalism could develop, once the territory had been cleared of the obstacles posed by the presence of its relatively few original inhabitants. The indigenous populations would be integrated into the social bases of the colonial class system in New Spain as slaves, laborers, peons, and peasants. The Spanish sought their labor. In the British areas, though, the dynamic would be different. The original inhabitants would always be outside of the evolving economic system. All that the new settlers wanted from them was their land.

If feudal and semifeudal institutions slowed the development of capitalism in part of North America, slavery, which existed in both the Spanish and southern British colonies, played a more supporting role. North American slavery, unlike peasant agriculture, was always related to capitalist development. The basic purpose of having a slave labor force was to produce products for which there was a market demand. Owners used slaves to mine silver and plant sugar, tobacco, and other crops for the world market. Slaves certainly produced profits for their owners and significantly contributed to the overall accumulation of capital that launched international capitalism. It is yet to be determined whether more primary capital accumulation came out of the compulsive labor of the frugal Puritans or the overexploitation of slaves.[3]

In sum, the sixteenth-century varieties of capitalism that the Europeans brought with them were hybrids of feudal, slave, and capitalist formations. Three major varieties developed: a capitalism with significant feudal features in New Spain and New France; a slavery-based capitalism in the British southern colonies; and an elementary agrarian capitalism in the British northern colonies.

SPANISH COLONIAL SOCIETY

Colonial New Spain, composed of present-day Mexico and Central America, represented both a radical uprooting and restructuring of Aztec society and an adaptation to it. The Spanish took over as the new ruling class and razed Aztec cities and churches in order to construct a new society in their own image. One of the most graphic monuments to this policy is at Cholula in Puebla where the Spanish constructed a church precisely at the apex of the ruins of a pyramid. The visual symbolism of this act of cultural domination would later be paralleled in the United States, when within a couple of decades of the final military conquest of the Sioux, the conquering power carved the faces of four of its presidents on the top of Mount Rushmore, a mountain sacred to the conquered. In both cases, conquerors through physical defacement of a cultural shrine attempted to symbolize their power while simultaneously erasing the cultural pasts of the conquered.

The sheer size and cultural depth of the conquered indigenous population, though, forced the Spanish to adapt to already-existing institutional arrangements as well. They had to include them within their institutions. They would not be able to simply keep pushing Indians to frontier areas, as was done in the areas that would become the United States. Spanish feudal institutions could fairly easily be transplanted and adapted to the new colonial conditions because the preexisting Aztec state and the Spanish feudal economies had had a number of similar features. Peasant labor was the base of both types of economies; and in both, peasants were accustomed to making tribute or rent payments to overlords. The Spanish, once they had lopped off the Aztec occupants of the ruling positions within the economic and social pyramids, simply took their places.

The Spanish initially implanted the *encomienda* system. The crown granted an individual, the *encomendero*, the right to collect tributes from the individuals, the *encomendados*, within an area. This was the first landlord-peasant economic class structure established by the Spanish in New Spain. The *encomienda* system though represented not so much a break from the old pre-Hispanic state society forms of collecting tribute as a continuation of them. As Bartra concluded, "During these first years after the conquest the Spanish simply substituted themselves for the old indigenous sovereigns and took advantage of the native systems of exploitation."[4] In that sense, it was an institutional form that could function in both state and feudal modes of production, which, while distinct, contained many similarities. Angel Palerm argues that not only were there institutional continuities between the pre-Hispanic and Spanish colonial economic class structures, but that there were also continuities of individuals. According to him, during this period substantial parts of the old Indian upper class remained largely intact. The Spanish allowed them to keep some of their properties and political authority and to continue collecting tributes from the Indian masses. In this sense, according to Palerm, the Spanish did not totally displace the old Indian upper classes at first but rather moved in alongside them in the class structure. "The Spanish and the superior indigenous class," writes Palerm, "lived over the mass of aboriginal agriculturalists from whom they wrested part of their product by means of tribute payments."[5] In time, though, the Indian component of the early colonial upper class would be almost completely edged out, with the Spanish taking over virtually all opportunities for acquiring upper-class incomes.

The *encomienda* system did not last long. Instead of being content with simply collecting tributes from Indians who continued their economic activities as they always had, the Spanish sought to directly develop and exploit the land and other natural resources. Toward that end they developed their own agricultural, ranching, and mining operations with an overall colonial economy based on haciendas (for both agriculture and ranching) and mining in the countryside, and based on state administration, commerce, and some production in the cities. The major economic actors were the hacienda owners, whose labor force consisted mainly of indigenous peasants; the church, which was a large landowner in its own right and holder of credit capital; and the colonial state, which controlled lucrative political and military positions. Men could make their fortunes and insure their upper-class membership from the exploitation of peasant labor on the land they owned or from the exploitation of income opportunities afforded by controlling state posts. Although the church was a powerful economic actor in its own right, it did not so much generate upper-class members as receive them. That is, because of celibacy vows as well as the corporate organization of the institution, rich priests could not pass on fortunes to heirs. However, it was customary for at least one son of a rich family to become a priest who would quickly move into the upper echelons of the church. In this sense the church was not immune to being a part of the colonial class society. Landlords, priests, and state authorities thus ran the economic structure.

Many writers, such as Palerm, have described the colonial labor force in dualistic terms.[6] That is, the core of the economy consisted of the hacienda, mining, and urban labor forces. But outside of that core economy existed peripheral subsistence-level villages and farms in which mainly Indians lived. These were in a double sense peripheral labor forces. First, they generated mainly subsistence products for household consumption. Such surplus products as they generated did not circulate beyond local markets. Second, they were outside of the control of the landlords and mine owners and thus outside of the main systems of exploitation.

A middle class of professionals and merchants sputtered into existence in the cities by the late colonial period. They were middle class in both the economic and social senses. That is, economically they were small business owners, and socially their businesses were prosperous enough to afford incomes above those received by the Indian and mestizo lower classes.

The New Spain colonial economy combined feudal, capitalist, and, to a much smaller extent, slave elements. It was feudal to the extent that a significant amount of peasant production was for self and household consumption rather than market sale; and it was feudal to the extent the church's power as a large land controller and accumulator of capital acted as a brake on capitalist development. It was capitalist to the extent that increasing amounts of production were oriented to both domestic and international markets; and it was capitalist to the extent that labor and capital markets were developing. Slave labor was employed in households, plantation fields, sugar mills, and mines. It was thus legal and existed for the entire colonial period, but it was never practiced as extensively as in the southern areas of British North America or other parts of the Americas.

The first slaves were Indians. Some had been slaves before the conquest and simply changed owners after it. Others were newly enslaved by the Spanish. Indian slavery legally ended in 1551 by order of the Spanish court. In practice, though, it continued in frontier areas of New Spain. But the burden of slave labor did pass from Indians to Africans, as in the rest of Latin America, by the middle of the sixteenth century. For the full colonial period as many as 250,000 African slaves would be imported through the ports of Veracruz and Acapulco into Mexico.[7] Some had already been slaves in Spanish possessions in the Caribbean. Others were directly imported from Africa. There was also a much smaller trade in Asian slaves transported from the Philippines, also a colony of Spain, to the Pacific port of Acapulco. These were all referred to as *Chinos,* though the majority were Filipinos.[8]

David M. Davidson calculated the distribution of Mexican slaves during the height of their use in the mid-seventeenth century. There were four main areas. The first, involving 8,000 to 10,000 slaves at the height of Mexican slavery, during the mid-seventeenth century, spread from Veracruz to Panuco along the Gulf coast and inland across the tropical lowlands to the Sierra Madre Oriental mountains. In the city of Veracruz itself there were about 5,000 slaves who worked mostly as transporters and dockworkers. Outside of Veracruz in the countryside the other 3,000 slaves worked on sugar plantations and ranches. The second area was north and west of Mexico City, where some 15,000 slaves worked in mines and as herders of cattle, sheep, and mules. The third area was in a belt from Puebla to the Pacific Coast, where some 3,000 to 5,000 slaves worked on sugar plantations, on ranches, and in mines. The fourth and largest area of slavery was in Mexico City itself, where between 20,000 and 50,000 slaves worked in urban occupations.[9]

Significant numbers of slaves rebelled and escaped during the colonial period. The fear of slave rebellion was always an undercurrent of colonial society. In 1537, as the African slave population of Mexico City was growing rapidly, rumors spread among the Spanish inhabitants that a rebellion was about to break out. They responded by publicly executing through quartering several dozen slaves.[10] That same year a number of escaped slaves—referred to collectively as *cimarrones* in New Spain—attacked a Spanish village.[11] Because New Spain contained many remote mountainous areas, *cimarrones* were able to establish themselves relatively easily and fend off attempts at recapture. Some of the mountain villages originally established by *cimarrones* in Veracruz, Oaxaca, and Guerrero continue today to be inhabited by their descendants.[12] The Spanish authorities attempted to deter escapes by establishing severely repressive punishments including castration.[13]

There was a close correlation between race and social class position in New Spain. As Alexander von Humboldt, who traveled extensively through New Spain, noted, "The skin, more or less white, decides the rank that a man occupies in society."[14] The upper classes were completely white, but not without divisions. The top social class positions belonged to leading landlord, political, and military families, as well as the top echelons of the clergy, who were Spanish born (*peninsulares*). Below them in status, but still upper class, were wealthy landlords and merchants who were creoles (Spaniards born in New Spain). The small middle class was made up of moderately prosperous creole merchants and landowners. The two lower classes were made up of the free poor (mestizos, mulattoes, and Indians) and black slaves.

Throughout the colonial period the Spanish authorities attempted to carefully categorize people racially, with people of mixed backgrounds being placed in what they called castes.[15] Europeans, Indians, and Africans constituted the three racial trunk lines and originating caste positions. Cross-racial unions produced three general mixed-race caste positions: *mestizos* (European-Indian), *mulatos* (European-African), and *zumbaigos* or *mulatos pardos* (Indian-African). The attempt to categorize the colonial population though did not stop with these six positions. Cross-caste unions among the different mixed race castes produced still new combinations, which received their own labels. The offspring of whites and mulattoes were called *moriscos*. The offspring of a particular type of mixed union could also be labeled differently according to which parent had one of the particular racial backgrounds, such as whether it was the father or the mother who was the white in a white-Indian union. In time, as new types of combinations increased, the number of labels generated to describe their offspring multiplied to as many as fifty-six in the highly race-conscious discourse of colonial society.

From the most positive point of view, the generation of an elaborate language of racial labels reflected a refined appreciation of how different combinations could produce an interesting mosaic of different physical types of people. Sor Juana Inés de la Cruz included mestizos and mulattoes in her seventeenth-century poetry, though most often as picturesque background characters. Racially mixed persons were the subjects of paintings, in some cases

TABLE 3–1   Population of New Spain, Various Years

	1570	1646	1742	1793	1810
Europeans	0.2	0.8	0.4	0.2	0.2
Africans	0.6	2.0	0.8	0.1	0.1
Indians	98.7	74.6	62.2	61.0	60.0
Euro-mestizos	0.3	9.8	15.8	17.8	17.9
Afro-mestizos	0.07	6.8	10.8	9.6	10.1
Indo-mestizos	0.07	6.0	10.0	11.2	11.5
Total	100.0	100.0	100.0	100.0	100.0
Total population (in thousands)	3,380	1,713	2,477	3,800	6,122

Source: Gonzalo Aguirre Beltrán, *La Población Negra de México* (Mexico City: Secretaria de la Reforma Agraria—Centro de Estudios Históricos del Agrarismo en México, 1981, originally published in 1946), p. 234.

in their own right as interesting subjects, in others to aid church officials in classifying the members of their parishes. Art historians have recently collected these types of paintings of the castes and established them as a focus of study.[16] Art historian Edward J. Sullivan notes that the paintings reflect the societal prejudices of the time. "Most of the depictions of the *castas* with the highest percentage of white blood show peaceful (even blissful) domestic scenes; some of those portraying people with predominantly black and Indian blood can be, from time to time, surprisingly violent."[17] The zoological origin of many of the names for castes—such as *mulato* (from mule), *coyote*, and *lobo* (wolf)—reflected the deep prejudice with which the white colonial upper class viewed racially mixed persons.[18]

Catholic missionary work moved in tandem with the consolidation of Spanish economic and political power. The Indians' fatalistic receptivity to the rule of new gods facilitated the work of the church. Nevertheless, the conversion of millions of Indians to Catholicism was an extraordinary ideological feat seldom if ever matched in world history, before or since. The depth of Catholic religiosity among the Mexican Indian population today, as evidenced by the huge crowds that turn out to see visiting popes, bears testimony to the success of the missionary effort.

A fortunate and, in the eyes of some colonial critics, suspicious miracle greatly aided the conversion effort. In 1532, just eleven years after the final conquest of Tenochtitlán, the Virgin Mary appeared in transfigured form as an Indian on a hill that today is within the limits of Mexico City. An Indian peasant, Juan Diego, witnessed her appearance. As evidence, she left her image on a piece of cloth. From that incident spread belief in the miracle of the Virgin of Guadalupe, which facilitated conversion of the indigenous population. Belief in the Virgin of Guadalupe continues to be deeply embraced in

Mexico, especially among Indians. In addition to allowing that divinity could take the form of an Indian, Spanish Catholicism had to adapt itself to some preexisting indigenous beliefs and practices while attempting to uproot those that were judged to be heathen. Celebration of the indigenous Day of the Dead could continue and even become a part of the church's customary festivities, but adoration of idols had to end.

From the 1530s onward the Spanish pushed northward, attempting to colonize frontier areas. The north was inhabited by a large variety of nomadic bands who spoke various languages. The Aztecs had pejoratively called them collectively Chichimecas—descended from dogs—and the Spanish inherited the term. When the Spanish first moved north of the Valley of Mexico—where the conquered Tenochtitlán lay in ruins—to establish ranching haciendas, they first encountered the nomadic bands. By the 1550s they had established farming haciendas and opened mines in Zacatecas. Most of the north was made up of mountains and deserts. The Spanish first developed the most desirable areas where fertile lands or minerals lay. Their main obstacles were the nomadic Indian bands.

The bands were nomads whose hunting and gathering technology required large areas in which to search, especially given the arid and semiarid characteristics of the Mexican north. The Spanish sought to use the land in a different way, that is, for agriculture, ranching, and mining. In a sense, two different technologies competed for land use. There is no question that the Spanish sought to use the land more efficiently in the sense that a square hectare of land used for agriculture can support more people than can the same unit of land used for hunting and gathering. At the same time, because the nomadic hunting and gathering bands required so much territory to survive, any intrusion by foreigners undercut their economic means of survival. The very presence of the Spanish therefore created problems for the Indians.

The Spanish colonization of northern New Spain followed a pattern. As haciendas, mines, and towns were established, the authorities established a presidio or fort near them for protection. The church in turn established a mission in its attempt to convert and pacify the nomads. As the frontier advanced and old towns disappeared, presidios moved. Their locations thus marked the progress of Spanish colonization toward the north. Huerta Preciado has described the general stages of colonization of the north as involving "exploration and possession of new lands, founding of population centers, exploration for natural resources, forced submission of the Indian, and once the enterprise was consolidated, defense of the acquired possessions."[19]

Spanish policy also attempted to make the Indians sedentary and transform them from hunters and gatherers into a labor force for haciendas and mining. None of these efforts proceeded peacefully. Almost continual warfare accompanied the Spanish colonization of the northern territories up through the nineteenth century. The sword and the cross were thus the primary Spanish instruments for overcoming nomadic Indian resistance and opening up the northern territories to agricultural, ranching, and mining exploitation.

CAPITALISM, FEUDALISM, AND
NEW FRANCE (1608–1760)

Almost a century after the beginnings of New Spain, Spain's northern neighbor, France, established its own colony in the northern reaches of the continent. There were many differences between these Latin country colonial enterprises, but the parallels that, at the same time, marked each region off from the Anglo-Saxon British colonies in between are most interesting here. Colonial New France was centered in Quebec and the St. Lawrence Valley, with its influence carried by French explorers, traders, and military outposts further west and south down through what is now the U.S. Midwest to Louisiana.

Since both Spain and France, unlike England, still had significant feudal economic vestiges slowing capitalist development in the sixteenth and seventeenth centuries, both of their North American colonies would be partially constructed according to both feudal and capitalist principles. An important part of agriculture in seventeen-century New France, like that of New Spain, remained firmly embedded in feudal customs. The colonial authorities followed the feudal custom by granting land as estates (*seigneuries*) to landlords (*seigneurs*) in the St. Lawrence Valley. The landlords inhabited the estates with French-origin peasants (*censitaires* or *habitants*). The estate economies followed almost completely French feudal precedent. The peasants owed rent (about 10 percent of their yearly income—less severe than in France), military service, and, in some cases, corvée labor, that is, compulsory work for the landlord. They were also required to work for the crown a few days a year to maintain roads and bridges. Approximately half of the peasants produced only enough for subsistence and rent payments.[20] At the same time, the fur trade was definitely organized according to capitalistic principles. French merchants bought pelts from Indian trappers that were then shipped for sale in France. The Indian was thus a kind of business partner in the development of the fur trade. The early fishing industry also was carried out on a profit-making basis, with the crews being paid wages.

New France, like New Spain, had a history of slavery on the margins of the economy, but it was even more marginal. No more than four thousand persons were slaves in the entire history of the colony. The majority of these were

Indians rather than blacks. There was even less of a basis for plantation slave systems in New France than there was in New Spain.[21]

Relations between whites and Indians developed in New France in a number of ways that paralleled those of New Spain. While there was no conquest comparable to that of Tenochtitlán, the early military history of New France saw French settlers aligning themselves with one Indian tribe against another to accomplish objectives rather than confronting the Indian per se, as most often occurred in the British areas.

There was significant intermarriage among French (and, to a smaller extent, Scots) and Indians, with the resulting offspring being called *métis*, who shared the same racial characteristics as Mexican mestizos. These established their own separate identities, developing settlements that spread across present-day western Canada beginning in the nineteenth century.

BRITISH COLONIALISM

British North America, after the 1763 defeat of France in the Seven Years War, included the thirteen original colonies that would make up the United States and the area from what is now Ontario eastward through Quebec to the maritime provinces and Newfoundland, which would become parts of Canada. The northern colonies economically functioned within elementary agrarian and mercantile capitalist structures, while an export capitalism based on slave labor grew in the southern colonies.

In one way or another whites, Indians, and blacks confronted each other in the colonial projects, and inevitably, as in the other areas of North America, racially mixed offspring emerged. The language that evolved to describe these persons differed in degree of elaborateness between the British colonies and those of Spain and France. This linguistic difference reflects the lack of integration of Indians in the development of the British colonies, in contrast to those of Spain and France. In the British colonies, Indians and mestizos were simply outside—in both the physical and linguistic senses—the evolving colonial project; in the Spanish and French colonies they were an integrated, internal part of it, however much they were perceived as inferiors. In terms of psychological perception theory, the further an object is from a perceiver, the more that it is perceived as an undifferentiated whole. Indians and mestizos, on the one hand, and slaves and mulattoes, on the other hand, tended to be perceived as undifferentiated wholes in British colonial society because they were essentially outside it, despite the fact that slaves were economically essential in the south. In the Spanish and French areas they were perceived as being inside the colonial project, and, since they were closer, distinctions could be perceived among them.

Agrarian Capitalism and the Northern British Colonies

The starting point of the northern British colonies was farther down the road toward capitalist development than either the Spanish or French colonies. Throughout the colonial period, farmers made up the majority of the labor force. From the beginning—unlike the Spanish and French areas—market production dominated colonial farming practices in the British areas. Farmers in these areas produced for household consumption as well, but that was never their primary goal. Only in remote areas, such as Appalachia, were there farmers who produced mainly for household consumption and built a corresponding peasant subsistence economic and cultural way of life. For that reason a peasantry never became an entrenched part of the class structure, in contrast to Mexico, which was characterized by subsistence-oriented farmers rather than market-oriented peasants. Because of the increasing production of market-oriented agricultural surplus products, there was enough food to support immigration and population growth in colonial cities such as Boston, New York, Philadelphia, and Halifax. Within the cities, in turn, important industries such as shipbuilding and rum distilling developed. These colonial industries were both the seeds of the later development of industrial capitalism and sites of the original development of the urban economic classes of capitalists and workers.

The northern colonies thus developed predominantly—but not exclusively—through the use of independent businesses and free labor. Not all labor was free, though, because the northern colonies made some use of black slaves and, more significant economically, they greatly depended on the use of indentured servants for labor. Indentured servants were temporary slaves who had to work off the payment of their passages to the colonies from England. (Seven years was the usual period.) They came from the ranks of the urban poor, most of whom or whose ancestors had been peasants squeezed off the land. Some voluntarily became indentured servants in order to escape poverty at home and eventually find land in the colonies. Others had been convicted of crimes and sold by the courts to ship captains for resale at a profit upon arrival in the colonies. A not insignificant number had been kidnapped. (The expression "spirited away" had its origin in the kidnappings associated with the indentured servant trade. Kidnappers in the English ports were euphemistically referred to as "spirits." When someone turned up missing, the comment would be, "He was probably spirited away.") The indentured servant trade was an important source of profits for a number of English ports as well as supply of labor for the colonies. As much as half of the white population in the northern colonies came originally as indentured servants.

The indentured servant trade eventually died out for three reasons. First, the investment in indentured servants was costly, considering that they would have to be freed in seven years. Second, many escaped, leading to an immediate loss of the investment. Third, England ceased to encourage the trade. Originally, mercantile policy had encouraged the trade as a way of resolving English unemployment. But economic policy changed when it was realized that the maintenance of an unemployed population at home had a salutary effect on wages from the point of view of employers. That is, the greater the relative size of the unemployed population, the greater the downward pressure on the wages of the employed population because of the law of supply and demand.

The northern economic and class structure, although it rested for a long period on unfree indentured labor, always developed in the context of the primary capitalist goal of profitability and, as Max Weber emphasized, insuring growth through reinvestment of profits.[22] Religious values motivated much economic conduct, as among the Puritans and Quakers, but their churches did not demand as much time or absorb as much capital as did the monopolistic church of New Spain. If in New Spain spectacular amounts of wealth were made and squandered episodically, in British North America capital was accumulated methodically. However, it was no less accompanied by violence. The Massachusetts and Pennsylvania colonies established scalp bounties for Indians who stood in the way; and once the many small streams and rivulets of methodical accumulation joined together into an institutionalized national economy and self-evident national purpose, means of violence on a far larger scale would remove other obstacles.

Slave Capitalism and the Southern British Colonies (1660–1782)

The southern slave system always functioned within a world capitalist context. Slave labor was used to produce particular crops, such as sugar, tobacco, cotton, and indigo, for which there was a strong demand on the world market. In this sense, new world slavery was a necessary complement to the early development of capitalism. The trade in slaves themselves was exceptionally lucrative, with the profits generating capital formation; slave products were profitably sold on the world market; and, in many cases, slaves produced the raw materials that free labor in factories transformed into finished products.

The three great slave areas of the New World were Brazil, the Caribbean, and the South. At first, Indians were used in Brazil and the Caribbean as slaves to meet the increasingly voracious demands of the world market. But no sooner had the plantation economies been established than the Indian labor supplies dwindled as diseases, mainly of European origin, took their toll. In order to replace their labor supplies, the plantation owners turned to the African slave trade, which had already been in existence since at least the tenth century. From the sixteenth to the eighteenth century the African slave trade expanded enormously. As many as ten million Africans were kidnapped and forcibly transferred to the Americas, thereby creating the bases of racial divisions.

In the New World as a whole, sugar was the most important slave-produced crop for the world market during the colonial period. But it was of minimal importance in the southern colonies because their climatic and soil conditions were not appropriate. For the entire colonial period, tobacco was the leading slave-produced crop. It was only after independence that the invention of the cotton gin facilitated the orientation of southern agriculture toward meeting the skyrocketing world demand for cotton. Because the demand for tobacco was considerably less than that for sugar, the southern colonies only counted a very small percentage of New World slaves. By 1700 the South had imported no more than 30,000 African slaves, a small number compared to, for example, Brazil, which had imported 500,000 to 600,000.[23] Nevertheless, the bases of the southern slave economy were established during the colonial period. These would allow the expansion of the system as world economic demands changed in the late eighteenth century.

Unlike the Spanish, Portuguese, or French, the English in their colonial areas, including the South, followed the practice of systematically separating slaves from the same tribe so that they would not be sold together for work in the same area. This practice forced to the slaves to learn English quickly, since each slave spoke a different African regional or tribal language from Africa. With no one to communicate with, the languages fell into lack of use and eventually were lost. So too were African regional and tribal customs. English policy thus led to a rapid cutting of the slaves' African cultural roots.

Colonial practices were different in the Spanish, French, and Portuguese areas where there was no attempt to separate Africans from the same regions and tribes. As a result, the African roots of black culture remained much more alive in the Caribbean and Brazil than the south. Black culture in the United States would therefore develop relatively autonomously, while in the Caribbean and Brazil much more of a hybrid culture with strong African influences in dance, religion, and music would develop.

CONCLUSIONS

The various European conquerors of North America—Spain, France, England, the Netherlands—implanted capitalistic and feudal colonial models according to their own stages of development. England and the Netherlands, being relatively more capitalistic, developed North American colonies with relatively more capitalistic features. Spain and France, being relatively more feudal, developed North American colonies with relatively more feudal features. In addition to the implantation of capitalistic and feudalistic colonial features, North America was also the site of the implantation of a type of capitalism that relied upon African slave labor.

CHAPTER 4

Three Societies, Two Worlds of Development

From the time of European conquest and colonization, capitalist market economies developed on the North American continent, but at different rates and accompanied by different degrees of success and prosperity, as is obvious from the great differences between living standards in Mexico and those in the United States and Canada. Put differently, if uneven development characterized Europe and North America at the outset of the conquest, the societies that emerged from this violent encounter would also develop unevenly, producing the third and first world areas of the continent. Contemporary economic differences between the three countries can only be understood against the background of this uneven capitalist development.

ACCUMULATION OF CAPITAL AND INDUSTRIALIZATION

In his discussion of Canadian economic history, Ronald Manzer concludes that early state economic policy was primarily based on the principle of "appropriation." That is, the early Canadian state encouraged labor force members to develop business activities by appropriating already-existing means of production, such as land, waters, and forests. Given Canada's bountiful natural resources, there were a large number of opportunities for the start-up of businesses. Farmers could appropriate already-existing land to grow crops; fishers could appropriate the waters; lumber cutters could appropriate the trees of the forests; fur trappers could appropriate fur-bearing animals. The result, according to Manzer, was an economy based on small units of production in which workers owned their own means of production and were driven by strong senses of competitive individualism in their pursuits of resource exploitation. The Canadian state's role in the appropriative period was to facilitate "access to natural resources" and encourage or direct "human effort toward their exploitation." Construction of transportation infrastructure (roads, railroads, canals, ports) to facilitate access to already-existing natural resources and marketing of the resulting products was the most tangible of the state's roles during this period.

The appropriative period, in Manzer's estimation, lasted until approximately 1900, when the state shifted to a capital accumulation strategy. Business activity that was based upon capital-intensive—as opposed to labor-intensive appropriative—means of production was now encouraged and supported. The start-up costs of these types of businesses were much higher than those of appropriative businesses, but their efficiency, productivity, and international competitiveness were much greater. This shift, according to Manzer, has been accompanied by three important consequences for the social organization of production.

> First, ownership and control of capital is progressively concentrated in the hands of a relatively small entrepreneurial class, and workers become dependent on capitalists to supply the means of their productive employment. Second, small individual business enterprise is displaced by large corporate business enterprise and the organization environment for work is progressively bureaucratized. Third, both the expansion of business enterprise and the dependency of bureaucratized workers necessitate the development of mass markets and the progressive replacement of production for personal consumption by production for mass consumption.[1]

Manzer's description of the two stages of Canadian development could as easily be applied to the United States' economic history, where small business activity has been progressively displaced in the twentieth century so that it occupies today no more than a marginal position in the economy. As late as 1880, 36.9 percent of the labor force owned their own businesses. Most were farm owners, followed by owners of commercial establishments, workshops, and professional practices. By 1920, the proportion of self-employed had slipped to 23.5 percent—similar to that of Mexico today—and the decline has progressed steadily since to just 9 percent in 1990.[2] In a parallel fashion, as small business ownership declined, corporations and governmental economic activities increased. Most of the markets formerly serviced by small businesses are now controlled by large private corporations. State-organized economic activities have also increased dramatically in the last hundred years. At the time of the Civil War public employees where a very small part of the labor force. By 1970 as much as one-third of the labor force was employed by the state either directly as civil servants, teachers, soldiers, and the like or indirectly as employees of private businesses that were financed by state contracts.[3]

There have also been sweeping changes in the capitalist character of the economy. The period following the Civil War was one in which many different corporations fought for control of particular markets. The logical outgrowth of this intense struggle was the elimination of weaker by stronger competitors such that most markets shifted toward oligopolistic control. Blair concluded that by 1970 two-thirds of all local and national markets were dominated in the United States, that is, that the largest eight firms operating in those markets accounted for at least 50 percent of sales.[4]

As the power and control of large corporations have grown, so too has the international expansion of their activities. Before 1900 the vast majority of private corporate activity took place within the confines of the country. Today, a significant component of the activities of virtually all large U.S. corporations takes place outside the country. Foreign activity has thus significantly supplemented domestic activity.

In the nineteenth century, most corporations were identified with single families. Today, control of corporations has diversified among many families through stock sales. Similarly, wealthy families have diversified their stock holdings among many different corporations. Thus there has been a shift largely from family to class control of corporations.

However, the same shift, or at least the same degree of shift, from an appropriative to a capital accumulation economy does not apply to Mexico, where small business activity continues to be very significant mainstay of total business activity. A full quarter of the Mexican labor force, as will be discussed presently, continues to be made up of independent business owners—the vast majority of whom own micro-sized farms and shops—compared to less than 10 percent in either Canada or the United States. If, following Manzer's account, economic development has proceeded on a continuum from one pole characterized by appropriative, small, and labor-intensive businesses to another pole characterized by large capital-intensive businesses, then the Mexican economy remains significantly closer to the former pole than either the Canadian or the U.S. economy.

One example will suffice to demonstrate the different timing of the stages of Mexican economic history. In 1917, at the conclusion of the major phase of the Mexican Revolution, the Carranza government instituted an agrarian reform program that over the next several decades distributed small parcels of land to thousands of peasants. In 1917, by contrast, the period of small farm expansion had long since been over in Canada and the United States, and ownership of farmland was beginning to be concentrated in fewer hands. In other words, at the very time that the Canadian and U.S. governments were pursuing development strategies that discouraged appropriative small-scale labor-intensive business activities, the Mexican government was attempting to promote them. The Mexican appropriative strategy conformed to what had been promoted north of the border, but a century earlier and in different international economic conditions.

The Mexican agrarian reform program was contained in Article 27 of the 1917 Constitution, which mandated the distribution of land to the landless, thereby creating over the next decades thousands of small landholders, and the creation of *ejidos* or rural communal organizations that held land which could not be sold.

The original designers of Article 27 made *ejido* land nonalienable (that is, forbade its sale) in order solve a classic peasant problem. In almost all agrarian conditions small landowners must take out loans to finance their operations, often putting up their land as collateral. When enough expected returns to retire their loans do not materialize, they forfeit their lands. The nonalienability of *ejido* land thus provided a fail-safe protection to the *ejitario*. No matter how badly he fared economically, at least the land—his essential means of production—remained secure.

Roger Bartra, in his 1970s study of the Mexican countryside, concluded that the *ejido* and land-distribution programs, especially during the Cárdenas period of the 1930s, because they impeded land concentration, were economically irrational from the point of view of capitalist developmental needs. But they were politically rational from the point of view of the state's need to build a base of peasant political support. In his words, "Today's bourgeoisie pays a high price for the radical bourgeois populism of the 1930's; of course, it gained something else that was priceless: the famous political stability of the Mexican system."[5]

The chapter on appropriative agrarian policies was only ended in 1991, when Mexican President Carlos Salinas de Gortari delivered a double blow against the 1917 agrarian reform by sponsoring legislation to rewrite Article 27 to formally end the distribution of new land to the landless and allow sale of *ejido* land.[6] The opposition press was quick to dub the president's reforms as the "counter agrarian reform." The only possible explanation why the Salinas administration dared to touch what had been previously untouchable in Mexican politics was that it felt secure enough to sacrifice political capital in order to achieve an economic goal: removing one of the remaining obstacles to the concentration of capital in the country. The president in fact proposed the constitutional reform only after his ruling Partido Revolucionario Institucional (PRI) had two months earlier won a sweeping victory in legislative elections.

Accumulation of capital parallels and facilitates technological development. A country's economy technologically develops through agricultural, industrial, and postindustrial stages. In the first stage, the majority of the labor force is absorbed in agricultural and associated primary sector activities (fishing and mining). In the second stage, as farmers become more productive, proportionately fewer of them are needed to feed the country, thereby releasing workers from the countryside who are now available for urban manufacturing and industrial employment. In the third stage, labor-saving technological advances in industry decrease the need for factory workers. This postindustrial stage is marked by tertiary service employment absorbing the majority of the labor force. There are thus two great shifts in labor force distribution in economic development: from farms to factories and from factories to services.

Both shifts have occurred in the United States and Canada, but not yet in Mexico. For the first century of the existence of the United States, farming absorbed the majority of its labor force. In 1800, the earliest year for which labor force statistics exist, three-quarters of the labor force was on farms.[7] As agriculture became more productive and capital intensive, surplus countryside labor shifted to urban factories. In New England in the 1830s and 1840s textile mills started up with labor forces made up mostly of young women who had grown up on farms. Manufacturing activities grew in fits and spurts up through the 1861–65 Civil War and then accelerated dramatically in its aftermath. Farming and other primary sector activities, though, still continued to absorb the majority of the labor force up through 1880. The 1880–90 decade was the first decade in which the United States could be properly described as an industrial society in the sense that agriculture and other primary sector activities no longer absorbed the majority of its labor force. Farming continued to account for the largest part—but no longer the majority—of labor force employment. In the industrial period (1890–1920), the majority of the labor force was absorbed in agricultural and industrial employment. The 1920–30 decade brought to a close the properly industrial period as the current postindustrial labor force pattern set in with the majority of workers beginning to be engaged in producing services in offices, hospitals, restaurants, schools, and other locations rather than physical goods on farms or in factories. The distribution of Canada's labor force went through similar historical changes that occurred relatively soon after those of its southern neighbor. The distribution of the Mexican labor force, though, has not yet fully gone through these stages. Today, less than 30 percent of the U.S. or Canadian—compared to over half the Mexican—labor force continues to be absorbed in primary agricultural or secondary industrial activities.

OBSTACLES TO INDUSTRIAL CAPITALIST DEVELOPMENT

That there have been different rates of accumulation of capital and technological change in North America seems apparent enough. Why those rates
have been different is not as apparent. In large part they have been different
because the countries of North America have faced different historical obstacles in the paths of capitalist and industrial development. Put differently, capitalist development requires rationalization in terms of its own logic through
the progressive removal of noncapitalist structural and cultural obstacles in
its path. Canada and the United States have been much more successful in removing those obstacles than has Mexico, in part because their obstacles have
been less formidable.

The United States

To a certain degree the economic history of the United States is a result
of the pure logic of economic development. But that logic could not have progressed as it did had it not been accompanied by at least three key historical
events and processes that resulted in the removal of obstacles to its development: the elimination of Indian resistance, the conquest of the Southwest, and
the northern victory in the Civil War.

The European colonists who came to the East Coast of what was to become the United States brought with them the attitudes of early capitalist development. The Europe that they left was in the late stages of its economic
transition from medieval feudalism to capitalism. When they arrived, they encountered sparse populations of indigenous peoples with communal modes of
production that were distinctly different from either feudalism or capitalism.
The Indians were mostly hunters and gatherers with no concept of private
property. Two different economic and social ways of life were thus set against
each other.

The colonists immediately sought land to develop into farms. In order
to achieve such a farming toehold on the continent, they had to, in one way
or another, push the indigenous peoples back from the shore lands. This push
immediately triggered resistance, touching off a series of coastal wars. By the
eve of the War of Independence, Indian resistance in the thirteen colonies had
been practically eliminated. But with more land-hungry settlers continually
arriving and with the most fertile lands already claimed, pressure mounted for
further expansion westward. The British colonial authorities, though, had negotiated a series of treaties with Indian tribes that limited further westward
expansion of the colonies. This was one of the background grievances of the

colonists that set off the War of Independence. After the War of Independence the new United States military was mainly preoccupied for the next eight decades, apart from the 1812 and Mexican wars, with pushing Indians westward in order to free up their lands for European settlement and market-oriented farming.

The Indian thus was always marginalized in U.S. history. Unlike in Mexico where the Spanish colonists encountered relatively densely populated areas, the labor of whose people they sought to exploit, in the United States there was virtually no attempt to exploit Indian labor. The only thing that the colonists wanted from the Indians was their land. The violent expropriation and appropriation of that land was the original condition for the economic development of what would become the United States.

By the third decade of the nineteenth century, Indian resistance had been largely eliminated east of the Mississippi. To the west lay a vast, though sparsely populated and lightly defended, territory belonging to Mexico. Increasingly in the 1820s and 1830s southern planters eyed Texas for expansion of the slave system. East Texas was geographically identical to Louisiana and thus suitable for growing cotton, the South's major cash crop. Increasing world demand for cotton, associated with the growing textile industries in England and the North, and soil exhaustion of some plantation lands already in production stimulated the need to find new fields. But Texas was a part of Mexico, which shortly after independence illegalized slavery. Texas presented an additional problem for the Southern planters. Because it bordered the slave South, it was a destination and safe haven for runaway slaves.

Shortly after Mexico achieved its independence from Spain in 1821, Anglo settlers, with permission from the new Mexican authorities, began moving into Mexico's northern territory of Texas. Most of these settlers came from the contiguous slave South. The Mexican authorities granted permission for them to settle because they saw in them a stabilizing force against Indians. From 1821 to 1836, some 35,000 United States citizens entered Texas and quickly outnumbered Mexicans ten to one.[8] They also brought their slaves with them and established plantations. By the fall of 1825, there were 443 slaves and 1,800 whites in Stephen Austin's colony.[9]

The Texas War of Independence broke out in 1836, and the Anglos, 75 percent of whom were from the South,[10] with help from other Anglos who streamed in mainly from the southern states, were quickly victorious. Mexico, still militarily weak after its grueling war of independence, was unable to hold onto its northern territory. The loss of Texas followed a pattern that has been often witnessed in world history. After revolutions, new governments often find that they are unable to defend border areas that are desired by powerful neighbors.[11]

One of the first acts of the new Texas government was to legalize slavery. The importance of slavery in the economy that the early Anglo settlers established in Texas is obvious from its first census as a state of the United States in 1847, which showed 38,753 slaves and 102,961 whites.[12] There was one slave for every three whites. It is thus no accident that today the overwhelming majority of Texas's black population lives in the eastern portion of the state, where in the 1820s to 1850s a slave economy was established on lands geographically contiguous and climatically similar to the original slave South.

When Mexico found itself obliged to grant independence to Texas, it did so with the understanding that Texas would remain an independent country, as a kind of buffer zone between itself and the United States. Unresolved was the actual border of the new republic. The Texan and U.S. governments recognized the Rio Grande, while Mexico recognized the Nueces River, 150 miles to its north, as the border. Between the Nueces and Rio Grande rivers lay a river valley that was potentially one of the most agriculturally productive in North America. The value of what today is called the Valley in Texas was well known at the time. Whether its produce would flow northward or southward depended on which country controlled it, and that was the vital issue that underlay the border dispute.

The Texas Republic lasted until 1845 when it was annexed, with the agreement of the Texas authorities and in violation of the understanding with Mexico, by the United States. The United States then claimed the Rio Grande as the border and sent troops to make good the claim. The U.S. troops marched across the Valley, fought a series of minor skirmishes, and made it to the Rio Grande, where Brownsville, Texas, is today, by early 1846. There they fought their first major battle with Mexican troops and were successful. They pushed southward and within months occupied Mexico City. They remained in Mexico City until 1848, when in return for their withdrawal, Mexico was obliged to sell for a token sum the rest of what today is the Southwest of the United States.

Among the historical consequences of these events was the transformation of Mexicans living in the Southwest into a minority living in the United States. The problematic nature of their new status in the eyes of their dominators was indicated by Stephen Austin, the namesake of Texas's capital city, who had earlier explained the Texas War of Independence as having been "a war of barbarism and of despotic principles, waged by the mongrel Spanish-Indian and Negro race, against civilization and the Anglo-American race."[13] The subsequent decades would see considerable violence between Anglos and Mexicans in the Southwest as the former moved into dominating positions and took over the land of the latter in New Mexico, California, and other territories and states.

The Southwest that was taken from Mexico amounted to some 814,145 square miles and now encompasses all of New Mexico, California, Nevada, Utah, Arizona, most of Texas, half of Colorado, and small portions of Oklahoma, Kansas, and Wyoming.[14] It represented more than half of Mexico's previously existing territory.

How instrumental was and is this area to the economy of the United States? In 1980 approximately 44 percent of the mining and 22.5 percent of the total gross national product of the United States were produced there.[15] If those products were a part of the Mexican rather than United States economy, the economic differences between the two countries would be considerably less. The objection can be made that even if the Southwest had remained with Mexico, Mexico would not have been in the position to develop it to the degree that the United States did. Nevertheless, even if that were the case, the United States still would not have been able to develop anywhere near the economic power that it has today, and its average standard of living would not have been so much higher than that of Mexico. One only has to think what United States economic development would have been without Texas oil, New Mexico and Arizona copper, the southwestern cattle industry, and California gold and agriculture.

The United States in the 1850s now controlled the land on which forty-eight of its fifty states existed or would be formed. Its external borders were essentially in place. But the internal contradiction between a growing industrial capitalism based on free wage labor in the North and plantation capitalism based on slave labor in the South was coming to a head. The issue was not so much the morality of slavery—though moral concerns fired the ire of the northern abolitionist movement—as it was the purely economic interests of the two different systems. Slave and wage labor capitalism had complemented each other during the early decades of the nineteenth century. Slaves toiled in southern fields to produce cotton that was spun and woven into textiles in English and northern factories. Northern and southern elites had joined together to wrest independence from the British.

By the 1850s, however, the interests of the two elites were diverging. The North was expanding the infrastructure for the marketing of its products and wanted to use the federal government to finance the construction of the railroad to the west coast. It wanted preferential access to southern raw materials and tariffs to protect its resulting products from foreign, especially English, competition. The South had little interest in financing a railroad to California because its raw materials went mostly east to be shipped to England and secondarily northward. The South with no industries to protect did not favor tariffs, which would only make its imports more costly. The South seceded when it lost control over the direction of federal policy. The North saw the southern territory as an integral part of the country's economic destiny. Loss of it would severely weaken its own developmental prospects.

The nation's most costly war in lives broke out in 1861. The northern victory settled the issue, and the United States embarked upon its most ambitious period of industrialization with the active support of the federal government. The Civil War removed the final obstacle, the slavocracy, in the path of the full industrial development of the United States. After the war, the United States was able to industrialize rapidly and become a world power by the next century.

It had taken two nineteenth-century acts of force parallel to the expropriation of Indian land to prepare the terrain for the emergence of the United States as a world industrial power—one directed against Mexico and the other against the southern slavocracy. In sum, the acquisitions through conquest of Indian and Mexican lands removed two key spatial obstacles to the development of what was to become the U.S. economy, and the northern victory in the Civil War removed the agrarian slave system that had been an organizational obstacle to corporate-led industrialization.

Canada

What is striking about Canadian economic history is its relative absence of obstacles to capitalist development. There were problems to be overcome, but none as formidable as those that confronted the United States. No war of independence was required to allow a domestic bourgeoisie to accumulate capital. Canada was after all created by the colonial subjects of British North America who did not go along with the War of Independence that created the United States; and its population was significantly increased by loyalists who fled north after the war. Even today Canada retains some colonial, albeit essentially symbolic, ties to England.

The English Crown established the principle that colonist settlement on lands over which Indians had traditionally hunted and gathered should proceed peacefully. In 1763 the Crown proclaimed that Indian lands were to be purchased through treaty negotiations *before* European settlers would be allowed to establish farms on them. At the same time the treaties would divide off nonalienable lands or reserves on which the Indians could continue their traditional hunting and gathering economies. That principle was continued by Canadian authorities after the British North America Act established home rule in 1867.

In the area that became the United States, however, the Crown's proclamation was fiercely opposed on the grounds that it kept settlers from acquiring needed lands for farming. The Declaration of Independence cited the

British policy as being oppressive. It was, therefore, logical that in the War of Independence most Indians would side with the British, since, of the Europeans who were fighting each other, they had the most favorable policy. Once the United States had secured its independence, it began its own policies of acquiring Indian lands through conquest and pushing Indians westward.

In the areas that became Canada, though, the more peaceful British policy of acquiring lands through treaty and purchase continued. As Canada expanded from east to west in the nineteenth century, its new territories were occupied relatively peacefully. Unlike the United States, Canada fought no large-scale wars against Indians. Lipset emphasizes that for that reason and general cultural reasons the Canadian frontier experience was significantly less violent than that of the United States.[16]

Though no civil war was necessary to unleash industrialization as it had been in the United States, in large part capitalist development in Canada proceeded in tandem with that of its southern neighbor, one step behind perhaps, but close enough to travel together into the ranks of the first world by the twentieth century. Canadian development proceeded in tandem with that of the United States because of a historically extremely close integration of the two economies. The vast majority of Canadians have always lived within a short distance of the border. As a result, much Canadian economic activity is oriented toward the United States, with the cities of Boston, New York, Buffalo, Detroit, Chicago, Minneapolis-St. Paul, Seattle, and Portland acting as economic and metropolitan hubs. Friedrich Engels visited Canada in 1888 and was struck by how alike it was to the United States. Engels viewed the border between the two countries as artificial and "ridiculous," even assuming that it would soon vanish because Canadians would want to be annexed by their more economically vigorous southern neighbor.[17] Though Canada was not annexed, its economic development was inevitably pulled along by United States economic developments. In this sense Canadian capitalist development directly benefited from the nineteenth-century removal of obstacles to capitalist development in the United States.

Mexico

There have been far more obstacles to capitalist development in Mexico than either of the other two countries. Aside from the current smallholding land tenure system established by the 1910–17 Revolution already mentioned, there have been other deep-seated obstacles. As in the United States, where the development of industrial capitalism in the nineteenth century was significantly slowed by the existence of a slave system in the South, in Mexico noncapitalist economic structures also acted as brakes on capitalist development.

It cannot be emphasized too often that, from the beginning, Mexican history and economic development proceeded differently than those of the United States or Canada because the Spanish, unlike the English, entered a territory that already contained a large population with its own noncapitalist economic institutions. Unlike in the areas to the north, Europeans could not so easily marginalize this population and its inconvenient institutions. There was, in brief, little virgin fertile soil available in which to plant the seeds of capitalist development. After the fall of Tenochtitlán many Indians stayed on the peripheries of the developing semifeudal and capitalist structures. Down to the present time, many Indians have preferred to stay out of the money economy as much as possible. They produce on small plots of land mainly for household consumption and reciprocally call on each other's labor as needed rather than resorting to hiring outsiders.[18]

The hybrid formation of capitalist and feudal features that the colonizers implanted created further problems for future capitalist development. Commodities were produced for, as well as bought on, domestic and world markets. But a significant part of the colonial economy was devoted to non-commodity production (rents, tithes to the church, and goods for household consumption) that was outside of the capitalist market and performed under at least semifeudalistic conditions. The rural economy was dominated by large landed estates in which landlords collected rents from otherwise largely self-sufficient peasants. Much agricultural production, therefore, was oriented toward the landlord's traditional household needs or the support of peasant households. There was little incentive to produce agricultural commodities for sale on open markets.

The church was an important pillar of the semifeudal structure, becoming the largest single institutional holder of land and an important source of credit. The church thus controlled enormous economic assets, but it did not manage those assets according to strictly capitalistic principles. It was more interested in using those assets to advance its spiritual mission. The church thus had the power to orient work and economic activities in general away from narrow ends of profit making and capital accumulation. The visual evidence of the church's enormous economic power during the colonial period is the large number of aesthetically and architecturally impressive churches that remain from that period in Mexico. A small village would devote an enormous amount of voluntary labor to constructing its cathedral. Quite clearly this work was diverted from the accumulation of capital. The accumulation of churches took priority over the accumulation of capital. Nothing similar existed in the British areas, where the Protestant churches were quickly built only to serve their strictly functional purposes of being places to meet and worship. They were not meant to be monuments to the Almighty. Finally, the colonial church mandated a large number of holy days when economic activities were suspended. There were fewer of these in the British areas.

The church's economic power was recognized as an obstacle to capitalist development and economic progress in general after independence in 1821. In 1856 the Mexican government took the most important step in curtailing the church's power, issuing the *Ley* Lerdo, which prohibited churches from owning properties not used in their directly religious activities. The struggle between church and state, however, did not end with the Ley Lerdo. The separation of church and state was consolidated in the 1910–17 revolution. The 1917 Constitution forbids church ownership of land and interference in politics, and it even forbids priest and nuns to be dressed as such on public streets. The final blow to church power was delivered in the Cristeros rebellion (1926–29), in which thousands of Catholics, under the cry of "Viva el Cristo Rey," rose up against the Calles government (1926–29) and its radical antireligious policies. The Mexican army defeated the Cristeros in a cruel war. The crushing of the Cristeros rebellion can be interpreted as having been necessary to end church-imposed obstacles to economic development in the same sense that the Civil War in the United States was necessary to remove the slave system as an obstacle to industrial development. But that would be overstating the parallel. The church's economic power had already been broken long before the war broke out. What it still exercised was political power, and that was what Calles sought to and did break. After the defeat of the Cristeros, the church retreated completely from Mexican politics.

If in U.S. history the logic of capitalist development always won and in Canadian history the logic of capitalist development moved forward without major impediments, in Mexican history the logic of capitalist development always had to accommodate itself to pre-Hispanic forms of organization and Spanish semifeudalism. In addition, its future economic development was further severely constrained when it lost its northern territories, which proved to be the most valuable, to the United States.

CAPITAL AND LABOR

The history of uneven development of North America's economies is nowhere more evident than in how capital and labor—the essential components of any economy around which class structures conform—are currently distributed within each of the economies.

As market societies develop, capital and business ownership in general become concentrated in fewer hands. Corporate and state ownership of means of production increasingly outcompete and drive out of the market independent farms, stores, workshops, and the like. This process has proceeded the furthest in the United States, resulting in a much greater concentration of private business ownership than in the other two countries. In the United States, after the Civil War, severe market competition from the owners of large farms and mounting debts forced successive waves of small farmers off the land. As a long-term result, by 1990 the average size of farms had grown greatly as the proportion of farm owners in the labor force shrank to less than 3 percent.[19] In a parallel fashion, competition from medium-size and large nonfarm corporations drove waves of nonfarm small businesses out of the market in such proportions that by 1991 only 9 percent of the labor force received its income from business ownership of any type.[20]

In Mexico, the historical process of concentration of business ownership has been somewhat retarded for a number of reasons. One of the largest reasons, as mentioned previously, was a direct consequence of the Mexican revolution. Since 1917 every Mexican government, with varying degrees of commitment and enthusiasm, has found itself politically obliged to maintain at least partially the interests of small landowners and *ejidarios* in the face of competition from larger owners. Government policies, by creating and guaranteeing the survival of *minifundios*, have retarded the process of land concentration and accumulation of capital in the countryside in large part to insure the political loyalty of the peasantry.[21] Thus, while over 50 percent of the land is in farms of more than 1,000 hectares (2,200 acres), over half of the farms, nearly two million, have less than 5 hectares (11 acres), reflecting the classic *latifundio-minifundio* pattern of Latin American land tenure.[22] In the United States, by way of contrast, the median farm size is greater than 100 acres. Only 188,000 farms in the United States, less than 10 percent of all farms, have less than 10 acres of land[23]—compared to the nearly two million in Mexico, whose population is only one-third that of the United States. As a whole, more than one-quarter of the Mexican labor force continues to operate farm and nonfarm independent businesses,[24] three times as high as the proportion in the United States and four times as that in Canada. Thus, in Mexico, small peasant farms dot large parts of the countryside, and small businesses and self-employed *ambulantes* (itinerants) crowd urban streets. While small farms and urban businesses continue to exist in the United States and Canada, they are not nearly as omnipresent as they are in Mexico.

A comparative examination of how capital income (that is, income generated from ownership of stocks, bonds, real estate, and businesses) is distributed in the populations of each of the three countries is somewhat revealing (see Table 4–1).[25] As expected, the poorest 20 percent receive proportionately the greatest amount of income from profits in Mexico because of the relatively large number of surviving micro and small businesses in that economy. At the other extreme, the richest 20 percent receive the greatest share in the United States. Calculation of Gini indexes allows us to rank the countries' distributions in terms of degrees of inequality. The indexes range between 0 and 1, with 0 expressing a situation of perfect equality in which all strata—quintiles in these distributions—receive equal amounts of income and 1 representing perfect inequality in which the top strata receives all of the income.[26] These indicate that capital income is significantly more unequally distributed in the United States than in Mexico or Canada.

How capital is distributed, both in the vertical sense of how it is concentrated and in the spatial sense of where it geographically exists, influences the distribution of workforces and populations in general. If capital becomes increasingly concentrated in large corporations rather than small businesses, greater proportions of labor forces become employees of those corporations. Where capital is spatially located influences demographic patterns. People generally move to where jobs are. If the balance of capital investment within a country shifts from the countryside to urban locations, the distribution of the workforce will follow accordingly. When corporations move their workplaces from one region to another, they also move their workforces.

The most generic and commonly accepted definition of a labor force or workforce is that it includes all of the people who are actively engaged in the

TABLE 4–1   Distributions of Capital Income

	UNITED STATES	CANADA	MEXICO
Poorest 20 percent	2.8	2.8	4.9
Second 20 percent	5.7	7.9	6.6
Third 20 percent	7.3	13.1	9.6
Fourth 20 percent	10.1	15.8	14.5
Richest 20 percent	74.1	60.4	64.4
Total	100.0	100.0	100.0
Richest 10 percent	49.3	50.5	51.9
Gini index	0.588	0.492	0.508
Year	1987	1990	1989

Note: Distributions of capital income were measured according to income received from interest, dividends, business profits, capital sales, rent, estates, and trust funds.

Sources: Calculated from U.S. Internal Revenue Service, Statistics of Income Division, *Individual Income Tax Returns,* 1987 (Washington, DC: U.S. Government Printing Office, 1990), p. 9; Revenue Canada, *Taxation Statistics* (Ottawa: Minister of Supply and Services Canada, 1992), Table 2; and Instituto Nacional de Estadística Geografía e Informática (INEGI), *Encuesta Nacional de Ingresos de los Hogares, 1989* (Aguascalientes: INEGI, 1992).

production of goods or services within a region, country, or some other unit.[27] The structural compositions of North America's labor forces differ dramatically in large part because of the different stages of capital accumulation and distributions of capital in the three countries.[28] In general, the structural distributions of the labor forces of the United States and Canada arc very similar and reflect their first world stages of development, while that of Mexico is very different and reflects its third world stage of development.

The most dramatic difference between the labor force of Mexico and those of its first world neighbors is the larger number, in relative terms, of small business owners and, consequently, the smaller number of wage and salary workers that it has. As mentioned earlier, more than a quarter (26.6 percent) of Mexican labor force members draw their main income from business profits compared to just 9 percent in the United States and 6.5 percent in Canada. With a population only one-third the size, Mexico has almost as many self-employed persons as the United States.

The self-employed in all three countries are highly stratified, ranging from extremely poor street vendors to billionaire capitalist owners. But Mexico's self-employed are much more likely to have only micro-sized businesses and be poor than their U.S. or Canadian counterparts. The vast majority of the Mexican self-employed (86.5 percent) operate businesses that are too small to have any paid employees.[29] In contrast, nearly 80 percent of the businesses of the self-employed in the United States are large enough to have paid employees.[30]

A substantial part of the Mexican self-employed population is made up of itinerants who peddle their wares or services from place to place. The existence of this very large floating labor force reflects two facets of Mexican underdevelopment. First, there has not been a sufficient accumulation of either private or public capital to create enough regular paying jobs to absorb them. Second, there is little or no public assistance or welfare to serve as an alternative source of income for the part of the labor force that cannot find regular employment. Many members of this itinerant population prefer to work as employees when and for as long as such regular jobs in the formal labor force can be found. When they cannot find jobs, they must hustle livelihoods as best they can as itinerant peddlers of goods and services. It is typical for a worker to be laid off, be unemployed for a period, and then start some type of itinerant business in order to generate an income. The business will then be abandoned if a better paying position as an employee opens up. There is also a substantial part of the itinerant population that earns an income higher than the low average wages prevailing in Mexico and thus prefers to remain in that position. These itinerants constitute a lumpen bourgeoisie. They are bourgeois by virtue of being owners of independent businesses but lumpen (from the German for "rag") by virtue of their businesses being so small. Their massive numbers reflect structural conditions in the nature of Mexican capitalism that are different, at least in degree, from those of the United States.

Of course, somewhat similar itinerant sellers exist in large U.S. cities such as Washington, New York, and Los Angeles, and the growing existence of weekend flea markets indicates that many people are at least part-time itinerants, but the significance of itinerancy is not nearly as great as in Mexico. Itinerant sellers are one of the largest components of the Mexican labor force. In the contemporary United States they are a distinctly marginal phenomenon. But they were not always marginal. In the late nineteenth and early twentieth centuries, many neighborhoods, especially immigrant neighborhoods, contained street markets and itinerant sellers. The relatively large Mexican itinerant population is thus a reflection of the country's preindustrial stage of development, a stage surpassed in the United States, Canada, and other first world countries decades ago.

Because of the sporadic employment pattern of a substantial part of the Mexican labor force, it is difficult to estimate the true size of unemployment in the country. Whether these itinerants are counted as employed, underemployed, or unemployed greatly affects overall estimates of unemployment in the country. Mexican government statistics, for example, do not count them as unemployed or underemployed, and this policy results in unrealistically low estimates of underemployment. In 1993, when the unemployment rate in the United States was regularly over 7 percent, the Mexican government claimed that its was only 2 percent, a claim that the *New York Times* uncritically reported in its international business statistics.

The relatively large percentage of mainly small—most often micro—business owners in Mexico explains a second difference in labor force compositions. Because there are proportionately so many more family-owned businesses in Mexico than in the United States or Canada, there are more family members working without pay. In Mexico, 2.6 percent of the labor force is made up of unpaid workers, compared to 0.3 percent in the United States and 0.5 percent in Canada. There are thus proportionately more than five times as many unpaid workers in the Mexican labor force. The large part of the labor force accounted for by unpaid workers is a logical consequence of the fact that farming and self-employment are still predominant in the Mexican economy. There is a high correlation between the existence of family small business ownership in a sector and the use of unpaid family labor. Traditionally, the family members, including children, of both farmers and urban small business owners have been called upon to supply labor when hired workers could not be afforded. To the degree that farms and small businesses decrease, as they have in the United States, such opportunities for employment of unpaid family labor decrease.[31]

The relatively large percentage of family business owners and unpaid laborers in the Mexican working population results in part, but not fully, from the fact that agriculture continues to absorb 23.5 percent of the labor force, compared to 2.7 percent in the United States and 4.7 percent in Canada (see Table 4–2). Over half of Mexican small business owners are farmers. But, as any citizen of or visitor to Mexico knows, the nation's urban streets and markets are also filled with small businesses—family-owned stores, restaurants, repair shops, and workshops for the most part. And significant numbers of independent itinerants peddle their goods or services from place to place—or subway car to subway car in the case of merchants who work the Metro. Mexicans are more likely to eat out in thousands and thousands of small independently owned family restaurants than chain operations such as McDonald's (which exists in Mexico but is not as omnipresent as in the United States).

TABLE 4–2   Structures of the Labor Forces

	MEXICO Number (percent)		UNITED STATES Number (percent)		CANADA Number (percent)	
A. By Classes of Activities						
Self-employed	6,001	(26.6)	10,491	(9.0)	928	(6.5)
Paid employees	15,936	(70.8)	106,288	(90.8)	13,227	(93.0)
Unpaid employees	587	(2.6)	331	(0.3)	66	(0.5)
Total	22,524	(100.0)	117,110	(100.1)	14,221	(100.0)
B. By Sectors of Activities						
Agriculture	5,300	(23.5)	3,181	(2.7)	675	(4.7)
Mining	261	(1.2)	697	(0.6)	192	(1.4)
Industry	4,493	(19.9)	20,368	(17.4)	2,084	(14.7)
Construction	1,595	(7.1)	6,955	(5.9)	933	(6.6)
Commerce	3,108	(13.8)	24,491	(20.9)	2,445	(17.2)
Transportation, utilities	1,200	(5.3)	8,289	(7.1)	1,061	(7.5)
Finances	360	(1.6)	7,646	(6.5)	810	(5.7)
Services	6,282	(27.8)	45,483	(38.9)	6,021	(42.3)
Total	22,599	(100.2)	117,110	(100.0)	14,221	(100.1)
Year	1990		1988		1991	

Notes: In thousands and excluding unemployed members. Percentages may not add up to 100 because of rounding.

Sources: Calculated on the basis of information from Instituto Nacional de Estadística Geografía e Informática (INEGI), *XI Censo General de Población y Vivienda, 1990* (Aguascalientes: INEGI, 1992); U.S. Department of Labor, Bureau of Labor Statistics, *Employment and Earnings,* vol. 38, no. 12, December 1991, Tables A–24 and A–25; and Statistics Canada, *Industry and Class of Worker,* 1991 Census (Ottawa: Minister of Industry, Science and Technology Canada, 1991), Tables 1 and 2.

They have their mufflers repaired or replaced in independent curbside shops rather than Midas-type franchises. They buy their clothes off of impromptu rods in market stalls rather than in department stores.

As is well known, Mexican labor is cheap compared to United States and Canadian labor. Calculations from the two most recent surveys of the Mexican labor force offer different estimates of income averages, but both are significantly lower than those prevailing in the United States and Canada. According to figures from the Mexican census, the median weekly income of the labor force in 1990 was $40.[32] According to the national survey of households, the median income of the labor force in 1989 was $25, and its mean income was $42.[33] Median incomes in Canada and the United States are at least ten times as high as the Mexican median. That difference, though, does not mean that the differences in standards of living are as severe. Substantial parts of the Mexican labor force receive forms of income that do not appear in the census estimations. Undoubtedly the one-quarter of the Mexican labor force that is self-employed underreports its income to avoid taxes. Many of those who are employees receive forms of nonmonetary income such as free medical care, subsidized loans for purchasing houses at below-market rates, and coupons that can be exchanged for food. While there is no question that the standard of living of the Mexican labor force is, on the average, much lower than those of the United States and Canadian labor forces, it is not as different as the disproportions in direct monetary incomes reported in official statistics would seem to indicate.

The current distribution of the Mexican labor force bears a resemblance to that of the United States in the 1920s before the full brunt of industrialization, monopolization, and urbanization had set in. In 1920, for example, 28.9 percent of the United States labor force was still occupied in primary-sector agricultural and mining activities, a figure which is close to what exists today in Mexico.[34] Correspondingly, small family-owned businesses lined and, in some cases, filled urban streets in the United States and Canada, as they do today in Mexico. The great difference is that the United States with that labor force distribution in the 1920s was still a rich society by world standards, but Mexico today with the same distribution is a poor society.

CONCLUSIONS

From the time of the implantations of European colonial rule with their particular class and racial structures to the present, the North American societies developed unevenly. The United States and Canada became first world and prosperous, while Mexico became third world and poor. This uneven development can be demonstrated and examined in three different ways.

First, North American economic development has moved in a continuum between appropriative and capital accumulation strategies. In the former, laborers use already-existing natural resources (land, forests, fish-bearing waters) to produce commodities for sale. This appropriative stage can also be referred to as simple commodity production. This type of economic activity takes place in small-scale units where the laborers have direct control over their means of production. In the latter strategy, economic activity is based on investments of accumulated capital and is organized in larger units in which laborers are employees who do not have control over the means of production. The U.S. and Canadian economies, in this respect, shifted to capital accumulation stages much earlier than did the Mexican economy; and, today, in the United States and Canada a much greater share of economic activity takes place within large units of production than in Mexico.

Second, economies progressively develop through agricultural, industrial, and postindustrial technological stages. In the agricultural stage, most of the labor force is absorbed in farming. As farming becomes more productive, laborers leave farms for urban factories. As industries become more productive, workers then shift into services. In this respect, the Canadian and U.S. labor forces evidence postindustrial patterns of development, but the Mexican labor force evidences that it has not completely advanced out of the agricultural stage of technological development.

Third, the specifically capitalist development of a country occurs through the progressive removal of obstacles to its internal developmental logic. In North America, the indigenous peoples and their forms of economic organization, semifeudalism, and southern slavery have been obstacles to capitalist development. In addition, the United States was able to significantly advance its own capitalist development by removing the obstacle of Mexican control of the Southwest. In comparing Mexico, the United States, and Canada in this respect, it is clear that Mexico has faced more formidable obstacles to capitalist development than either of the other countries.

The notion of uneven national economic development, although of paramount significance, should not obscure the reality of uneven development within countries. There are high and low capitalist circuits and rich and poor within as well as between the countries.

The history of uneven development of North America's economies has resulted in remarkably similar distributions of labor forces in the United States and Canada, both of which are markedly dissimilar from the distribution of the Mexican labor force. At the same time, the rate of concentration of distribution of capital income is more similar between Canada and Mexico than between either one and the United States. The configurations of the U.S. and Canadian labor forces largely conform to economies with more advanced accumulations of capital that are at the postindustrial technological stage of development, while the configuration of the Mexican labor force conforms to an appropriative economy that is largely at the agricultural technological stage of development. The greatest difference in the labor force configurations is that agricultural activities still absorb a substantial part (23.5 percent) of the Mexican labor force, while they absorb less than 3 percent in the United States and less than 5 percent in Canada. The second greatest difference is that the Mexican labor force contains proportionately three times as many self-employed members as do those of the United States and Canada. Finally, because small family businesses continue to occupy a substantial part of the Mexican economic structure whereas they no longer do in the United States or Canada, there are relatively more unpaid, usually family, laborers in Mexico than in the United States or Canada. In sum, the Mexican labor force, compared to that of the United States and Canada, has a much greater proportion of its members working in agriculture and a much greater proportion of its members who draw their incomes from independent small business ownership.[35]

An increase in agricultural productivity utilizing labor-saving innovations that would result in the need for fewer agricultural workers is thus a critical hurdle still to be cleared in the development of the Mexican economy. The obvious problem confronting Mexico, therefore, is how to release labor from the countryside into desirable jobs as opposed to massive unemployment, which would increase even more the economic misery of the rural masses and most likely ignite severe social unrest. Mexico is thus caught between an anachronistic present that maintains the majority of the rural population in misery and a future that could be even worse. Present agricultural institutional arrangements only work in the respect that any tampering with them, such as the reform of Article 27 of the Mexican constitution described previously, could produce an even worse situation.

If we follow the technological mode of classification,[36] then we would have to conclude that Mexico remains an essentially agricultural society because agricultural activity absorbs the largest part of its labor force, while the United States and Canada are postindustrial societies in the sense that services now absorb by far the largest parts of their labor forces.

The proportion of the Mexican labor force employed in industry (17.1 percent) is deceptively similar to the proportions similarly employed in the United States and Canada. It is deceptively similar because substantially fewer of these members than in the United States or Canada are fully industrial, with substantially more remaining manufacturing workers. The difference is that industrial workers use power-driven machines as tools while *man-u*facturing workers use hand tools. Much of Mexican production is still accomplished with hand tools and is thus preindustrial.

For the Mexican labor force structure to approximate that of the United States and Canada, two great related changes would have to occur. First, there would have to be a tremendous shift from agricultural to industrial employment. Indeed, peasants have left the countryside over the past several decades in search of better opportunities in urban areas, thus reducing the proportion of agricultural laborers in the labor force. But, what is problematic is that more of these former peasants are finding work in tertiary service than industrial occupations. Second, there would have to be a massive accumulation of capital in the country capable of developing enough reasonably well paying positions to absorb both laborers shifting out of agriculture and much of the currently itinerant self-employed population.

✳ CHAPTER 5

Contemporary Classes

The contemporary labor forces of North America are divided into the *economic* classes of workers, small business owners, new middle-class professionals and managers, capitalist owners, and—to a very small extent and only in Mexico—peasants. At the same time, the populations of North America are divided into lower, working, middle, and upper *social* classes. If economic classes are based upon shared positions or roles within labor forces, social classes are made up of families and individuals who share the same general standards of living within populations. Clearly there is some correspondence between economic and social class positions, but it is far from a complete correspondence. While the source of virtually all upper-class income is capital ownership, social middle-class incomes, for example, can come from prosperous working-class or new middle-class professional or managerial positions.

ECONOMIC CLASSES

Given Mexico's significantly lower level of economic development compared to the United States or Canada, which is reflected in the configuration of the Mexican labor force, it is not surprising that Mexico would have an economic class profile that is also significantly different from that of the continent's first world countries. Uneven development produces different economic class profiles, as well as different labor force bases from which they arise.

The labor forces of market societies are classified in official statistics, as we saw in Chapter 4, into the general "classes of activities" of the self-employed, the employed, and unpaid employees. Though official statistics clearly separate these categories, they do not distinguish economic classes within them. Therefore, in order to estimate proportionate sizes of economic classes in labor forces, it is necessary to employ operational definitions for each of the classes and regroup official governmental statistics according to those categories.

The self-employed class of activity is made up of the economic classes of capitalists and small business owners in all three countries. In Mexico it also includes peasants. The employee class of activity includes the new middle class (professional and managerial employees) and the working class. Unpaid employees are members of the working class.

The first class of activity to be examined for its division into internal economic classes is the self-employed. For the self-employed economic classes in Mexico, the extremes of capitalists and peasants can first be ferreted out. Once the size of those classes has been determined, it is then a simple matter to consider the remainder of the self-employed to be small business owners. In the cases of Canada and the United States, where peasants no longer exist, once the size of the capitalist class has been estimated, the remainder of the self-employed can be counted as small business owners.

In the most general of terms, what distinguishes a capitalist from a small business owner is that the former is an employer in addition to being an owner, while the latter is not. At what point, though, is a business owner enough of an employer to constitute a capitalist? Clearly an owner with only unpaid family workers or at most a few paid laborers does not constitute a capitalist. Theoretically, we have to conclude that a business owner becomes a capitalist when the majority of his or her income derives from profits made from the labor of employed workers. But, unfortunately, there is no source of information on the exact number of capitalists in any of the North American countries who conform to this definition. Most researchers, therefore, have counted as capitalists those employers who had more than a certain minimum number of employees. Some include as capitalists employers with as few as five employees; others require higher thresholds.

The economic distinction between peasants and other agricultural laborers is that the peasant produces outside the money economy, principally producing for self-consumption rather than market sale. Any member of the agricultural labor force who, along with household members, consumed 50 percent or more of what he or she produced would therefore be a peasant. Such economic peasants continue to exist in Mexico. Riding, for example, without citing evidence, maintains that "around 80 percent of *ejidos* consume almost all of their food production."[1] Unfortunately, though, Mexican government statistics are not categorized in such a manner as to permit estimation of the number of economic peasants in the self-employed fraction of the labor force.

Among the employee classes, what distinguishes a new middle-class member from a worker is that the former occupies a position that requires the exercise of a professional skill or managerial ability for which the employer is willing to pay a significantly higher salary. The new middle class exists in the employment hierarchy between, on the one hand, owners and top managers, and on the other, ordinary workers. In brief, relatively highly paid employed professionals and managers make up the new middle class. For calculation purposes, employed professionals, managers, and supervisors were included as members of the new middle class. Once the size of the new middle class has been estimated, the remainder of paid and unpaid employees in each of the labor forces can then be counted as workers.

With these operational definitions in mind, we can proceed to portray the economic class structures of each of the North American countries.

Estimates of the proportionate size of the capitalist class in the United States vary considerably. Recent estimates have ranged from 1 to 2.1 percent of the population.[2] In order to calculate an estimate for this study I assumed that a labor force member had to have a total yearly income of at least $75,000—over seven times the minimum wage in the United States—to make it into the bottom rungs of the capitalist class. I then calculated on the basis of income tax data[3] the percent of total income accounted for by interest, dividends, rent, profits, and estates (that is, income from capital properties) of all those who received over $75,000 in 1987. This percentage was then multiplied by the total number of income tax returns with total incomes of over $75,000 to estimate the number of capitalists in the labor force. According to this form of estimation, capitalists make up approximately 1 percent of the labor force, which conforms to the minimum estimate cited previously.

Members of the highest stratum of the capitalist class have yearly incomes of more than $1 million. An examination of this stratum is revealing. In 1987, 34,944 returns were filed with million-dollar incomes. Over three-quarters (76 percent) of the income of this stratum came from capital properties (stocks, bonds, business profits, rents, etc.). By far, the largest single source of capital income—some 52.7 percent—for this stratum came from the sale of capital assets. That is, speculation on the rise in value of capital properties remains the largest single source of income for the richest stratum of the labor force in the United States.

Subtracting capitalists from self-employed members yields the estimate that the small business class makes up approximately 7 percent of the labor force (see Table 5–1). Independent professionals, such as physicians and lawyers, represent the largest occupational fraction of small business owners, followed in descending order by craft workers, such as plumbers, electricians, mechanics, and carpenters; storekeepers; farmers; and owners

TABLE 5–1   Economic and Social Class Profiles

	UNITED STATES	CANADA	MEXICO
A. *Economic Classes*			
Capitalist	1.0	1.0	0.2
Small business	7.0	5.4	0.4
New middle	22.4	24.3	7.2
Working	69.6	69.3	66.2
Peasant	—	—	1.5
Total	100.0	100.0	100.0
B. *Social Classes*			
Upper	1.8	1.1	0.5
Middle	24.5	26.5	16.5
Working	60.2	63.7	42.0
Lower	13.5	8.7	41.0
Total	100.0	100.0	100.0

Note: Approximately 45 percent of the Mexican lower class is made up of the urban poor. The remaining 55 percent are peasants.

Sources: Estimates based on data in U.S. Department of Labor, Bureau of Labor Statistics, *Employment and Earnings,* vol. 38, no. 12 (December 1991), Tables A–24 and A–25; U.S. Internal Revenue Service, Statistics of Income Division, *Individual Income Tax Returns, 1987* (Washington, DC: U.S. Government Printing Office, 1990); U.S. Bureau of the Census, *Poverty in the United States, 1991* (Washington, DC: U.S. Government Printing Office, 1992); Statistics Canada, *Employment Income by Occupation,* 1991 Census (Ottawa: Minister of Industry, Science and Technology, 1993), Table 1; Revenue Canada, *Taxation Statistics, 1990* (Ottawa, Minister of Supply and Services Canada, 1992), Table 2; Brigitte Buhmann, Lee Rainwater, Guenther Schmaus, and Timothy M. Smeeding, "Equivalence Scales, Well-Being, Inequality, and Poverty: Sensitivity Estimates across Ten Countries Using the Luxembourg Income Study (LIS) Database," *The Review of Income and Wealth,* series 34, no. 2 (June 1988), pp. 115–142; Instituto Nacional de Estadística Geografía e Informática (INEGI), *Encuesta Nacional de Ingresos de los Hogares, 1989* (Aguascalientes: INEGI, 1992); and Programa Nacional de Solidaridad, *El Combate a La Pobreza* (Mexico City: *El Nacional,* 1990).

of service establishments, such as barber and beauty shops, restaurants, and the like.

Among the employee classes, new middle-class professionals and managers constitute approximately 22.4 percent of the labor force. Managers account for a little more than half of the class and professionals for a little less. The distinction between managers and professionals refers more to position than occupation. That is, many middle- and top-level managers began as professionals and then were promoted into managerial positions. They thus occupationally combine both managerial and professional characteristics in their positions.

The majority, nearly 70 percent, of the labor force is made up of workers. Unskilled and semiskilled workers constitute the largest occupational fraction of the working class, followed in descending order by clerical workers, sales persons, crafts persons, and technicians. If we follow the traditional blue-collar–white-collar distinction, then the majority, 57.3 percent, of the working class is still made up of blue-collar workers. These represent nearly 40 percent of the entire labor force.[4]

In sum, the economic class structure of the United States is made up of 1 percent capitalists, 7 percent small business owners, 22.4 percent new middle-class professionals and managers, and 69.6 percent workers.

Application of the same techniques of estimation to the Canadian labor force reveals the existence of an economic class structure that closely resembles that of the United States—1 percent capitalists, 5.4 percent small business owners, 24.3 percent new middle-class professionals and managers, and 69.3 percent workers. Both of these class structures, though, significantly differ from that of Mexico.

The 1990 Mexican census identified the self-employed members of the labor force but did not provide a clear basis for distinguishing the capitalist, small business, and peasant classes among them. Capitalists, as indicated earlier, have the double identity of being both business owners and employers. In this respect, the census found 535,008 business owners, 2.4 percent of the labor force, who had employees. But it did not subdivide those individuals according to the numbers of their employees. Business owners with as few as one employee were included as employers. It is thus impossible to directly distinguish capitalist from small business employers. In order to estimate the size of the capitalist class, it was necessary to find an indirect manner of distinguishing small business from capitalist employers. The *Encuesta Nacional de Ingresos y Gastos de los Hogares, 1989* (The National Survey of Household Incomes and Expenditures, 1989) distinguished employers according to the amounts of their income.[5] In its highest income category, equivalent to $8,800 a year, it found 180,340 employers. If that were the number of capitalists, it would represent 0.8 percent of the labor force. But we can safely assume that capitalists receive far more income. Unfortunately, though, the official statistics do not distinguish employers who have those higher incomes. At most, capitalists probably represent no more than half of those employers who receive $8,800 a year or more. They therefore make up no more than 0.4 percent of the entire labor force.

The remainder of the self-employed—26.2 percent of the labor force—is made up of the small business and peasant classes. As discussed previously, there is no way to directly estimate the number of these who are peasants. Almost every small farm in Mexico, though, operates on both sides of the line dividing production for household consumption and production for sale, but in different proportions. Most produce the majority of the food that they consume—corn tortillas, beans, eggs, chicken, pork. They sell their surplus products in order to get money needed to buy the items that they cannot or do not wish to produce directly themselves such as clothing, soft drinks, and gasoline. The larger and more prosperous the farm, the less likely that there will be production for household consumption. The national survey of households just cited found that in the poorest two strata of farm households, which represent 3.2 percent of all households, the total value of products produced for self-consumption exceeded monetary income.[6] From those figures, we can hazard a guess that economic peasants—farmers predominately outside of the money economy—probably make up 1.5 percent of the labor force.

The remaining 24.7 percent of the self-employed labor force is made up of small business owners. But that is a very highly stratified class, ranging from itinerant sellers of foods on the streets to owners of fixed places of business. All technically operate profit-oriented small businesses. But the livings that they can derive from them vary greatly. It would be a mistake, therefore, to view small business ownership in Mexico as necessarily conferring a middle-class standard of living or social status.

The categories of the census do allow us to readily identify the proportions of new middle-class and working-class members in the labor force. The new middle class of employed professionals and managers makes up 7.2 percent of the labor force. However, this figure should be treated with caution. Half of the country's professionals are schoolteachers whose very low average wages are not sufficient to afford a socially middle-class standard of living. If we defined new middle-class members to be those who had both an employed professional and managerial position and a middle-class salary, then the size of that class would shrink to no more than 3 to 4 percent of the labor force.

The working class constitutes 66.2 percent of the labor force. Farm laborers make up the largest fraction of the working class (30 percent), followed in order by service (38.9 percent) and factory (31.1 percent) workers.[7]

In sum, the Mexican economic class structure is made up of approximately 0.4 percent capitalists, 24.7 percent small business owners, 7.2 percent new middle-class professionals and managers, 66.2 percent workers, and 1 to 2 percent peasants.

Quite clearly, as in the case of the labor force configurations, there are dramatic differences between the economic class structures of Mexico and those of the United States and Canada. In relative terms, there are significantly more capitalists and new middle-class members in the United States and Canada, while there are more small business owners in Mexico. These differences occur because Mexico is at a different stage of capital accumulation than the United States and Canada. On the one hand, capital accumulation is more advanced in the United States and Canada in the simple sense that quantitatively more of it has been formed, on the basis of which a relatively larger capitalist class can subsist. But capital accumulation is also more advanced in the United States and Canada in the sense that capitalist businesses have been able, as we saw in Chapter 4, to take over greater percentages of economic activity at the expense of small businesses than have their Mexican counterparts. As a result, the small business class continues to control very significant parts of the Mexican economy, while in the United States and Canada most of the professional and managerial skills formerly exercised in small business contexts are now exercised in corporate and state bureaucracies. Put differently, because there is a relatively much smaller accumulation of private capital in Mexico than the United States or Canada, the relative sizes of both the capitalist and new middle classes are correspondingly much smaller. Only 0.4 percent or less of the Mexican labor force are capitalists, compared to 1.0 percent in the United States and Canada, which are proportionately five times as large.

The relatively smaller accumulation of private Mexican capital has meant that there has been less possibility of financing large-scale capitalist businesses, hence the smaller number of capitalists that can be supported. The existence of fewer large-scale businesses has also meant that there are fewer positions for a new middle class of middle-level managers and professionals. They make up only 7.2 percent of the Mexican labor force, compared to 22.4 percent in the United States and 24.3 percent in Canada, over three times as large. Finally, a peasant class—in the economic sense of farmers whose households consume the majority of what they produce, making them largely independent of the market economy—continues to exist in Mexico but not in the United States or Canada. Peasants in this economic sense account for perhaps 1.5 percent of the Mexican labor force. It is a small percentage, but their economic way of life continues as a reminder of a previous precapitalist economic stage through which the first world passed and the third world is passing.[8]

The great difference in the relative sizes of the self-employed components of the labor forces has far-reaching consequences for the economic class profiles of the two countries. The small business class, because of the large number of self-employed in the labor force, is much larger in relative terms in Mexico than the United States or Canada. The capitalist class of large business owners is smaller, though. Large businesses in the United States have been more successful than their Mexican counterparts in monopolizing markets, as is indicated by the relatively small amount of small business activity that continues to exist on the margins of the national economy. As a result of medium- and large-size private and public units monopolizing the economic landscape, over 92 percent of both Canadian and U.S. labor force members are employees. Because large units in Mexico have not absorbed as much of the economic landscape as have those in the United States or Canada, there is relatively more economic space to operate a small business, and consequently a quarter of the labor force is still self-employed. The comparatively high percentage of self-employed workers in the Mexican labor force also affects the profiles of the employee classes, that is, the new middle and working classes. Because of the large number of small businesses in Mexico compared to the United States or Canada, the economic space occupied by businesses, either public or private, that are large enough to have significant numbers of employees is relatively smaller. As a result, both the new middle and working classes are relatively smaller. Put differently, because of the disproportionately large size of the small business class in Mexico, all other classes—capitalists, new middle-class professionals and managers, and workers—are disproportionately smaller in relative terms.

MANAGERS

In all three North American economies the role of managers has been increasing. In large part the growth of a separate role for managers is the result of long-term trends in all market societies. The earlier the period of capitalist development and the smaller the company, the more likely that ownership and management roles were fused; that is, the owner ran the company directly. But as companies develop into large-scale corporate bureaucracies, the roles became divided and were occupied by different people. Generally, the role of management increases as corporations grow larger and direct ownership control declines. It becomes increasingly impossible for owners to be involved in all decisions. Hence, they must delegate those powers to trusted managers. This inevitable development has given rise to two questions: What is the class positions of managers? And have managers displaced owners as the real holders of corporate power?

Managers in general terms are employees who organize and direct other employees. The larger and more complex the economic organization—either public or private—the greater the need for the coordinating function of management. In one sense, thus, managers are simply coordinators in the production process who exist under all complex systems—be they capitalist or socialist, public or private sector. For that reason, there is some circulation of managers between top public and private positions in the United States, Mexico, and Canada. In another sense though they are intermediaries between centers of economic power and workers. In the formerly socialist societies, managers transmitted the directives of central plans that had been developed by ruling communist parties. In market societies, managers in the public sector transmit the general directives of those who control the state. Managers in the private sector transmit the directives of the owners of the corporations. Private corporations are thus organized as bureaucracies with managers in the top positions of presidents, vice presidents, treasurers, and so on, but above them are boards of directors who represent the interests of owners. The whole occupational role of managers is highly stratified, rising in positional terms from foremen on factory assembly lines and managers of franchised convenience stores to top officers of transnational corporations. In economic-class terms, the bottom rungs of the managerial hierarchy exist in the working class, its middle levels are in the new middle class, and its peaks are in the capitalist class. Many working capitalists identify themselves in occupational terms as managers. Many top corporate managers, who did not start out as capitalists, become capitalists in the course of their career developments by virtue of receiving very high salaries that are invested in profit-making activities. Many professionals, as they advance in their careers, take on managerial responsibilities.

While it is clear that more and more decisions in the private sector are completely within the prerogatives of managers, it is also clear that hiring and firing power over managers is still held by owners. The top manager survives only so long as he or she carries out the management role to the satisfaction of the owners. If profit rates begin to slide dangerously or the corporation begins to lose its competitive footing, owners, as represented by boards of directors, will replace top managers.

Because accumulation and concentration of capital are more advanced in the United States and Canada than Mexico, the growth and development of private management in these countries are also more advanced. The proportion of Canadian and U.S. labor force members who identify themselves as managers is greater than the proportion in Mexico. The separation of the roles of owner and manager is also much more advanced in the United States and Canada than Mexico, where the private manager is much more likely to be the working owner. The expansion of the separate role of private sector management, that is, separate from that of ownership, in the United States and Canada is one of the reasons why the occupants of its top positions often receive million-dollar and more incomes that are sufficient to propel them into the ranks of the wealthy. In Mexico, in contrast, it is rare for private sector management to be the road to wealth.

The three countries differ in the extent to which appointments to state managerial posts are politically determined. Politically based appointments reach further down into the administrative hierarchies of national and local governments of the United States than Canada.[9] They reach much further down in Mexico, where patronage appointments, even for clerical positions, are customary. Middle-level managers in Mexico attach themselves as team members to particularly powerful or upwardly mobile individuals. As the patrons change positions, they take along their team members. The patron can arrange for the appointment of relatives of the managers to other positions.

In the United States and Canada very few managers in the public sector become wealthy. These are generally new middle-class positions whose incomes peak in the top ranks of the social middle class. In Mexico, however, management within the public sector has for many been the source of capital formation, which later financed private ventures. Mexican state managerial positions have been sources of capital accumulation for a significant number of capitalists. Salaries, which are not high, have not been the source of this accumulation. Rather, what made state managers in Mexico into wealthy men was the opportunities to make money that their positions afforded. In the most crass of cases, they received large payoffs for special uses of their powers. The famous payment of the *mordida* ("small bite") to traffic police to avoid larger fines and problems is only the most visible base of a pyramid of corruption that reaches into the heights of the state apparatus. Kickbacks are a second type of corrupt profit-making opportunities from state positions. A state manager can facilitate the awarding of a contract to a private company which will then show its appreciation financially. The most spectacular profits come from insider knowledge that allows top managers to turn small investments into fortunes. It would be naive to believe that top state managers have not reaped superprofits for themselves during the wave of selling off of state-owned companies to the private sector initiated by the Salinas de Gortari government's privatization policies.

It is relevant in this context to consider Max Weber's (1905) distinction between booty capitalists and "sober bourgeois" capitalists.[10] The former grab wealth through taking advantage of a series of one-time opportunities for spectacular profits. The latter produce wealth through slow but methodical circulations of production, profit, and reinvestment. Political corruption, like the slave trade, the contemporary drug trade, and the pillage of indigenous treasures after the Conquest, belongs in the category of booty capitalism.

Corruption of public managers and officials has not been unknown in the history of the United States, the Tammany Hall scandals being just one example. Payoffs of public officials for special favors and the use of insider knowledge for private ends continue. The difference, however, is one of scale. Payoffs of public officials for favors continue to be taken for granted in Mexico, whereas they are now considered to be exceptional in the United States.

This corruption occurred most often when the United States was at a stage of economic development similar to Mexico's today. But it would be a mistake to assume that corruption is an inevitable feature of particular stages of development, since Canada's history with corruption was not nearly as scandalous. The real economic difference lies in the respective balances of pubic and private capital. Mexico, unlike the United States or Canada, developed a form of state capitalism in which the state was the main accumulator and director of development. That system has continued to give opportunities for public corruption because the state is where money and power are. In the United States and Canada, most of the money and power belong to private corporations. Corruption could be used to bilk public monies in Mexico without causing the state itself to collapse economically no matter how much public cynicism it might leave in its wake. However, continual embezzlement of a private corporation would lead to bankruptcy. Hence private corporations have a greater purely economic interest in controlling corruption than does the state. The private corporation can bilk the public as much as it wants without directly undermining its own financing, but it cannot allow embezzlement. Thus, if we are to seek out an economic explanation for the greater public sector corruption that exists in Mexico, we would have to conclude that it has rested in the greater use of the state as an accumulator of capital and director of the economy. At the same time, stating this conclusion is not the same as concluding that state-directed economic development inevitably produces corruption. A general anticorruption cultural ethic can act to keep opportunities for corruption in check, as can strong political or accounting control measures.

SOCIAL CLASSES

Economic classes refer to groups of people who share similar roles within labor forces, but each country's lower, working, middle, and upper social classes are made up of families and individuals who share similar standards of living. In each of the North American countries there are four general social-class standards of living: upper, middle, working, and lower. In addition to shared standards of living, the concept of social class also indicates popular recognition; that is, unlike the concept of economic classes which refers to research categories of analysis, the concept of social classes refers to labels that are widely recognized and identified with by populations. Because popular conceptions are at the core of the meanings of social-class terms, in order to define a social class for measurement purposes, it is necessary to begin with the popular conception of its meaning.

The popular conceptions of upper and lower class are fairly straightforward. By "upper class" most people mean the rich, and by "lower class" they mean the poor. Exactly where to draw the line between rich and middle-class incomes, though, is a matter that varies between countries and is highly subjective. Nevertheless, rough estimates of rich income thresholds can be established for each country and proportionate sizes of upper classes accordingly estimated. For the estimation of the proportionate size of the lower class in each country, we can accept the estimations of government studies of the number of poor in their populations. In the case of Mexico, we can easily distinguish the peasant and urban lower classes simply according to where the poor are geographically located. These urban and rural poor populations in Mexico can be considered either as separate social classes or fractions of one and the same lower social class.

For the middle and working classes, the great divide lies between the standard of living that can be afforded with an average professional or managerial income and that which can be afforded with an average manual or support occupational income. By middle class most people assume a standard of living that is supported by an "average" professional or managerial income— we consider the "average" income because "very high" income professional and managerial incomes support upper class standards of living and "low" professional and managerial incomes only support working class standards of living. In a related sense, the highest paying positions of working class occupations support middle class standards of living. We will therefore estimate the size of the social middle class by using as our base figure the proportion of professionals and managers in the labor force and then from it: (1) subtract the proportion of professionals and managers already assigned to the upper class; (2) subtract professionals and managers with working class incomes; and (3) add the proportion of working class occupations that afford incomes above the lower levels of professional and managerial incomes. Once the proportionate size of the middle class has been determined, the social working class will then be estimated by process of elimination. That is, the working class equals the proportion of the population that is not in the upper, middle, or lower classes.

We can begin by estimating the proportionate sizes of the upper and lower class extremes in the United States. If we consider rich or upper-class families to have a minimum income of $100,000, they are, according to 1986 income tax returns, the top 1.8 percent of the population.[11] The lower class of the poor constitute, according to official government estimates, the bottom 13.5 percent.[12]

For the middle class estimate, our first step is to subtract the 1.8 percent in the upper class from the proportion of professionals and managers in the labor force, which yields 24 percent. The remaining steps are to: (1) subtract persons with managerial or professional occupations—kindergarten teachers, social workers, painters, and photographers—that are paid salaries below the median income of technicians, the highest rung of working-class occupations; and (2) add persons with working-class occupations—computer programmers, securities sales, supervisors of protective services and mechanical repair shops, telephone and electric power installers and repairs, tool and die makers, railroad and ship workers, and airline pilots—that are paid salaries above the median income of managerial/professional occupations.[13] This operation resulted in a net increase of the relative size of the middle class by 0.5 percent to 24.5 percent of the population.

By process of elimination—that is, by subtracting the sizes of the upper, middle, and lower classes from the total—the relative size of the social working class was then estimated to be 60.2 percent of the population.

In sum, according to this estimate, the relative proportions of social classes in the United States population are as follows: upper, 1.8 percent; middle, 24.5 percent; working, 60.2 percent; and lower, 13.5 percent (see Table 5–1).

Employment of the same procedure to Canada yields an upper class of 1.1 percent, a middle class of 26.5 percent, a working class of 63.7 percent, and a lower class of 8.7 percent. The Canadian social-class profile is somewhat similar to that of the United States, but there are significant differences at the extremes: the Canadian upper and lower classes are proportionately smaller because there is a more equal distribution of income, as we will see. Canada does not contain proportionately as many poor people as does the United States. The Canadian poor make up 8.7 percent of the population compared to 13.5 percent in the United States.[14] Most of the reason for the smaller numbers of Canadian poor is that the Canadian government more aggressively favors them through use of redistributive taxation policies than does the U.S. government. In 1989, for example, the lowest 20 percent of Canadian households only received 1.2 percent of the total national income. However, that share was raised to 5.6 percent, almost five times as high, by transfer payments financed through redistributive taxes. In the United States, during the same year, the bottom 20 percent also received 1.2 percent of total national income before transfers. Their share of national income rose to 5.1 percent after transfers, which was a significantly smaller increase than that received by their Canadian counterparts.[15]

Our source of empirical information for Mexico, the national survey of household incomes and expenditures cited earlier, unfortunately stopped at distinguishing the richest 8 percent of households—unfortunately, because the incomes of this upper 8 percent begin well below that of the country's rich. In 1990 an income of $810 a month, eight times the monthly minimum wage, in

Mexico qualified a family for membership in the upper 8 percent, but it was hardly enough to make them rich. For the approximation purposes of this study it was assumed that a family had to have a yearly income of at least $60,000, which is six times the minimum income of the upper 8 percent, to be socially recognized as rich. It follows that the upper class has to be a very small percentage of all income recipients, most likely much less than 1 percent.

In 1977, 36 percent of Mexicans lived at or below the poverty line as defined by the World Bank.[16] Current Mexican government studies estimate that the proportion of poor people has risen to 41.3 percent of the population.[17] On the other hand, the latest Mexican census reveals that 52 percent of Mexicans do not have running water or toilets in their houses.[18] If we were to consider not having access to indoor plumbing to be a minimal mark of poverty in the last decade of the twentieth century, then we would have to conclude that at least 50 percent of the Mexicans live in conditions of poverty. Nevertheless, we will follow the government's conservative conclusion that at least 41 percent of its population lives in poverty and is therefore lower class. The national survey of households provides information about the location of the poorest 40 percent of Mexican households. About 55 percent are in rural areas, with 30 percent operating their own farms. The remaining 45 percent are in urban areas.[19] It follows that a little over half of the Mexican lower class is made up of peasants and a little under half is made up of the urban poor.

How large is the Mexican middle class? The answer depends upon how it is defined. Wilkie and Wilkins, in an influential analysis, calculated that the Mexican middle class in 1970 represented 23.4 percent of the population.[20] Some analysts argue that it is much larger, encompassing as much as one-third of the Mexican population.[21] But employment of our method for determining the size of the middle class yielded a somewhat lower figure of 16.5 percent.[22]

By process of elimination, the social working class—whose incomes and standards of living are situated between the lower and middle classes— was estimated to make up the remaining 42 percent of the Mexican social class structure. Approximately three-quarters of working-class household incomes derive from wages or salaries with the remainder coming from small business profits.[23]

In sum, the proportionate sizes of Mexican social classes are upper class, less than 1 percent; middle class, 16 to 17 percent; working class, 42 percent; and the lower class of peasants and the urban poor, 41 percent.

The most dramatic difference between the social class structures of Mexico and those of the United States and Canada is the disproportionately large size of the lower class in Mexico—41 percent of the population—compared to 13.5 percent in the United States and 8.7 percent in Canada. As in the case of the disproportionately large size of the economic small business class in Mexico affecting the relative sizes of all other economic classes, the disproportionately large size of the lower class of the poor in Mexico results in all other social classes being disproportionately smaller. Hence, the Mexican working, middle, and upper classes are relatively smaller than their counterparts in the United States or Canada. The disproportionately large size of the Mexican lower class results from the country's low accumulation of capital, which is incapable of generating sufficient employment opportunities that pay greater than poverty-level wages.

There are two reasons why the middle class is relatively smaller in Mexico. First, despite there being relatively more small businesses in Mexico than the United States or Canada, the vast majority of these are micro businesses that are not profitable enough to produce middle-class incomes. Their owners most often have working- and lower-class, rather than middle-class, standards of living. Second, large-scale public and private bureaucracies, which contain positions and pay levels for new middle-class professionals and managers, have not developed as much in Mexico as they have in the United States or Canada, thereby precluding one of the key labor force sources of social middle-class incomes.

INEQUALITY

Income distribution statistics are one of the most useful indicators of social-class inequality in a country. "Income" refers to everything that is received by individuals, families, or households. Sources of income include wages, salaries, interest, dividends, rents, and profits. North America's countries all have unequal distributions of income, but they differ according to the degrees to which these are distributed unequally. In Canada and the United States the richest 20 percent strata receive respectively 9 and 12 times as much income as the poorest 20 percent, while in Mexico that stratum takes 15 times as much. Every 20 percent income stratum from the poorest to the next to richest gains relatively (as well as absolutely) more income in the United States and Canada than Mexico. The richest 20 percent, on the other hand, gain relatively more income in Mexico than in the United States or Canada, indicating that income in Mexico is much more disproportionately skewed in favor of the rich than in the other countries. Mexico's Gini index of inequality is at a high of 0.489, significantly above those of the United States and Canada (see Table 5–2).

Mexico's severely unequal distribution of income is well known. All of the country's main political parties—the Partido Revolucionario Institucional

TABLE 5–2   Distributions of Household Income

	UNITED STATES	CANADA	MEXICO
Poorest 20 percent	3.8	4.7	3.6
Second 20 percent	9.6	10.4	8.1
Third 20 percent	15.9	16.9	13.0
Fourth 20 percent	24.2	24.8	20.4
Richest 20 percent	46.5	43.3	54.9
Total	100.0	100.1	100.0
Gini index	0.428	0.365	0.489
Year	1991	1990	1989

Sources: U.S. Bureau of the Census, Current Population Reports, Series P–60, No. 180, *Money Income of Households, Families, and Persons in the United States, 1991* (Washington, DC: U.S. Government Printing Office, 1992), Table B–3; Statistics Canada, *Income Distributions by Size in Canada, 1990* (Ottawa: Minister of Industry, Science and Technology, 1991), Table 55; and Instituto Nacional de Estadística Geografía e Informática (INEGI), *Encuesta Nacional de Ingresos de los Hogares, 1989* (Aguascalientes: INEGI, 1992), p. 39.

(PRI), the Partido de la Revolución Democrática (PRD), and the Partido de Acción Nacional (PAN)—agree that Mexico's income is badly distributed. Pedro Aspe, PRI minister of the treasury in the Salinas de Gortari administration, and Javier Baristain observed that every recent Mexican administration has come into office publicly endorsing redistribution of income in favor of the poorer classes. Nevertheless, according to the results of their investigation, the distribution of income remained essentially the same from 1940 to 1980—the last year that they examined.[24] Studies such as that of Aspe and Baristain indicate that in Mexico the configuration of income distribution results more from the structural characteristics of the country than stated governmental goals. In this context, it is relevant to consider Weisskoff and Figueroa's conclusion, made in the 1970s, that if 20 percent of the income of the richest 5 percent of Peruvians, Brazilians, and Colombians were redistributed to the poorest 40 percent, it would effectively double the latter's share of national income and thus significantly improve their standard of living.[25] The result of a similar hypothetical redistribution in Mexico would be almost as dramatic, increasing the income share of the poorest 40 percent by approximately 40 percent.[26]

During the 1980s a correspondence of neoliberal PRI rule, supply-side Republican administrations, and Tory governments produced redistributions of income upward all over North America. The top income strata increased their shares of total national incomes in all three countries. Overall, Gini indexes increased in Mexico from 0.454 to 0.489, in the United States from 0.403 to 0.428, and in Canada from 0.360 to 0.365.[27] Income inequality thus rose in all three countries, but it rose the least in Canada.

CLASS, POWER, AND POLITICS

Generally those who exercise economic power seek to at least influence if not directly control the exercise of political power. All three countries have institutional mechanisms by which economically powerful individuals and corporations influence state policies.

C. Wright Mills' *The Power Elite*, published in 1956, included the most influential postwar sociological explanation of the relationship between economics and state power in the United States. According to Mills, in the United States power is exercised by a power elite composed of the occupants of the command positions of the economic, political, and military institutional bureaucracies. In the United States the economic members of the power elite included the members of the boards of directors and top managers of the largest corporations; the political members of the power elite included the president, vice president, members of the cabinet, governors of important states, and powerful members of the Senate and House of Representatives; and the military members of the power elite included the Joint Chiefs of Staff and other top military officials.

Mills proposed that these individuals be studied sociologically like any other group in terms of their family backgrounds and values. One of his findings was that individuals often moved in their careers from one type of elite position to another. A military leader could move to a top political position, as did General Dwight Eisenhower when he became president. A corporate manager could be appointed to a cabinet post, as was Robert MacNamara. Mills also concluded that the majority of the power elite came from upper-class families, attended exclusive private prep schools, went to private colleges, and belonged to the same private clubs. Their common socialization experience, which was different from that of ordinary members of the population, produced common values and outlooks that they carried with them into the command positions of the power elite.

Mills' study and theory of power initiated subsequent studies and debates. Ralph Miliband and G. William Domhoff have been the most prominent followers of his approach in studying the individuals who occupy powerful positions.[28] Among Domhoff's many useful contributions to the study of power in the United States has been his uncovering of the role of private-foundation think tanks, such as the Council on Foreign Relations and the Heritage Foundation, in grooming corporate leaders for top political leadership positions. According to his portrayal, think tanks play the crucial intermediary role in translating corporate into state power. The think tanks bring together corporate, academic, and political leaders to study political problems. These seminars perform the functions of developing working and social relations among powerful individuals who come from geographically dispersed cities and providing an atmosphere within which corporate leaders with political potential can develop. The contacts necessary to launch serious presidential campaigns are developed within the think tanks, as are the pools from which subsequent cabinet appointments are drawn.

What Mills' *The Power Elite* was to subsequent power structure studies in the United States, John Porter's *The Vertical Mosaic*, published in 1965, was to subsequent power structure studies in Canada. Porter followed Mills' general approach by concentrating on elite wielders of power in Canadian institutional orders, including as institutional orders the economy and politics, as had Mills for the United States, but not the military. In addition, he included the federal bureaucracy, labor unions, mass media, higher education, and religion, which he considered to be other key functional parts of the society. Unlike Mills, who saw the various elites in the United States as coalescing into one power elite, Porter allowed for much more contention within and between Canadian elites. This included both the British and French differences and problems between the economic, political, and other elites. In terms of the class origins of elite members, Porter found upper-class descendants to be heavily overrepresented in the corporate elite. By his calculation at least 37.8 percent and possibly as much as 50.1 percent of the 611 members of the economic elite came from upper-class backgrounds, 32.2 percent came from the middle class, and 17.7 percent possibly rose from working- or lower-class backgrounds. As in the United States, Porter found that members of the economic elite formed a common worldview through attending the same private schools, where they developed friendships and kinship ties. However, the upper class was not as heavily overrepresented in the other institutional elites (politics, education, etc.), which tended to draw their recruits more from the middle class. On the key question of how economic elites influenced state policy and action, Porter concluded that this influence was usually achieved when members of the economic elite were appointed to various political boards and commissions, and when elite individuals moved back and forth between economic and political positions in the course of their careers, as in the United States.[29]

Mills continues to be widely read and studied in Mexico. In part his popularity results from his critical portrayal of power in the United States. But in another part it results from the relevance to his method of analysis to the study of power in Mexico itself. The focus on a tripartite elite of political, economic, and military leaders can be usefully applied to an interpretation of twentieth-century Mexican history. The 1910–17 Revolution was carried out against the political elite that surrounded the Porfirio Díaz dictatorship. It produced a new military elite that essentially ran the country for two decades before institutionalizing itself into a political elite with a monolithic political party, which today is the PRI. The Mexican political elite thus grew out of a military elite. The holders of state power, in both their military and political elite incarnations, have built strategic alliances with the country's economic elite. The Mexican upper class can also be studied in the same way that Mills studied their counterparts in the United States. They send their children to exclusive private schools such as the American School and belong to clubs such as the Club Alemán. Through the 1970s the upper class sent its offspring to universities in the country. The major private universities were the Colegio de México in Mexico City and the Instituto Tecnológico de Estudios Superiores de Monterrey in Monterrey. The major public university was the Universidad Nacional Autónoma de México in Mexico City. But now the preferred path is to send them outside of the country to universities in the United States, England, or France.

The general orientation of power research represented by Mills, Miliband, and Domhoff was not without its critics. To their right, pluralists accused them of erroneously conceptualizing monolithic power in the United States. Paul Sweezy (1956), the dean of Marxian economists in the United States, praised Mills' study but found its theoretical framework lacking. Instead of seeing the military, corporate, and political components as being co-equal in power, Sweezy argued the classic Marxist position that power was ultimately held by a capitalist-based ruling class.[30] Nicos Poulantzas argued that emphases on the individual occupants of powerful positions ignored the systemic features of power.[31] That is, no matter who occupied positions of state power in capitalist societies, even if they were committed to socialist reforms, the economic logic of the capitalist system would institutionally constrain their actions. Hence state power was directed in the way it was not just because of the upper-class values of the occupants of its top positions but also because it functioned within a specifically capitalist institutional environment.

Despite the common influencing of state policies in all three countries by holders of economic power, it functions differently because of the differences in party politics. The United States functions with two parties, the Republicans and Democrats. Other parties exist but rarely attain political office, because Congress and the state legislatures have mandated winner-take-all elections. That is, each occupant of a congressional or state legislative seat is the majority winner of an election from a particular district. There is no representation of losing parties, even if their candidates win as much as 49 percent of the vote, as there is in countries that have proportional representation. The winner-take-all provision of U.S. elections with its need to win more than 50 percent of the vote has effectively blocked the emergence of third parties.

The two major parties thus compete for the votes of centrist voters, even if they must significantly modify their ideological stands, to carry them over the 50 percent mark. This provision works doubly against third parties that maintain consistent ideological positions. First, they are less likely to attract the majority of voters to attain representation, since they do not change their programs to go after other voters. Second, even voters who agree with their programs may not vote for them out of fear that the vote will be wasted, since there is little likelihood that they will win.

Politics in the United States are also based on very loose relationships between parties and ideologies and parties and candidates. Because each party, as mentioned, seeks to win over centrist voters, it is willing to significantly modify its ideological position. With each of the two major parties fighting for the center, it is often difficult to distinguish them ideologically. Once the candidates win, the parties have little control over their votes within the various legislative bodies. Democratic and Republican legislative officeholders often vote with the other side on particular issues. Money influences politics in the United States in this individualistic climate in two ways. First, running an effective electoral campaign is expensive. Candidates must raise large sums of money from donors, who see their donations as investments in having the candidate, if he or she wins, support their particular concerns. Second, corporate and other special interest groups hire lobbyists to convince legislators to vote in particular ways.

Despite the relatively loose ideological basis of politics in the United States, there are clear class voting patterns, with support for Republican candidates rising with income. In every presidential election since 1976, the earliest year for which this information was available, there has been a direct relationship between social class and voting behavior: the higher the family income class, the greater the proportion of Republican Party votes, and vice versa for Democratic Party votes.[32]

The Canadian system is constitutionally organized to be relatively more pluralistic and ideological than that of the United States. There are three major political parties that offer voters clear choices between conservatives (the Progressive Conservative Party), liberals (the Liberal Party), and social democrats (the New Democratic Party). Canadian voters choose among candidates for legislative seats to represent their districts. They do not vote directly for national leaders. This provision of the Canadian constitution has favored the emergence of third parties within districts. Since there are no national candidates on the ticket, the Canadian voter is not as influenced by the strongest national parties as is the voter in the United States. Third parties can thus develop within particular provinces. Canadian national governments with their prime ministers are then formed by the party or coalition of parties that has the majority of seats within the national parliament. Unlike in the United States, there is firm party discipline over the voting of legislators.

Mexico is essentially a one-party state. But, it is not so much a question of one party controlling the state as the state being a self-reproducing institution that uses one party for its electoral and legitimacy needs. This is not to argue that the Mexican state party, the PRI, is without ideological differences. The Mexican state and the PRI are composed of a number of ideological currents. For example, the ideological differences between the nationalistic, somewhat social democratic government of Luis Echeverría Álvarez (1970–76) and the conservative Salinas de Gortari government (1988–94) are greater than anything witnessed in recent U.S. governments. Nor is it to argue that the PRI is the only party represented within the Mexican state. There are a number of oppositional parties, the two most important being the Partido de Acción Nacional (PAN), to the right of the PRI, and the Partido de la Revolución Democrática (PRD), to the left. But unlike in the United States or Canada, where most people assume that votes are counted honestly, most people assume that the state, when needed, alters electoral results. The 1988 presidential elections are the most well known recent example; there continues to be widespread belief that the actual results were reversed to avoid a victory by Cuauhtémoc Cárdenas over the PRI's candidate, Carlos Salinas de Gortari. From time to time and place to place, electoral victories by opposition parties are recognized, and they share in the governance of the country as distinctly minor partners. The Mexican constitution also allows for limited proportional representation of minor parties, unlike the constitutions of the United States or Canada. In 1978 the Mexican constitution was reformed to expand the Chamber of Deputies to 400 seats, with 100 to be distributed proportionately to opposition parties according to voting strength. The Senate, however, remains without proportional representation of minority parties.

As in many other Latin American countries, Mexico experienced guerrilla warfare in the 1960s and 1970s as a number of small groups attempted through armed actions to ignite a general revolution. The most significant rural guerrilla groups operated in Guerrero (the Partido de los Pobres, led by Lucio Cabañas) and Chihuahua (led by Arturo Gamiz), and there also were urban groups, the largest being the Liga Comunista 23 de Septiembre and the Movimiento de Acción Revolucionaria, operating in Mexico City, Monterrey, and Guadalajara. The Mexican Army, after several years of counterinsurgency warfare, in which as many as 3,000 were killed and 500 disappeared, largely extinguished the rebellion.[33] Carlos Montemayor in the late 1980s traveled through the mountains of Guerrero, where most guerrilla activity took place, and interviewed witnesses. He then wove those reminiscences into an impressive novelistic description of guerrilla leader Lucio Cabañas, the group that he led, and the war.[34] Also in the novel are descriptions of other guerrilla groups that were active in Mexico during that period. Among other long-suppressed facts brought to light by Montemayor's research is that the Mexican army in its counterinsurgency campaigns pushed suspected guerrilla prisoners from helicopters high above the Pacific. Their bodies washed ashore just north of the beaches of Acapulco, the international resort, and were discovered by fishermen.

CONCLUSIONS

As in the case of the labor forces, the economic class profiles of Mexico, the United States, and Canada reflect their different stages of capitalist development. Compared to Mexico, the United States and Canada have relatively larger capitalist, new middle, and working classes. Mexico has a relatively much larger small business class and a very marginal peasant class, which does not exist in the countries to its north.

What is comparatively most notable about the class stratification of the Mexican labor force is the relatively large number of small business owners and the small number of capitalists. Over a fifth (22.3 percent) of the labor force is made up of small business owners. Most are itinerants and owners of micro businesses with no employees. Most are thus more of a lumpen than a petite bourgeoisie. They exist in such large numbers because neither state nor large businesses have yet been economically strong enough to displace them. In the United States and Canada, by way of contrast, where the concentration of business power is much more advanced, not more than 8 percent of the labor force continue to maintain businesses of any size.

By far the largest source of contrast between the social-class profiles of Mexico and the United States or Canada is the relatively (and absolutely) much larger size of the lower class in the former. That is, the lower class, with 41 percent of the population, is the largest social class in Mexico, whereas in the United States the lower class, with 13.5 percent of the population, is a relatively small minority. But, while the lower class is certainly relatively smaller in the United States than Mexico, it is relatively larger in the United States than in Canada, where it constitutes 8.7 percent, or other first world countries. Because the United States is the first world country that has been least willing to redistribute income and services in favor of its most disadvantaged citizens, it has tolerated most the continued existence of poverty in its midst.

Income is more equally distributed in Canada than in the United States or Mexico, which has one of the most unequal distribution of income in Latin America. Brazil has the most unequal. During the 1980s income distributions became significantly more skewed toward the rich in the United States and Mexico, while in Canada the overall pattern of distribution changed very little.

✳ CHAPTER 6
Race and Pigmentocracy

The cities of North America mirror the racial realities of their respective national cultures. The South Side of Chicago stretches for miles, and its inhabitants are almost all black, evoking the title of Drake and Cayton's 1945 classic, *Black Metropolis*. One can board the El, Chicago's major public transportation system, on the southern edge of the South Side. The El rolls through the black ghetto until it reaches the downtown Loop and then passes into north Chicago, which is mostly white. As the train passes through the Loop, white passenger faces systematically replace black faces. Black passengers feel a certain uneasiness if they stay for the white section of the run, and white passengers feel a corresponding uneasiness if they ride through the South Side. Some Canadian cities also contain neighborhoods where particular racial minorities predominate. In Toronto and Montreal, for example, recent black immigrants from Jamaica and Haiti have established their own neighborhoods. But there is nothing in Canada that approximates the scale of U.S. black ghettos, in large part because the black population is infinitesimally small by comparison. In large Mexican cities there can be racial differences between residential areas. Some areas have relatively more whites than others. But there are no areas in which whites alone reside. The racial complexion of Mexican neighborhoods can differ with rich areas being relatively whiter, but the racial tension that exists is much more latent than in the United States.

These urban ecologies of race in part reflect the racial composition of each society. More importantly, they reflect how each society has institutionally structured its racial relations. In order to comparatively understand these different racial realities, it will first be necessary to comparatively establish the demographic facts of the different racial compositions of the North American societies. We will then examine how each country has historically evolved different patterns for handling its race relations.

POPULATION COMPOSITIONS

The national populations of the North American countries are composed of indigenous-, European-, African-, and Asian-descent individuals, but in different proportions and combinations, resulting in significantly different overall racial textures (see Table 6–1). In the parts of North America that became the United States and Canada, the indigenous populations were relatively small, allowing white European immigrants to establish numerical superiority quickly. That numerical superiority has carried over to today, with white European-descent people predominating in Canada (91 percent) and the United States (80 percent). The part of North America that became Mexico, though, was densely populated by indigenous peoples, and white, mainly Spanish, European immigrants were never able to establish numerical superiority. Today, whites do not make up more than 4 percent of the Mexican population. The United States experienced slavery in its history to a much greater extent than either Mexico or Canada. For that reason, blacks are a sizable minority in the United States (12 percent) but very small minorities in Canada (1.1 percent) and Mexico (0.4 percent). Asians have migrated to all three countries, but their numbers are slight compared to Europeans. Most live in

TABLE 6–1   Estimates of North American Racial Groupings, Percent of Population

	UNITED STATES	MEXICO	CANADA	TOTAL
European	80	5	91	63
Indigenous	1	15	2	4
Mestizo	4	79	1	23
African	12	< 1	1	8
Asian	3	< 1	6	2
Total	100	100	101	100

Note: Because of rounding, percentages may not total to 100.

Sources: Estimates based upon information in U.S. Bureau of the Census, *Census of Population and Housing: Summary Population and Housing Characteristics* (Washington, DC: U.S. Government Printing Office, 1992), Table 2; Luz María Valdés, *El Perfil Demográfico de los Indios Mexicanos,* 2nd ed. (Mexico City: Siglo Veintiuno Editores, 1989); and Statistics Canada, *Ethnic Origin,* 1991 Census (Ottawa: Minister of Industry, Science and Technology, 1993), Table 1A.

the United States, but they are proportionately the largest minority in Canada, where they constitute 5.5 percent of the population—compared to 3 percent in the United States and much less than 1 percent in Mexico.

In addition to the main racial trunk lines of the North American population—Europeans, Indians, Africans, and Asians—a half millennium of coexistence has produced a very statistically and socially significant fifth-race population of combined racial descent. Nearly 80 percent of the Mexican population exists somewhere on a continuum between the poles of fully indigenous and fully European descent. There are also significant mestizo minorities in the United States and Canada. Most Mexican-origin individuals in the United States are mestizos, along with those produced through contacts between domestic whites and Indians. In Canada there is a significant cultural as well as racial minority of métis who combine Indian and French ancestry. In the total North American context, mestizos are the largest racial minority, making up nearly a quarter of the continent's population. In a parallel sense, much of the continent's population that is socially identified as black is in reality technically mulatto, combining both European and African ancestry. A much smaller population of Eurasians also exists.

Racial interaction patterns differ in the three countries in part because of the different racial compositions of the respective national populations. Mexicans become minority members only when they travel to the United States and Canada. Whites are a minority in Mexico. In the United States, blacks are the largest minority, with Indians being far less than 1 percent of the population. In Mexico, however, Indians are the largest minority, with blacks being far less than 1 percent. The United States could promote legal segregation of races in education, housing, public transportation, and public accommodations until 1964 in large part because it was a segregation imposed against a demographic minority. Canada also segregated blacks from whites at various times in its history. Mexico, during its colonial period (1620–1821), largely segregated Indians, mestizos, mulattoes, and blacks from the white minority. But, it would have been very difficult for Mexican whites to maintain that segregation after independence, since they were the demographic minority. They would have had to develop a social system along the lines of South African apartheid. The experiences of race, racial interaction, and racism differ in the three countries in large part, therefore, because of these different racial proportions and compositions. The experiences differ also because they are culturally perceived differently, with each national culture containing a set of norms and values that filter the perceptions of racial relations.

HISTORICAL AND CULTURAL TRENDS

Each country's racial relations have evolved and developed according to a distinct logic. The different logics result from both the different racial compositions and the different ways in which each country has constructed ideologies of national self-identity.

There is no common definition of racial identity in North America. In the United States and Canada, racial identity tends to be defined genetically, that is, according to biological descent. In Mexico, it tends to be defined according to appearance, that is, according to skin color. The issue is further complicated for African-origin individuals in the United States, who have a social definition that overrides their actual biological identity. That is, most blacks in the United States are technically mulattoes, and a number of these carry more European than African genes. Nevertheless, for reasons to be explored in Chapter 12, these predominantly white individuals are socially defined as blacks. In Mexico, a number of very-light-skinned individuals, who are biologically mestizos, define themselves and are defined by others as whites.

The United States

The history of race relations in the United States is intimately connected with conquest and labor exploitation. It began in the colonial period with the violent usurpation by European settlers of the lands of indigenous peoples and the importation of African slaves to work many of those lands. Up through independence, race relations were played out between a dominating white majority, conquered and resisting Indians, and enslaved blacks.

In the nineteenth century, the U.S. victory in the Mexican-American War opened up the Southwest for exploitation. It also resulted in the formation of two new racial minorities: mestizos and Asians. The takeover of Mexican territory meant that the mainly mestizo citizens would become a racial minority under white domination. Exploitation of that land required the importation of Chinese contract laborers, the origin of the Asian minority, to work mines and build railroads. By the end of the century the United States victory in the Spanish-American War would add colonial subjects—Puerto Ricans and Filipinos—to the already-existing categories of dominated racial minorities.

Voluntary immigration from the 1870s to the present, especially of Latin Americans and Asians, has also contributed significantly to the formation of the minority populations. Most Latin Americans and Asians in the United States today came as a result of voluntary immigration. But it was migration in the context of international inequality. The directions of international migration patterns are almost always from poorer to richer regions. Regions become richer for a variety of reasons, including their ability to outcompete poorer regions in production and trade. In this sense, the ability of the United States to outcompete economically most of the countries of the world has had the unintended effect of stimulating many of the citizens of these poor countries to attempt to migrate to the United States. Economic deprivation, in part caused by the economic success of the United States, has thus driven many Latin Americans and Asians in the last few decades to leave their countries for perceived better economic opportunities in the United States.

Because of its history of conquest and exploitation of minority labor forces as well as its attractiveness to third world immigrants, the United States has been and continues to be the most racially heterogeneous of the North American countries (see Table 6–2). The relations between these different groups, therefore, have been one of the most critical problems in U.S. history. Racism could develop as strongly as it did in the United States because it had an ideal climate within which to grow. The white majority psychologically rationalized its harsh treatment of first Indians and blacks and later Latinos and Asians by accepting the belief that these were inferior races. With racism being a vital component of the belief system or ideology embraced by most of the white majority, it is no wonder that up through the first half of the twentieth century the United States evolved and institutionalized an elaborate system to separate and segregate the races in housing, schooling, and other areas. With the passage of the 1964 Civil Rights Act the United States made an official break with legally sanctioned racial segregation. Racial discrimination did not come to an end that year, but it ceased to be officially promoted and tolerated.

TABLE 6–2   Race, Income, and Poverty in the United States, 1991

	AVERAGE HOUSEHOLD INCOME	PERSONS BELOW POVERTY LEVEL (PERCENT)
White	$31,569[a]	9.4[b]
Asian	$36,449	13.8
Hispanic[c]	$22,691	28.7
Black	$18,807	32.7
All	$30,126	14.2

[a]Includes Hispanics.
[b]Does not include Hispanics.
[c]Persons of Hispanic origin may be of any race.
Sources: U.S. Bureau of the Census, *Poverty in the United States, 1991* (Washington, DC: U.S. Government Printing Office, 1992), p. x, and *Money Income of Households, Families, and Persons in the United States, 1991* (Washington, DC: U.S. Government Printing Office, 1992), p. xi.

Racial discrimination continues to permeate economic and social life in the United States. With over 85 percent of U.S. history having been lived with either slavery or legally promoted segregation and only 15 percent since the 1964 official break with racial discrimination, it is not surprising that the institutionalized racism that developed during more than 300 years of colonial and postcolonial history could not immediately end and completely disappear with the passage of a bill. The passage of the Civil Rights Act was an absolutely necessary but not a sufficient step for achieving racial justice. The relations between whites and the other racial minorities—Latino mestizos, Asians, and Indians—also continue to be problematic, though not as contentious as they were in earlier historical periods.

Since 1964 there thus have been significant changes in relations between whites and blacks in the United States. Whites perceive blacks and other racial minorities very differently than they were before 1964. Most white politicians are careful to not make directly racist statements. When former Secretary of Agriculture Earl Butz told a racist joke that was overheard and reported by reporters, he created a public furor and was obliged to resign from office. Before 1964 blacks appeared in television programs only as happy-go-lucky menials and not at all in commercials. There are now a number of programs with blacks in dignified leading roles, and they regularly appear in commercials.

The civil rights movement opened up opportunities for blacks with higher education to move into new middle-class economic roles. One of the unintended consequences, however, was that many then moved out of the traditional black communities and into integrated suburbs, leaving a dearth of leadership and role models in those communities. In a sense, the solidarity that was forced by common racial oppression on all classes of the black community has broken down. William Julius Wilson thus argues that increasingly class inequality is becoming a more important issue for most blacks than racial oppression per se.[1]

Mexico

The logic of racial relations in Mexico begins with the Spanish conquest of the large indigenous population. From that time on, European-descent whites, either first-generation Spaniards or their *criollo* full descendants, though always a small minority, have exercised economic and political dominance over the majority nonwhite population. During the colonial period, as described earlier, the Spanish authorities practiced clear discrimination and segregation against the nonwhite population and, in official records, carefully categorized it into castes according to its proportions of European, indigenous, and African ancestry.

Following independence in 1821, Mexico adopted the liberal position that all citizens regardless of race or ethnic background were equal. This position was largely in reaction to the colonial practice of categorizing people racially into castes. It was also in reaction to black slavery in the United States. That position has continued to exist in virtually unaltered form ever since. A number of Mexicans point with pride to the fact that the country's most revered president, Benito Juárez, was a full Indian as indicating that racism either does not exist in Mexico or exists least there of all of the countries of North America. As a consequence of the official position, the government considers the very compilation of public statistics on racial minorities to be racist. If all Mexicans are equal regardless of skin color, according to the official position, then it is a contradiction to divide them by skin color for statistical purposes.

In the 1921 census, however, the government did include a question about racial identification. Some 60 percent of the population identified themselves as being of mixed racial descent, 29 percent as indigenous, 10 percent as white, and 1 percent as other.[2] Projecting from those and other statistics, we can estimate that today approximately 79 percent of the population is mestizo, 15 percent indigenous, 5 percent white, and less than 1 percent predominantly black or Asian.

The failure of the Mexican government to distinguish racial groups in its contemporary statistics frustrates research attempts to document the degree to which discrimination and inequality exist or do not exist in the country.[3] At most, the government admits that its indigenous population constitutes minorities—but cultural minorities. Indians exist in official discourse as a socially definable group primarily because they practice a culture that differs from the national culture. The color of their skin is theoretically irrelevant as a definer. The official view of the country's small black population, on the other hand, is that it does not practice a culture that is significantly different from the national culture. Blacks are therefore not officially recognized as a distinct minority.

The problem with the official view is that it is belied by everyday experience.[4] In fact, racial differences do count in Mexico. One Mexican psychiatrist states offhandedly, "All you need to get ahead here is blue eyes." A Mexican economist makes the observation that people with dark skin who have professional or managerial positions generally dress better than people with light skin. The reason, she states, is that dark-skinned people feel subtly obliged to compensate for the low status of their skin color with high-status clothing. Everyday terms in the country, such as *negritos* and *chinos*, carry at least some racist connotations.

On the level of official discourse, Mexico scrupulously takes pride in its Indian foundations. Unlike Canada or the United States, the sense of history in Mexico begins with the large-scale Indian civilizations that preceded the arrival of Europeans. Mexican schoolchildren are taught to take pride in the accomplishments of these civilizations. In reality, however, the predominantly European-descent population continues to be disproportionately represented in positions of power and the middle and upper classes. It maintains its position of racial privilege by practicing considerable discrimination against the predominantly Indian-descent population, and it is not immune from indulging in racist-tinged discourse against them too. The term *nako*, which has somewhat the same connotations that "nigger" has in the United States, is often used in discourse among the predominantly European-descent population as a code word for dark-skinned Indians. *Nakos* are usually described, in addition to being dark skinned, as uncouth, dirty, and ignorant. Expressions such as *nuestros inditos* are also common and condescending.

Mexican sociologist Jorge Bustamente reports that there are more cases of Mexican police brutality against undocumented workers waiting to cross the border in Tijuana (across from San Diego, California) than Ciudad Juárez (across from El Paso, Texas). He believes that the reason is racial. Most of the undocumented persons who pass through Ciudad Juárez are from northern Mexico and light skinned. Most of the undocumented people that pass through San Diego are from central and southern Mexico and darker skinned. In Bustamente's estimation, the relatively light-skinned Mexican police in San Diego and Ciudad Juárez are more likely to abuse the dark-skinned Indians than those that are somatically light skinned and more like themselves.[5]

The consciousness of race permeates everyday life not only between people of different skin colors and shades, but also possibly in the psychology of individuals. Mexican authors, such as Samuel Ramos[6] and Octavio Paz,[7] have long argued that the mixed Indian and European descent of most Mexicans has not been without problems for their psychological identities. They argue that, despite the official pride in the Indian descent, there is in fact a complex of inferiority because of it. Mexican racism, therefore, is in part a racism of self-denigration, according to this view, with the mestizo majority feeling shame about the Indian part of its descent and somatic appearance.[8]

Not surprisingly, race is often associated with class in generalizations about Mexican society. In a half-century debate over the Mexican national character that included Samuel Ramos, Octavio Paz, and Roger Bartra,[9] the class structure was presented in tripartite Indian, mestizo, and *criollo* terms. These writers either associated the Indian with the rural peasantry or as being marginalized and outside of the main drift of modern Mexican history—"like a chorus that silently accompanies the drama of Mexican life."[10] Mestizos make up the urban proletariat—Ramos's and Paz's *pelados* who suffer from inferiority complexes and excesses of violence in the *cantinas* (bars). The bourgeoisie in these accounts is assumed to be, if not openly stated to be, essentially white. Although this description cannot be taken as absolutely or literally true, it does highlight the tendency for racial and class positions to cohere that is taken for granted in Mexico. The existences of poor whites and rich Indians are exceptions that do not invalidate the main tendency.

But because official statistics in Mexico are not categorized according to race, they cannot be directly used to document the extent to which race and social class are correlated, that is, the extent to which whites, mestizos, and Indians have different social-class standards of living. Not only can they not be used to document the inequality of nonwhites, they cannot be consulted to document the extent to which white *criollos* continue to dominate. White domination is both officially denied and statistically hidden.

The relationship between race and social class position can be seen by comparing the racial compositions in three neighborhoods located on different sides of the Universidad Nacional Autónoma de México in Mexico City (Table 6–3). Pedregal de Santo Domingo on the eastern side is what is called in Mexico a *colonia popular*, meaning that it is made up of poor and working-class people. Its streets are filled with mestizos and Indians. Copilco, on the northern side, is by everyone's account a middle-class neighborhood, which contains both ordinary and upscale stores. Since it is adjacent to the national university, it also contains several coffeehouses and two of Mexico City's best stocked bookstores. A systematic observation of one of its condominium complexes indicated that a little over half of the residents were white. Jardines del Pedregal, on the western side, is, along with Lomas de Chapultepec, the most exclusive neighborhood in the city. To enter its streets and view its walled mansions, one must pass the guardhouses of private security

TABLE 6–3   Race and Social Class in Mexico City: Three Neighborhoods

| | LOWER AND WORKING CLASS | | MIDDLE CLASS | | UPPER CLASS | |
	Number	Percent	Number	Percent	Number	Percent
Whites	4	2.1	37	53.6	34	75.6
Mestizos and Indians	191	97.9	32	46.4	11	24.4
Total	195	100.0	69	100.0	45	100.0

Source: based on the author's observations of inhabitants in residential parts of the lower- and working-class area of Pedregal de Santo Domingo, the middle-class area of Copilco, and the upper-class area of Jardines del Pedregal.

forces. Observing the race of who lives in those houses is difficult because, unlike in the other two neighborhoods observed, the true residents of the area are not observable from the street. They rarely walk outside their walled enclaves. Most of the people who do walk Jardines del Pedregal's streets are employees of those who live within the walls. By peering from a distance into cars as they arrived at the houses, it was possible to get a sense of who the residents are. About three-quarters of them were white.[11] Racial inequality exists not only between whites and nonwhites in Mexico but also among nonwhites according to the relative lightness or darkness of their skin colors. In the lower- and working-class neighborhood of Pedregal de Santo Domingo, the mestizos and Indians clearly had dark somatic features. In the middle-class area of Copilco and the upper-class area of Jardines del Pedregal, though, a substantial number of the people who appeared to be mestizos had sufficiently light skin to make it difficult to distinguish them from whites. The neighborhoods surrounding the National University are thus a microcosm of the larger pattern of racial and class correspondence in Mexican society.[12]

Canada

In Canadian history the main axes of racial relations have been between whites and Indians and between whites and Asians. The dynamics of race relations in Canada begin with French trappers and farmers establishing a toehold on the continent by adapting themselves to the reality that this was land occupied by Indians. The first generations of Europeans, who also soon included English, were minorities. But because the number of Indians in the area that would become Canada was relatively small and because the promise of free land lured so many English and French immigrants, within a short period of time Europeans became the majority. Canadian history then became the history of greater and greater white domination over the Indian peoples. Unlike in the United States and Mexico, however, the establishment of white domination proceeded relatively peacefully. There were no large-scale frontier wars. Today, Indians make up a proportionately larger minority in Canada than in the United States, and they continue to adhere to separate identities and press for land and cultural rights.

The largest racial minority today is made up of Asians—Chinese and Indians being the largest components. These began to arrive in Canada in the middle and late nineteenth century and they encountered considerable racist hostility from the European-origin population.

Canada also has other less pronounced racial axes. As in Mexico, but not the United States, mestizos have a defined identity that is neither Indian nor European. As in colonial Mexico, relatively few women accompanied the first

European inhabitants. The first mestizos thus resulted from French settlers and trappers of necessity taking Indian wives. In time, sizable communities of métis developed. They often established separate communities and identities and even in the nineteenth century attempted rebellions to secede from Canada. Today, the métis continue to be recognized as a separate minority.

The number of blacks in Canada has always been very small. There was a brief period of slavery, but it was nowhere near as significant as it was in the history of the United States or Mexico. There were never plantations, in large part, because of the unsuitability of climatic and soil conditions. Most blacks who entered Canada entered as free persons, often fleeing the slave condition in the United States. Nevertheless, it would be a mistake to believe that whites in Canada necessarily welcomed blacks. Throughout Canadian history there have been acts of hostility toward the black minority. In the nineteenth and twentieth centuries immigration officials attempted to discourage and block black immigrants. In the nineteenth century Nova Scotia and Upper Canada segregated their schools.[13] The Ku Klux Klan has been active at various times in Canada as well as the United States. Labor unions have in the past barred blacks from membership or accepted them only in separate segregated locals.[14] In 1992 there was a major disturbance involving blacks in Toronto.

Canadians use the metaphor of a mosaic to evoke the image of the type of multicultural society that they wish to preserve and promote. John Porter in an influential work, though, dubbed it as a vertical mosaic in which racial and ethnic differences were hierarchically structured.[15] Lautard and Guppy found that the verticalness of the mosaic has continued in terms of labor-force positions down though the 1980s, but less so. Their study indicates that whites on average occupy higher-status positions than, in order, Asians, blacks, or Indians, but the degrees of inequality are not as great as in the United States or Mexico. Two white ethnic groups—Portuguese and Greek—occupy lower-prestige positions on average than any of the racial minorities.[16]

In general, perceptions of race in Canada tend to follow the pattern in the United States, but not entirely. The differences occur because the protagonists are different—Indians and Asians rather than blacks have been the main minorities. But, more importantly, postindigenous Canada was established by two charter European populations rather than one. The necessity of accommodating the separate cultural identities of French- and English-origin citizens was then extended to racial minorities. It has also been pointed out that Canada's multiculturalism resulted in part from the dominant English-origin population's need to retain its ethnic attachment to Great Britain during the colonial period in order to maintain a national identity that was separate from that of the United States.[17] Hence, there is now more of a sensitivity toward preserving the separate cultural identities of all minorities, including languages, in Canada than in the United States or Mexico.

NATIONALITY AND ETHNICITY

At the same time that North America's cities spatially manifest underlying racial inequalities to different degrees, they also often manifest ethnic and nationality differences as well, with ethnic or national minorities that share the same racial identity living in different neighborhoods. San Francisco has a Japantown as well as Chinatown. The New York metropolitan area has predominantly Irish and Italian neighborhoods. Even where ethnic differences within racial groupings have not generated distinct ecological patterns within cities, they have been sufficient to generate subcultures within and sometimes to crosscut racial groupings.

Common racial position thus does not necessarily produce a common cultural outlook. Italian- and English-origin Americans, while sharing the same racial grouping, are culturally different. It would be a mistake to assume that common racial position unites Chinese- and Japanese-Americans. In 1906 the Japanese community of San Francisco protested vigorously when a racist and culturally ignorant school board attempted to segregate its children in Chinatown schools.[18] And, certainly, no one could maintain that common racial position makes English and French Canadians culturally indistinguishable.

What differentiates the concepts of ethnicity and nationality is the degree of separateness. The concept of nation is intimately related to the concept of state. A nation is a people that shares a common identity that is or has the potential of being manifested in the formation of its own separate government.[19] In this respect, minority nationality identities have existed in North American history among recently arrived immigrants who still carry the identities of their originating countries. They also exist among those minorities, such as the French in Canada, for whom the possibility of formation of a separate state exists. Ethnicity, as opposed to nationality, refers more to the identities of immigrant groups that are on their way toward being integrated into one multiethnic identity and for which formation of a separate state or society does not appear to be likely. Contemporary Italian-Americans or Chinese-Mexicans, in this respect, would be more ethnic than national minorities. Whether a minority is defined as being an ethnic or a national minority is thus a preeminently political issue, since the latter implies separate loyalty. In either case though, ethnic and national minorities are cultural minorities.

What race and ethnicity or nationality share in common as categories of analysis is that they are bases from which groups develop senses of common identity. By being black one shares a common racial identity with other blacks that is not shared with whites and other racial groups. By being Polish-American one shares a common and distinct identity that is not shared with other European-, Asian-, Native, or African-Americans. However, the degree to which a common racial or ethnic position evokes a common identity and consciousness varies historically and socially.

Racial and ethnic differences are sometimes directly related, as when blackness in the United States is associated with both a common racial and ethnic subculture. But they are not always directly related, as when one racial grouping, such as Asians within North America, contains a number of culturally different ethnic groupings. Race and ethnicity can also crosscut each other, as when black and white Puerto Ricans in the United States feel a common ethnic and nationality bond despite their racial differences.

In terms of national origins, the majority of North America's European-origin or white population came from the British Isles, Spain, France, and Germany. Different combinations of these nationalities produced different cultural patterns in the three countries. British immigrants were significant in the United States and Canada, but not Mexico. Spanish immigrants were significant in Mexico, but not in the other two countries. French immigrants were significant in Canada but not as much in the United States and not in Mexico—though French influence was great there in the early nineteenth century, and the country even had a French emperor for a short time. Correspondingly, the Latino population of the United States is a culturally heterogenous combination of Mexican, Puerto Rican, Cuban, and other nationalities. The same can be said for the Asian populations, which have originated for the most part in China, Japan, and the Philippines. The indigenous population is also culturally heterogenous, containing many different language and tribal groups. Only the African-origin population in the United States lacks major internal ethnic or nationality differences.

Throughout the nineteenth and a good part of the twentieth centuries, the national self-identity of the United States was largely molded by the cultural values of its British-descent population. Their culture was the norm to which other European white immigrants, such as the Irish, Poles, and Italians, had to conform. One omnipotent national identity thus developed in the United States for whites according to the cultural values of its dominating British-descent population. English became the official language, with immigrant groups quickly learning that maintenance of their languages would be a liability to their own economic success and social acceptance. Large numbers of immigrants even anglicized their names in order to fit into the typical (white) American image.

The forging of one unified national self-identity for whites out of the different European immigrant groups evoked the analogy of a melting pot. European immigrants came to the United States to be thrown into a melting pot of nationalities. Within one or two generations they would come out as indistinguishable Americans. The image of the melting pot, though, was imperfect because it was more of a process in which "non-American" elements were separated out and discarded than a process of true fusion of different European cultural elements. It was more of an Anglo conformity than truly a melting pot process. The attempt at cultural homogenization of the white population was never complete, with traces of Polish, Irish, Italian, and other identities continuing to maintain and reproduce themselves. Nevertheless, the basic thrust of United States history has been toward developing one homogenized national identity at the expense of minority cultural values and languages. For most of its history, the United States excluded blacks, Indians, Latinos, and Asians from this cultural homogenization process. They were thought to be inassimilable for largely racial reasons and subjected to discrimination and prejudice. At one time or another all of the racial minorities were subjected to segregation, with blacks being the most systematically segregated.

The metaphor of a melting pot applies to Mexico as well as the United States, but with important differences. The United States experienced a *cultural* melting pot among its dominant white population in which southern and eastern European immigrants submerged their separate cultural identities and adopted the dominant British-origin cultural characteristics of the white majority. The products of this melting pot became the dominating racial majority. In Mexico there was *racial* melting pot among substantial portions of the indigenous and immigrant European populations, resulting in the creation of a mestizo majority. But the products of this melting pot became a dominated rather than dominating racial majority.

Canada, unlike the United States or Mexico, has never adopted a melting pot goal to eliminate the cultural differences between its major European-descent populations. Canada has for most of its history developed policies based on the reality that it contains two large and powerful language communities, English and French. The majority speaks English, but there is enough of a minority that speaks, and is fully committed to continuing to speak, French, that any attempt to impose one language would provoke immediate resistance. Such an attempt would be somewhat similar to the U.S. attempt in the 1930s to make English the official language of a Spanish-speaking colony, Puerto Rico. There was so much resistance that the project was quickly dropped. Canada, therefore, has had to adopt a policy of cultural pluralism.

The policy includes not only the English- and French-descent communities, but also indigenous and other communities. The acknowledgement that these communities maintain separate cultural identities within the context of overall Canadian identity, however, has not resolved all of the outstanding issues, as is obvious because a substantial proportion of the French-descent population wants independence for Quebec.

Carey McWilliams, in his pathbreaking writing of the history of Mexicans in the Southwest, compared their condition to that of the French in Quebec. Both were oppressed minority language and cultural communities within the contexts of their respective countries.[20] But the analogy is limited because there is an important demographic difference between the two. The French quickly outnumbered the indigenous population in Quebec and have maintained that majority position to the present. The Spanish and Mexicans, on the other hand, were never the majority in the Southwest. Before 1848, they were outnumbered by Indians two to one. After 1848, waves of Anglos swept into the newly conquered territories and quickly became the demographic majority. Largely as a result of this significant demographic difference, Canada and the United States have pursued different policies with these respective minorities. In Canada, the French-origin community could easily reproduce its language because it was the majority within a large territory and the issue of possible political separation was realistic. In the Southwest of the United States, the Spanish-speaking community faced increasing difficulty reproducing its language because of its minority position and the penetration of roads and television. These influences have been only partially offset by family ties to Mexico and new immigrants from there. Despite some fledgling attempts during the height of the Chicano movement in the 1970s to project a separate national identity, there has never been a serious prospect of Mexican-origin people in the Southwest forming a politically separate entity.

CONCLUSIONS

The four racial trunk lines of the North American population originated in North America itself, Europe, Africa, and Asia. Intermixture of these races produced a fifth, synthesis race. Significant racial combination or mixture has occurred in the United States and Canada as well as Mexico. In the United States, however, the reality of racial mixture has been hidden by a Manichean view that each person belongs to one and only one race, with, most strikingly, any evidence of African ancestry, no matter how slight, resulting in being socially classified as black. In Canada the métis population of combined Indian and French descent is recognized as a culturally distinct minority.

Pigmentocracy exists in each of the North American countries, but its dynamics differ owing to different population compositions, cultural perceptions, and historical experiences.[21] In the United States and Canada the overwhelming majorities are European-descent whites. But while the United States has pursued the melting pot policy of forging one culturally unified national identity from its European immigrants, Canada has had to pursue a pluralistic policy of promoting the maintenance of separate cultural identities within the context of an overall national identity because most of its original European immigrant population came in nearly equal numbers from England and France, and neither one was willing to abandon its cultural identity and language. In Mexico the overwhelming majority are nonwhite mestizos, descended from Indians and Europeans. Mexico, in this sense, is an essentially mestizo country, with its mestizo character being alternately interpreted as a source of strength or of unresolved problems. Spanish-descent whites, though, have exercised disproportionate domination over this majority since colonial times. Pigmentocracy prevails in differing degrees in all three countries, with European-descent whites generally occupying the top economic, political, and social positions.

In all of the racial encounters and intermixing, in all of the centuries of racial prejudice, discrimination, and tension, with their different dynamics in the three countries, what stands out as a constant theme is the extent to which African-origin individuals have been most the targets of prejudice and discrimination. Indians were also enslaved, but the condition of enslavement was in the long run more associated with blacks. The cultural legacy of slavery produced a greater bar against assimilation of slave descendants in all three countries. Mixed European, Indian, and Asian-descent individuals have fewer problems being accepted as social equals than individuals with partial or full African descent. Even in Mexico, which has had the greatest racial tolerance, the Crown during the colonial period clearly frowned more on marriages between Spanish immigrants or creoles and Africans than on marriages with Indians.

The special burden of racism borne and suffered by African-descent individuals in North America grew in large part out of economic reality of slavery. But while slavery may account for most of the explanation for the racism against blacks, it does not provide all of the explanation. To some extent whites and blacks have always been perceived to be racial antitheses in North America, and Asians and indigenous peoples to be in-between races. Partly for that reason, whites in the North American societies have been more willing to accept Asians and Indians on socially equal terms than they have blacks.

Partly for that reason, whites have been more willing to accept miscegenation with Asians and Indians than with blacks. To some extent it is also true, though, that opposites attract and that antitheses eventually merge to produce new syntheses that overcome the old antagonisms. But of North America's historically discriminated against peoples of color blacks continue to suffer the most social injustice.

✷ CHAPTER 7

Euro–North Americans

The vast majority of North America's whites live in the United States and Canada (Table 7–1). The United States has the greatest number in absolute terms. Canada, with over 90 percent of its citizens being of European descent, has the most in proportional terms. It is the most white and racially homogeneous of the populations. In Mexico, whites are a small minority. In all three countries whites dominate positions of power and privilege.

The internal dynamics of the majority white United States and Canadian populations differ. In U.S. history, whites have been ethnically divided. In Canadian history, they have been both nationally and ethnically divided. That is, in the United States immigrant whites have been ethnically distinguishable because of their cultural differences from native-born whites; Canadian history, though, has experienced national as well as ethnic differences among its white residents in the respect that political separation and independence for the French-speaking part of the white population has long been a realistic possibility.

The three predominant sources of the white North American cultures have been England, Spain, and France. For that reason, today, English, Spanish, and French are the predominant languages of the continent, being spoken, respectively, by 71, 27, and 2 percent of its occupants.

THE UNITED STATES

Approximately 80 percent of the United States is made up of people with a white racial identity. A number of different European immigrant groups came to the shores of North America and combined to make up this white majority

TABLE 7–1   Distribution of Euro–North Americans

	NUMBER[a]	PERCENT	PERCENT OF OWN POPULATION
United States	199,686	87.5	80
Mexico	4,050	1.8	5
Canada	24,463	10.7	91
Total	228,199	100.0	

[a]In thousands.

Sources: U.S. Bureau of the Census, *Census of Population and Housing: Summary Population and Housing Characteristics, United States, 1990,* Table 2 (Washington, DC: U.S. Government Printing Office, 1992); Statistics Canada, *Ethnic Origin,* 1991 Census (Ottawa: Minister of Industry, Science and Technology Canada, 1993), Table 1A; for Mexico, based on estimate.

(see Table 7–2). Their diversity is most apparent in East Coast and midwestern cities where ethnic neighborhoods or their remnants still exist. In general, though, as you move westward in the United States—the city of San Francisco being an exception—visible ethnic differences in the white population dissolve.

At the time of the War of Independence, more than 90 percent of the white population had English origins. Small minorities had German and Dutch origins. For that reason, English rather than another European language became the language of the United States. The predominance of English-ori-

TABLE 7–2   Nationality Origins of Euro–North Americans

	UNITED STATES Number[a]	Percent	CANADA Number[a]	Percent	MEXICO Number[a]	Percent
British Isles	101,476	49.0	10,269	42.0		
Germany	49,224	23.8	912	3.7		
France	12,892	6.2	6,610	27.0		
Italy	12,184	5.9	750	3.1		
Eastern Europe	14,678	7.1	947	3.9		
Scandinavia	9,317	4.5	174	0.7		
Spain	95	0.1	83	0.3	3,450	85.2
United States					200	4.9
Other	7,378	3.6	4,718	19.3		
Not ascertained					400	9.9
Total[b]	207,244	100.2	24,463	100.0	4,050	100.0

[a]In thousands.
[b]Because of rounding, percents may not sum to 100.

Sources: Calculated from U.S. Bureau of the Census, *Statistical Abstract of the United States, 1989* (Washington, DC: U.S. Government Printing Office, 1989), p. 41; Statistics Canada, *Ethnic Origin,* 1991 Census (Ottawa: Minister of Industry, Science and Technology Canada, 1993), Table 1A; for Mexico, based on estimates.

gin individuals in the population was bolstered by the fact that most immigrants up through 1840 came from Great Britain. Thus, from the beginning of the colonial period it was a specifically English cultural identity that forged the predominant national identity of the United States. Non-English immigrants would have to conform to that identity and would often feel oppressed by it in the subsequent course of United States history.

Historians divide non-English European immigration to the United States into two periods. The first, from 1830 through 1882, was composed of Northern and Western Europeans—Irish (the most numerous), Germans, French, and Scandinavians. Most of the Irish were unskilled workers and peasants who left their homeland because of the potato famine. By 1847 the famine had produced over a half million starvation deaths.[1] The immigrants arrived in the United States to occupy the lowest rungs of the newly forming industrial working class. The traditional cultural and religious cultural tensions between the English and the Irish were reproduced in the United States during this period between native-born English-origin whites and Irish immigrants, with the former occupying more privileged economic and social positions than the latter.

The first wave of Irish immigration coincided with the Mexican-American War (1845–48), and the tensions between the English-origin population and the Irish immigrants would play a role in the war. At the onset of the war a number of unemployed Irish immigrants joined the U.S. army that invaded Mexico. The desertion rate of 8 percent for the U.S. Army was the highest of any war in its history. Among the deserters were at least 200 men, about 40 percent of whom were Irish immigrants, who, in addition to deserting, changed sides and formed a special unit in the Mexican army, the Saint Patrick's Battalion. It was the only case in U.S. military history where deserters actually changed sides and formed a special military unit in an enemy army. On August 20, 1847, the U.S. Army secured control of Mexico City by defeating the Mexican Army, which included the Saint Patrick's Battalion, at the battle of Churubusco. Thirty-five members of the battalion were killed, 85 were taken prisoner, and close to 90 escaped. Of the prisoners, 68 were sentenced to be hanged and two to be shot, with 18 of the sentences being later reduced. On September 10 and 12, the U.S. Army hanged 50 of the Saint Patrick's prisoners as deserters and traitors. The members of the battalion who had escaped capture continued to fight with the Mexican Army until the end of the war, with the battalion increasing its size as new deserters joined its ranks. The example of the Saint Patrick's Battalion, while largely forgotten in the United States, or if remembered, remembered only as a negative example of wartime betrayal, remains firmly embedded as a positive act in the Mexican national consciousness. The Mexican view is that these soldiers had been oppressed as Catholics in an army commanded by Protestant officers and had changed sides after seeing the invasion as an injustice. A special public plaque honoring 71 of the *San Patricios* was placed in the Mexico City *colonia* of San Angel in September 1959, near the site of the hangings, containing in Spanish the words "With the gratitude of Mexico, 112 years after your sacrifice." Each year on the anniversary of the hangings and on Saint Patrick's Day public commemorations of the Saint Patrick's Battalion are held there. Also, a public elementary school in Mexico City is named Battalón de San Patricio.[2]

In addition, 1848 was a world historical year. Revolutions and civil wars swept across France, Germany, and other countries. The German revolution was initially successful but then lost momentum, and repressive authority was restored. Many Germans, fed up with repressive conditions at home, then left for the United States to form the nuclei of German-American communities.[3] The communities attempted to preserve their separate cultural and language identities by educating their children in private schools where German was the language of instruction. The schools lasted until World War I, when anti-German sentiment provoked by the war caused their closing.

During the second large period of immigration (1882–1930) the source countries shifted from Northern and Western to Southern and Eastern Europe. Poles, Czechs, Italians, Russians, and others came to the United States. By 1920, a full 13.2 percent of the U.S. population was composed of foreign-born individuals.[4]

As non-English-origin immigrants entered the country, they encountered prejudice and intolerance toward their different languages, religions, and customs. They were the butt of jokes and suffered from derogatory nicknames. Not only were they considered to be culturally different, but they were often considered to be *racially* different. As late as the 1890s it was common to see references to Southern and Eastern European immigrants as not belonging to the same race as the English-origin population. Both as a result of being outcasts and in order to preserve their own cultural identities, Irish, Italian, Polish, and other non-Anglo European minorities developed ethnic neighborhoods in eastern and midwestern cities.

The Polish immigrant experience was somewhat typical. By 1914, there were about three million Poles in the United States, virtually all living in the East and Midwest. Chicago in that year was the third-largest Polish center in the world. The Polish immigrants saw themselves first and foremost as a subculture rather than individuals to be assimilated into the dominant culture. Most had come from conservative peasant villages with the intention of returning home after making enough money in the United States. The most important institution around which immigrants oriented their social lives was the Polish-American Catholic parish, which provided a setting where Polish could be freely spoken. When a large number of Poles would begin to settle in a city, the church would establish a parish in an inexpensive working-class neighborhood. The parish would then draw a concentration of Poles, other nationalities would leave, and the area would then become solidly Polish.[5]

Ethnic and class identity largely overlapped in these neighborhoods. Ethnic minorities—the Irish and Southern and Eastern Europeans—made up a majority of the late-nineteenth- and early-twentieth-century factory working class. Ethnic neighborhoods were thus, for the most part, also working-class neighborhoods.

The growing multiethnic, not to mention multiracial, nature of the working class became a source of division that frustrated attempts of organizers to promote class solidarity in the face of capital. Friedrich Engels, who visited the United States in 1888, was immediately impressed by the immigrant character and consequent internal ethnic diversity of the working class, which he saw as an obstacle to the development of class solidarity. First, there was a division between native-born workers, who mainly were Protestants with English-origin ancestors and cultural values, and immigrant workers, who were mainly Catholics—and to a much lesser extent Jews—from Ireland and continental Europe, which gave rise to the famous identification of "real Americans" with white Anglo-Saxon Protestants, or WASPs for short. And, second, among the latter, there were internal nationality and ethnic differences.[6] Being culturally Irish or continental European, no matter how hyphenated with American, or being Catholic or Jewish, no matter how white, marked one with a foreign identity. To be "100 percent American" one had to literally be a WASP, that is, someone descended from the English nation.

Throughout the nineteenth and the first part of the twentieth centuries cultural hegemony in the United States revolved around the values and identity of so-called WASP citizens. Ethnic minorities had to conform to WASP values and images if they wished to be successfully transformed into "100 percent Americans." To look and speak "like an American" meant looking and speaking like a WASP. Hence, within two generations Italians, Czechs, Poles, and other immigrants from other non-English-speaking countries learned to speak English without an accent and correspondingly lost the ability to speak their original languages. The predominance of the WASP norms was so strong that, until the 1960 election of John F. Kennedy, no Catholic could be elected president. Yet, as more Catholics and Jews from Ireland and continental Europe entered, the actual proportion of literal WASPs among the white population steadily declined. Today, less than a quarter of native-born whites in the United States are predominantly of English descent or literally WASPs.

The distinction between WASPs and non-WASPs among whites in the United States is most often not apparent to Mexicans, as the distinctions between whites, mestizos, and Indians among Mexicans are most often not ap-parent to whites in the United States. In the Southwest of the United States, the preferred term used by Mexican-descent residents is "Anglo," which, at this point in history, is a misnomer in terms of nationality, if not culture, for the majority of whites. In Mexico itself there is also a strong tendency to as-sume that all whites coming from the United States are WASPs.

In sum, the white population of the United States, unlike that of Mex-ico, was drawn from a number of European ethnic and national sources. This cultural multiplicity created an initial barrier to the forging of a unitary na-tional identity. Social scientists and others often evoke the image of a melting pot to indicate how the immigrant ethnic groups were assimilated into the na-tional identity of the country. If we follow the image, the different immigrant groups had their initial ethnic and national characteristics melted down and then they were all blended together to create what today is the national iden-tity, at least of whites, in the United States. The analogy accurately evokes the pressure that immigrant groups experienced to shed their original cultural identities if they wanted to be perceived as unhyphenated citizens. But it con-veys the misleading impression that all national identities were equally sub-jected to this process of nation building, when to the contrary those with Eng-lish ancestry were largely spared the ordeal. The process of assimilation and nation building in the United States was much more of a process of Anglo conformity than of an egalitarian melting pot.

Today, white incomes are, on the average, significantly higher than those of Indians, blacks, and Latinos.[7] For that reason, the Republican Party, which takes a conservative approach to racial issues, enjoys a significant advantage over the Democratic Party among white voters in presidential elections. In the elections from 1976 to 1992, Republican Party candidates outpolled Demo-crats among white voters by an average margin of 54 to 39 percent. Democra-tic Party candidates won two of those elections—Jimmy Carter in 1976 and Bill Clinton in 1992. But in both, the Republican Party candidates outpolled the Democratic Party candidates among white voters. Put in another way, in 1976 and 1992 the Democratic Party won the White House by virtue of black and Latino votes. If the election had been restricted to whites, the Republican Party would have won.[8]

CANADA

With 91 percent of its citizens being of European origin, Canada is the most racially white country of North America. But, it is not a unified white coun-try. It contains the continent's only nationality difference within the European component of its population. This difference is the most outstanding example of a firm contemporary division within a white population.

The origins of the dispute go back to Canada's colonization by both France and England, who provided the original migrant pools, which have been called by Porter, among others, the "charter" populations.[9] After Britain defeated France in the French and Indian War (1756–63) and removed France from governing power in North America, French immigration declined greatly. The decline in immigration was partially offset, though, by the generally higher birth rates of French-origin citizens; and French-descent citizens remained the majority in Quebec and maintained their own separate cultural identity. That Canada was at least officially a bicultural country has been assumed throughout its history. In 1867, at the time of confederation, 92 percent of the population had either English or French backgrounds. The British North America Act recognized the country's bicultural nature by allowing French as well as English to be used in courts and Parliament. Today, three-quarters of Canadians have British, French, Irish, Welsh, or Scottish backgrounds. Predominantly British Canadians (including, Irish, Welsh, and Scottish) make up 42 percent of the population, while predominatly French Canadians make up 27 percent.

While today French-descent citizens are a minority in the country as a whole, they make up a full 85 percent of Quebec's population, with almost all of them continuing to speak French in the home.[10] The possibility that Quebec might break off from Canada and form its own country has always been at least a latent issue in politics. Porter, in his pathbreaking and exceptionally influential study of ethnicity and class in Canada, argued that in Quebec, "because British and French live as largely separate social groups there are two class systems, each bearing the stamp of its own culture. Both French and British have their old aristocratic families as well as their lower classes." In the terms of this study, Porter essentially concluded that there were separate French and British social-class systems. At the same time, he was careful to point out that "these two class systems while operating side by side are also firmly interlocked in the economic system."[11] In other words, the implications of Porter's study were that Quebec contained one overall economic-class system but two separate social-class systems.

It would therefore seem that French Canadians clearly meet the objective test of being a nationality as opposed to ethnicity: They occupy a definable territory. They continue to speak their own unique language. They practice a unique culture that is different from overall Canadian culture. They have even established their own separate social-class system. Finally, as a result, there is a significant political tendency that seeks to establish Quebec as a separate country.

Part of the reason why self-determination or political independence is perceived to be a viable option for Quebec is that the province now enjoys prosperity similar to that of the country as a whole. Regions of countries generally are reluctant to pursue independence if it will result in economic decline. They pursue independence when they perceive that it will bring about economic as well as cultural advantages. In this respect Quebec is like the Basque land in Spain. Both are located in relatively prosperous regions of their respective countries, and many within them believe that their prosperity would increase further if they did not have part of their taxes redistributed to poorer regions. Quebec and the Basque land are also close to richer countries—the United States and France—which can provide good trading partners.

French Canadians on average have traditionally occupied lower positions in the labor force and have earned lower median incomes than English Canadians. Lautard and Guppy found that as of 1986 the overall occupation status of French Canadians still lagged behind that of English Canadians.[12] These differences, though, have been significantly narrowing over time. Nevertheless, the economic differences between the English and French in Quebec have been sufficient to provoke severe resentment among the latter, which at various times has led to violence.

There are two main explanations for the history of English and French Canadian economic inequality. The first is that England's defeat of France in the French and Indian War insured that its citizens would have privileged access to economic opportunities in the colony. But even if France had become the colonial power, another cultural factor possibly would have attenuated the extent to which the roles could have been reversed. English Canadians are Protestants, while French Canadians are Catholics. These religious differences immediately recall Max Weber's study of the different roles of Protestants and Catholics in the development of capitalism in Europe. Weber began his study noting that across Europe, Protestants tended to occupy higher ranks in the labor force than Catholics. He further argued that Catholic education prepared students more for humanistic than industrial occupations, and for that reason, among others, Catholics were underrepresented among industrial owners and managers.[13] The same observations, as Porter noted, could have been made of Quebec.[14] That is, to some extent, even if English Canadians had not had privileged colonial access to economic opportunities, they may have been more culturally predisposed than French Catholics to pursue acquisitive capitalistic occupations.

Not all of Canada's white population, however, has either directly English or French backgrounds. That population has also been significantly increased by migrants from the United States. In 1910 there were 304,000 U.S.-born persons living in Canada, and between 1910 and 1988 a total of

1,601,665 U.S.-born persons took up residence. However, for every one of these immigrants, at least two Canadians left for the United States. There have always been more Canadian-born persons in the United States than U.S.-born persons in Canada.[15]

The other, and more important, noncharter source of the Canadian white population has been immigrants from Germany, Italy, Russia, Poland, and other European countries. The percentage of European immigrants who came from non-Anglo, non-French backgrounds increased from 7 to 18 percent of the population between 1881 and 1931.[16] Today, close to one in four white Canadians comes from these backgrounds; and they have felt the stings of prejudice and discrimination from both the English and French communities. They came in three waves. The first, mainly East European peasants, came between 1896 and 1914. By 1911, 40 percent of the population of Saskatchewan and a third of the populations of Manitoba and Alberta were made up of people with non-British and non-French origins. The second wave came in the 1920s and resulted in the proportion of the total Canadian population that was non-English or non-French rising to 18 percent by 1931. The third wave came in the late 1940s and 1950s. By 1961, 26 percent of Canadians had non-English or non-French backgrounds.[17]

Those who put together confederation in 1867 had recognized the different needs of the English- and French-speaking communities, but they did not contemplate the cultural rights of other European immigrants. European immigrants from countries other than France or England faced considerable pressure, as in the United States, to assimilate into the dominant Anglo-defined Canadian culture. Thus, according to Palmer, it is a myth that Canada has always adopted a mosaic approach to minorities that was in contrast to the melting pot approach of the United States. Palmer notes, "Perhaps immigrant groups did not 'melt' as much in Canada as in the United States, but this is not because Anglo-Canadians were more anxious to encourage the cultural survival of ethnic minorities." Quite the contrary, he argues, "There has been a long history of racism and discrimination against ethnic minorities in English-speaking Canada, along with strong pressures for conformity to Anglo-Canadian ways." The same derogatory ethnic slurs that were used in the United States, such as dagos, wops, and Polacks, were also common in Canada; and the Ku Klux Klan, as in the United States, actively opposed new immigrants in the 1920s.[18]

Canada's informal policy toward non-Anglo, non-French immigrants shifted considerably in the twentieth century. An Anglo-conformity expectation prevailed up through World War II. The majority of native-born Canadians expected non-English-speaking immigrants to assimilate into an Anglo-defined Canadian culture and shed their original languages and cultural practices. The Anglo-conformity view lost favor in the public mind by World War II when it was replaced by a more evenhanded melting pot expectation in which Canadian national identity would be forged from the merged identities of its constituent groups. In the last couple of decades a cultural pluralism model has emerged in which it is deemed valuable for minority languages and cultural practices to be preserved in the context of an overall multicultural Canada. *Multi*culturalism itself arose in reaction to the assertion of *bi*-culturalism (English and French only). In October 1971, Prime Minister Pierre Trudeau proclaimed Canada to be a *multi*cultural country.[19] The Canadian public, however, has not yet been completely convinced of the desirability of multiculturalism.[20]

MEXICO

Less than 5 percent of Mexico's population is white, whether whiteness is defined by appearance or full European descent. The vast majority of members of this population are of Spanish descent and are referred to by Mexicans as *criollos*. There are much smaller numbers of whites who migrated from other European countries, the United States, and Argentina. There are also a small number of white enclaves, mainly in rural areas, where Italian, French, and Mennonite communities exist.

Two realities stand out about this white population. First, it is numerically small. Whites, unlike in the United States and Canada, have never been the largest racial group. Second, despite its proportionate smallness, the white population continues to dominate. The true extent of its domination, though, is hidden by official statistics, which, as discussed in Chapter 6, do not distinguish income and occupational data according to race.

Mexico's European-origin population has long maintained cultural ties to Europe and, according to Ramos, Bonfil Batalla, and others, attempted to remold the Indian and mestizo populations with European-origin institutions.[21] During the nineteenth century, especially during the Porfiriato, the Mexican government defined the country as underpopulated and actively attempted to encourage immigration. Many in the white upper classes held the additional hope and racist belief that immigration of European whites would alter the country racially by diluting the proportion of Indians and mestizos in the composition of the population. These efforts were largely a failure; relatively few immigrants were attracted to the country, and many of those who came later migrated to the United States or returned home. What stands out about immigration to Mexico is that it was and is so small. The percentage of the foreign born in the population reached its height in 1930 at 1 percent.[22]

By way of contrast, in 1930, 12 percent of the U.S. population was foreign born. Today only 0.4 percent of the Mexican population is foreign born,[23] compared to 6 percent in the United States[24] and 16 percent in Canada.[25]

Most of the twentieth century's foreign-born population has been made up of whites from the United States and Spain, with much smaller numbers from England, Canada, and Argentina. In 1980, 60 percent of the foreign born were from the United States, followed distantly in order by 5 percent from Spain and smaller percentages from Argentina, Germany, Cuba, and Chile.[26] But despite their smallness, immigrant generations have often had a significant impact in particular institutions. In the late 1930s and early 1940s, Mexico welcomed large numbers of loyalist exiles from Spain. Many of these and their children went on to establish prominence in the country's university and intellectual life. Mexico has also had a tradition of providing haven for Latin American revolutionaries in exile, the most prominent recent examples having been Fidel Castro and Ernesto "Che" Guevara in the mid-1950s. In the 1970s and 1980s, significant numbers of white Chilean and Argentinean exiles from right-wing military dictatorships found refuge in Mexico, as did larger numbers of mainly Mayan Guatemalans fleeing harsh, repressive conditions.

Not everyone in Mexico welcomes foreigners, however. In part because of the nationalism that developed in the postrevolutionary period, many Mexicans have viewed immigrants with the same disdain with which they have been viewed in the United States and Canada. In Mexico, though, the disdain has a different dynamic. If in the United States and Canada immigrants from the colonial power England were excepted from antiforeigner prejudice, in Mexico immigrants from the former colonial power, Spain, have borne the brunt of a special type of prejudice, being referred to as *gachupines*, a term that carries about the same amount of opprobrium as *gringos*, the term for white U.S. citizens. In the 1990s white Argentineans living in Mexico City must bear the burden of being the butt of immigrant jokes. There is a strong racial undercurrent to the jokes that reflects the widely held Mexican perception that white Argentineans view themselves to be racially superior to mestizo and Indian Mexicans. For that reason, in contrast to U.S. immigrant jokes where the target group is presented as stupid or disgusting, in Mexican jokes Argentinean immigrants are always presented as arrogant or vain.

Anti-Jewish sentiment is clearly present in Mexico. There are approximately 65,000 Jews in the country, with most living in Mexico City. As in the United States and Canada, most Mexicans perceive Jews to be disproportionately rich and resent it to some degree.[27] In comparing anti-Jewish sentiment in Boston and Mexico City, historian Barbara Driscoll notes that in the former it is a composite of both negative and positive stereotypes—for example, "Jews are clannish, but they contribute to the arts and education." In Mexico City, though, there appear to be only negative stereotypes.[28] It is not uncommon to hear references to the thieving "Jewish merchants and doctors in Polanco" (a neighborhood in Mexico City). In some ways, anti-Jewish sentiment in Mexico resembles the open prejudice that prevailed in the United States up through the 1940s. Whereas today expressions of anti-Jewish feelings have been largely driven underground in the United States, in Mexico they have not been.

The United States community in Mexico can be divided according to permanence of their residence in the country. There are students and tourists who live in the country for a few months and then leave. There are employees of U.S. government offices and multinational corporations assigned to the country for periods ranging from one to several years. There are large communities of retired people in Guadalajara, Cuernavaca, and San Miguel de Allende who live in the country for several years. There are people who have married Mexicans and moved to the country for permanent residence. Finally, there is a group that have lived for generations in Mexico, usually having intermarried with Mexicans, and are Mexican citizens, but who maintain ties with their country of origin by speaking English and maintaining contacts with relatives. The relatively permanent U.S. community in Mexico City has a clear ethnic consciousness of itself, having created its own churches, clubs, and schools in addition to having access to English-language media, including a newspaper and radio station. It even has its own telephone book, the *Anglo American Directory of Mexico*, where, for a fee, any citizen from the United States, Canada, or England can have a listing.[29]

Some of the U.S. and Canadian citizens living in Mexico are working there illegally. Mexico has the same prohibition of foreigners working within the country without explicit permission as do the United States and Canada. However, as in the United States and Canada, this provision of Mexican law is virtually impossible to fully enforce. It is, in fact, more difficult to enforce in Mexico than in Canada and the United States because of the relatively larger amount of work that is carried out through self-employment rather than in bureaucratic settings, which are easier to regulate by the state. U.S. and Canadian citizens living in Mexico can hence make an income from giving private English lessons with little fear of being caught.

The extent of overall white domination in Mexico is impossible to document because of the country's policy, discussed earlier, of not recording statistical information according to race. Despite the official view that race is irrelevant, there is a widely held public perception that whites continue to dominate. A columnist in one of Mexico City's leading newspapers, for example, made the following claims:

One thousand *criollos* govern from the highest levels of the state. It is now very unusual for mestizos to rise to the ranks of undersecretaries or ministers of state, governors, or high-level advisers to the president of the Republic. The five hundred most important business owners in the country are almost all *criollos*. The same is also true for the five hundred most important intellectuals, almost all of whom live in Mexico City.[30]

Whether exaggerated or not, the columnist's claims reflect widely held public beliefs.

White domination can be seen symbolically by the overwhelming use of white actors in television commercials. An examination of commercials on Channel 2, Mexico's major network station, during prime time on one evening revealed that 81.8 percent of the actors were white. A full 98 percent of the actors appearing in commercials for foreign, multinational corporations, such as Coca-Cola and Nestlé, were white. Even in commercials advertising national products, such as tortillas and video centers, 76 percent of the actors were white. The only counterbalance to the preference for white actors was in government-sponsored commercials for public programs, where 89 percent of the actors were mestizos or Indians. Government-sponsored commercials more accurately reflect the country's racial makeup, but since they are only a small minority of all commercials, their presence is not enough to offset the overall white bias in television commercials. This bias partially reflects the economic reality that whites have more purchasing power than mestizos or Indians in the country, and advertisers therefore prefer to use white actors as model consumers of their products. It also reflects the perception of advertisers that nonwhites will believe that if a product is being used by a white it must be good enough for them too.

Racial bias in media projections, though, no matter how much it is based on rational economic calculations, harms the self-esteem of those who are implied to be inferiors. It is relevant in this context to recall Kenneth and Mamie Clark's classic doll experiment, which was influential in the 1954 *Brown* v. *Board of Education* Supreme Court decision that mandated integration of education in the United States. The Clarks showed black schoolchildren four dolls. Two were brown with black hair, and two were white with blond hair. They then asked the children to identify which doll they liked the best, which looked "bad," which had a "nice color," and which looked the most like themselves. Most of the black children picked white dolls as looking "good" and black dolls as looking "bad." The Clark's experiment documented the extent to which racist cultural values undermined the self-esteem of black children.[31] Certainly commercial television, which began after the Clark's experiment, continued the attack on black identity. Blacks were either shut out from roles or restricted to undignified ones as fools or buffoons, as they had been in Hollywood movies. In the early 1960s, basing themselves on the conviction that commercial television's racial biases were psychologically harming the black population, which the Clarks' experiment had so dramatically documented, civil rights groups then began to pressure network stations to include blacks in more dignified roles in both commercials and regular programs. The parallels between this black experience with media in the United States and the experiences of Indians and Indo-mestizos with media in Mexico are obvious.

CONCLUSIONS

A half millennium ago European whites began their conquest of the native peoples of North America in order to remold the continent in their own image and for their own interests. Today the effects of that process can be clearly seen in the correlation between race and privilege that continues to exist. In all three countries whites occupy the top positions of economic power and privilege. The domination of whites in the United States and Canada is not surprising, since they are large majorities in the populations of both countries—80 percent in the United States, over 90 percent in Canada. But even in Mexico, where whites make up less than 5 percent of the population, they dominate. Pigmentocracy continues.

White domination was violently imposed over the indigenous peoples during the conquests of the different areas of the continent. Once the continent had been opened up, large numbers of European whites, attracted by free land and economic opportunity, streamed in, quickly outnumbering the native peoples in the United States and Canada, but never in Mexico. During the late nineteenth century large numbers of European immigrants came to the eastern United States and western Canada, but relatively few Europeans wanted to migrate to Mexico, and of those that did, many soon left for the United States. Thus, while the white populations of the United States and Canada were largely composed from nineteenth- and early-twentieth-century European immigrants, most of Mexico's white population has roots that go back to the colonial period.

The white populations that dominate in the United States and Canada have thus been made up from successive waves of European immigrants. Those populations, though, have not been completely unified culturally. Certainly an important theme in U.S. history has been the sometimes antagonistic cultural relations between native-born English-origin citizens and those who immigrated from Ireland and continental Europe. Two different cultural communities—English and French—reproduced themselves separately in

Canadian history; and immigrants from other parts of Europe have suffered prejudice and discrimination from both. The minority white population that dominates Mexico, unlike those of the United States and Canada, has developed largely in isolation because relatively few European immigrants have increased its numbers. In general class terms, whites in all three countries are disproportionately in the capitalist and new middle economic classes and the upper and middle social classes.

✴ CHAPTER 8

Indians after the Fifth Sun

There are slightly more than fourteen million indigenous (Indian and Eskimo) people living in North America today. The vast majority, over 84 percent, live in Mexico. Most of the rest live in the United States. The proportion of Indians in the total Canadian population, however, is larger than that in the total U.S. population (see Table 8–1).

In all three countries the indigenous peoples have historically suffered from racism and discrimination. In all three they are the poorest of the minority groups. However, despite the common experiences of racism, discrimination, and economic deprivation, there are significant differences in how indigenous peoples have been treated in the histories of the three countries since European contact and conquest.

MEXICO

Because of their numbers, Indians in Mexico could not be shoved aside quite to the degree that they were in the United States and Canada to make way for European settlers to take over and develop the land. As late as 1810, the beginning of Mexico's independence revolution, Indians still made up 60 percent of the population.[1] Indians had to be incorporated into the base of the postindependence labor force. But, as in the colonial period, not all Indians were willing to accept a subaltern role in the *criollo* nation-building project.

The vast majority of Mexico's Indian population has lived in the center and south of the country since pre-Hispanic times. Large numbers of Indian farming villages, surrounded by communal lands, dotted that part of the coun-

TABLE 8–1   Distribution of Indigenous Peoples in North America

	ESKIMO		INDIAN		PERCENT OF
	Number[a]	*Percent*	*Number*[a]	*Percent*	*OWN COUNTRY*
Mexico	—	—	12,000	84.3	15.0
United States	57	65.5	1,878	13.2	0.8
Canada	30	34.5	365	2.6	1.4
Total[b]	87	100.0	14,243	100.1	

[a]In thousands.
[b]Percentages may not total 100 because of rounding.
Sources: For Mexico, based on estimate, see Luz María Valdés, *El Perfil Demográfico de los Indios Mexicanos,* 2nd ed. (Mexico City: Siglo Veintiuno Editores, 1989); U.S. Bureau of the Census, *Census of Population and Housing: Summary Population and Housing Characteristics* (Washington, DC: U.S. Government Printing Office, 1992), Table 2; Statistics Canada, *Ethnic Origin,* 1991 Census (Ottawa: Minister of Industry, Science and Technology, 1993), Table 1A.

try. Throughout the nineteenth century, as large *criollo*-owned haciendas grew, they encroached upon these lands and touched off sporadic Indian up-risings, the most serious having been in Guerrero, Hidalgo, Morelos, Oaxaca, Veracruz, and Yucatán.[2] Clashes were more frequent in the north, though, de-spite the much more sparse indigenous population. The Indians of the north, as they had been in pre-Hispanic times, were nomadic warrior hunters and gatherers, while those of the more developed center and south tended to be sedentary horticulturalists. Unlike the uprisings in central and southern Mex-ico, which were touched off by encroachments on communal lands that were used for farming, the fighting in the north was mostly with nomadic bands, such as the Apaches and Comanches, who were resisting habitation of their hunting lands by outsiders moving up from the center and south. The Indian problem of the northern frontier dogged the Spanish for the entire colonial pe-riod. The Spanish, for example, never were able to develop stable colonies in western Nuevo México, which then contained Arizona, because the Indians kept wiping them out.

The intensity of Indian resistance on the northern frontier led the colo-nial authorities to carefully restrict gun trading in the area. By the end of the eighteenth century the Spanish had achieved a delicate peace with most of the Indians of the north. But that peace broke down in the early decades of the next century. Following independence in 1821, Indian fighting increased in Sinaloa, Sonora, Chihuahua, and Nuevo México with Utes, Apaches, Co-manches, Navajos, Mayos, Yaquis, and Arapahos.[3] The westward advance of the United States contributed to the increase. In 1821, the same year that Mex-ico gained independence, the Santa Fe Trail opened between Independence, Missouri, and Santa Fe, then in the Mexican north. Increased trade stimulated non-Indian immigration from both the south of Mexico and the east of the United States to take advantage of new economic opportunities. As more people entered the area, they competed with the nomadic Indians for use of the land, and frictions grew. Adding to the problem was a practice of newly arrived U.S. citizens—trading guns for property that Indians had stolen from Mexicans. The effect was to both encourage the Indians to resume raiding and give them the means to do so. In 1826 the Mexican government formally complained to the U.S. government that the trading practices of its citizens were instigating Indian violence in the frontier areas.[4]

The newly independent Mexican government was ill-prepared to insure order in its northern territories as fighting intensified between Indians and the increasing populations of non-Indians. The government reacted by developing extreme policies, including offering bounties in Chihuahua and Sonora for Apache scalps.[5] From the 1820s to the end of the Mexican-American War in 1848, some of the sharpest fighting took place in northern Sonora, including the areas that would become southern Arizona around Tucson, as the Mexican army sought to protect beleaguered outposts of Mexican settlement from Apache raids.[6] The Apaches were divided into a large number of small bands. Some lived in the Mexican settlements and sided with the Mexican army in defending them from other Apaches. The Spanish and Mexicans referred to these as *mansos* (tame ones). Most though—the *broncos* (wild ones)—were outside of the settlements, living in nomadic bands that practiced hunting, gathering, and herding. At earlier times they had practiced horticulture, but this was abandoned of necessity as fighting developed with the Comanches in the 1700s.[7] Raiding developed as an important adjunct to the Apache economy. Livestock raided from Mexican ranches could be used for the Apaches' own purposes or sold to U.S. citizens.

The 1836 Texas war of independence and the 1846–48 war with the United States resulted in Mexico losing the problems of pacifying the warring Indian peoples within the territories that were ceded. However, particular nomadic bands, such as the Apaches and Comanches, did not let the new border detain them from raiding on both sides. For that reason, in the Treaty of Guadalupe Hidalgo, which ended the Mexican-American War, Article XI specifically dealt with trying to control Indians who crossed and raided on both sides of the border.

The Indian wars in Mexico continued into the beginning of the twentieth century. Apache raids through the 1880s delayed the development of mining in Northern Sonora. The most sustained resistance in Sonora, though, was waged by the Yaquis, who staged major uprisings in 1885 and 1895.[8] Unlike the Apaches and Comanches, they were a mainly farming people. As late as 1905 some 500 Yaqui guerrillas staged raids on Hermosilla, Ures, and Guaymas.[9] Even in the 1920s there was still fighting between Yaquis and government troops.

To the *criollo* leaders of nineteenth-century Mexico, the Indian was not only a real or potential military problem but also a social problem. Most of Mexico's European-descent upper class saw the Indian as backward and an obstacle to their plans for national development. In order to overcome this perceived obstacle, they developed a series of cultural, demographic, and economic policies. In cultural terms, they pressured Indians to adopt Western manners. European, especially French, cultural and liberal ideas greatly influenced the upper class, which sought to model Mexico's constitutions and other institutions after those of modern European countries. But the majority of Mexicans were Indians, not Europeans, with different cultural traditions and institutions. Samuel Ramos advanced the hypothesis that the country suffered so much political instability in the decades following independence precisely because, if its Indian reality was always at variance with the provisions of European-inspired constitutions, then the reality was always illegal.[10] The policy of Europeanizing the Indian failed to transform the millennia-old culture of most of the population, and this failure continues to frustrate upper-class goals.

If Indians could not be transformed into dark-skinned Europeans, then the next logical solution was to alter the country's racial mixture demographically by encouraging immigration of enough whites so that eventually the Indians would be outnumbered, as they were in the United States and Canada. This policy also failed, however, as most migrants from Europe preferred to go to the United States, where they perceived economic opportunities to be more promising.

From independence in 1821 to Juárez's liberal constitution of 1867, Mexico's landowning upper classes also sought to transform the nature of Indian land tenure. During the colonial period, the Spanish Crown had protected the legal existence of Indian communal lands. These lands remained nonalienable properties of Indian villages. That is, they were neither owned by individuals, nor could they be sold like private properties, remaining outside of the market and capitalist development in general. The landowning upper classes, therefore, sought to transform them into individually owned properties, and the Indians into family farmers. Various states between the 1820s and 1860s began the encroachment on the legal existence of the communal lands, and the liberal 1867 constitution culminated the process. However, the process failed to turn Indians into middle-class family farmers, turning them rather into landless peasants. The main beneficiaries were large hacienda owners, who quickly were able to buy up the communal lands. The liberal and well-intentioned expropriation of Indian communal lands helped to set the stage for the 1910 Revolution, one of whose outcomes was to legally reinstate most of the Indian communal lands, an action which in turn created a new obstacle to the capitalist development of rural Mexico.

It is difficult to estimate the true proportion of Indians in Mexico today because of the large number of mestizos. At one pole are people who are, in biological terms, fully indigenous. Then there is a continuum of mestizos who range from mostly indigenous to mostly European, with people of fully European background at the other pole. Complicating the issue further is the interrelationship of people of African and Asian descent with the Indian population.

Investigators have used two other criteria, apart from the biological, to distinguish the Indian population. The first is to consider as Indians those who identify themselves as Indians and continue to uphold indigenous cultural values and practices. In this respect, Bonfil Batalla distinguishes Indians and de-Indianized Indians. That is, one part of Mexico's biologically indigenous population is easily identifiable because its members live together, usually in small towns and rural areas, speak a common language that is different from Spanish, and live a culturally distinct style of life. But members of another part of that population have, both culturally and physically, left their homes and integrated into the outside national culture.[11] The second criterion for distinguishing the indigenous population is linguistic, that is, to classify as Indians those who continue to speak an indigenous language. In this respect, the 1990 Mexican census found more than thirty-seven indigenous languages still spoken in the country by 5,282,347 persons, who represented 7.6 percent of the Mexican population over the age of five. Of these, 836,224 persons were monolingual, speaking only their indigenous language and not Spanish. Over 90 percent of the speakers of indigenous languages are in the center and south of Mexico—historically part of Mesoamerica. Just over half the indigenous language speakers speak one of the four major languages, which are, in order, Náhuatl (also called Mexicano), Maya, Mixteco, and Zapoteco. At a minimum, then, the Mexican population contains this 7.6 percent of indigenous language speakers. But the real percentage is higher because there are considerable numbers of Indians who do not speak indigenous languages. Various governmental agencies calculate that 15 percent of the population is composed of Indians, and a number of Indian organizations estimate the proportion to be 18 percent.[12]

The core of the population that is fully Indian in both the cultural and ancestral senses lives in some 373 *municipios*—a geographical unit equivalent to a county—where 70 percent or more of the population speak an indigenous language. These *municipios* contain 43.6 percent of all of the people within Mexico who speak an indigenous language. They are all located within eleven states in the center and south of the country—Campeche, Chiapas, Guerrero, Hidalgo, Nayarit, Oaxaca, Puebla, Quintana Roo, San Luis Potosí, Veracruz, and Yucatán. All are in the area of Mexico that was classically a part of Mesoamerica. Other states, such as México, Michoacán, and Chihuahua also contain *municipios* with significant proportions—as much as 60 percent—of speakers of Indian languages. Within each of the eleven states the Indian *municipios* are generally located outside of the larger cities. That is, the larger the city, the lower the proportion of Indians within it. The reverse, though, is not always true, since there are small municipios that contain few or no speakers of Indian languages. In general, then, the Indian population is disproportionately located outside of the larger cities in peripheral smaller towns and rural areas within the center and south of Mexico.

The collective labor force of the Indian *municipios* (Table 8–2) is disproportionately self-employed and agricultural. Over 60 percent of the Indian labor force is self-employed, compared to 36 percent of the total labor forces of their states; and three-quarters of the Indian labor force works in agriculture, compared to 42 percent for the states as a whole. The disproportionate representation of the Indian labor force in agriculture follows from its disproportionate location in rural areas. However, the Indian labor force is disproportionately self-employed not only in the rural areas within which it exists but also in the larger Indian towns. In general, the more urbanized a labor force is, the more its members become employees. This tendency is true for both the non-Indian and Indian labor forces, but less so for the latter. That is, Indians in the larger towns are more likely than non-Indians to be self-employed. The Indian predilection for self-employment follows from their resistance to complete integration into the national economy.

If we follow Max Weber's observation that one of the most significant trends of modern times is that more and more people work within organizational, that is, bureaucratized, settings,[13] then it is clear that the collective labor force of the Indian *municipios* is distinctly premodern because nearly two-thirds of its members still work outside of bureaucratic settings. The Indian economy, as reflected in the distribution of its labor force, has the same disproportions that exist between the national economy and those of the United States and Canada, but more extreme. If the national labor force is disproportionately made up of self-employed and agricultural members compared to those of its first world continental neighbors, the Indian labor force within the national economy contains disproportionately more self-employed and agricultural members than does the non-Indian labor force.

With some hesitation, we can attempt a comparative estimate of the economic class structure of the Indian labor force within the eleven states in question. Given our knowledge of its general profile and how it differs from the

TABLE 8–2   Labor Forces and Living Conditions in Mexico, the Eleven-State Region that Contains the Indian *Municipios*, and the Indian *Municipios*

	MEXICO		ELEVEN-STATE REGION		INDIAN MUNICIPIOS	
	Number	*Percent*	*Number*	*Percent*	*Number*	*Percent*
A. Labor Forces						
By Position:						
Self-employed	6,000,902	26.6	2,422,566	36.2	429,944	60.6
Employed	15,936,229	70.8	3,975,560	59.4	227,843	32.1
Unpaid	587,429	2.6	294,091	4.4	51,721	7.3
Total	22,524,560	100.0	6,692,217	100.0	709,508	100.0
By Sector:						
Agriculture	5,300,114	23.5	2,835,810	41.5	556,265	75.5
Mining	99,233	0.4	26,119	0.4	438	0.1
Petroleum	161,282	0.7	70,259	1.0	1,430	0.2
Industry	4,493,279	19.9	853,629	12.5	51,858	7.0
Electricity	154,469	0.7	42,505	0.6	915	0.1
Construction	1,594,961	7.1	425,651	6.2	23,850	3.2
Transport	1,045,392	4.6	249,156	3.6	6,614	0.9
Commerce	3,108,128	13.8	731,230	10.7	28,791	3.9
Finances	360,417	1.6	53,437	0.8	698	0.1
Services	6,282,266	27.8	1,552,593	22.7	65,907	8.9
Total	22,599,541	100.1	6,840,389	100.0	736,766	99.9
Median monthly income	$133		$103		$30	
Percent below minimum wage		27.7		42.6		77.0
B. Living Conditions (percent)						
Literate		87.6		80.4		55.2
With electricity		87.5		76.2		52.4
With indoor piped water		48.8		30.0		10.7

Notes: For labor forces, does not include unspecified members. Median monthly incomes calculated in U.S. dollars. Literacy rate is for population 15 and older, and it is defined as persons who report that they can take and read a message. Percentage totals may not equal 100 because of rounding.

Source: Calculated from Instituto Nacional de Estadística, Geografía e Informática (INEGI), *XI Censo General de Población y Vivienda, 1990* (Aguascalientes: INEGI, 1992).

average for the states in question, we can deduce the directions of some of its differences. Since the Indian labor force has relatively more self-employed members, it will have relatively more members of the joint self-employed classes (peasants, small businesses, and capitalists). Unfortunately, though, the census data do not permit us to determine the proportions of each of those classes. We can at best assume, but not empirically document, that the Indian labor force contains relatively more peasants and small business owners and relatively fewer capitalists than the non-Indian labor forces. We can, however, with some statistical accuracy estimate that the working class makes up approximately 36 percent and the new middle class approximately 3.5 percent of the Indian labor force, both of which are significantly lower than the corresponding proportions for the eleven-state region.

In social-class terms, the Indian population is, as is well known, significantly poorer and therefore lower class than the average. Over three-quarters (77 percent) of the Indian labor force receives less than the Mexico's minimum wage, compared to 42.6 percent for the region and 27.7 percent for the country as a whole; these statistics indicate that the Indian *municipios* contain disproportionately more lower-class members. There are a number of indicators of the poor, lower-class living conditions that prevail in the Indian *municipios*. Housing and living conditions are significantly below the national average, as well as the average for other non-Indian rural communities. For houses to have the bare essentials of modern standards of living, they must be hooked up to electricity and plumbing systems. Great progress has been made over the last few decades in Mexico in bringing electricity to the Indian communities. The vast majority of houses nationally now are hooked up to electricity (see Table 8–2). But almost half of the Indian houses are still without electricity. The state of plumbing systems in the Indian communities is a much more serious problem that is not likely to be resolved any time soon. Nearly 90 percent of the Indians live in houses without indoor plumbing, having neither running water or toilets. Potable (that is, safe to drink) running water is important for obvious reasons. But, perhaps more important, the lack of running water for sanitation greatly increases the likelihood of gastroenteritis and other infectious diseases. Without water to easily wash hands and dishes, all types of bacteria are ingested, especially by children, causing digestive disorders that range from mild bouts of diarrhea to life-threatening dysentery and cholera. Compounding the problem is the remote location of the communities and lack of access to medical facilities. The combination of lack of indoor sanitation facilities, susceptibility to digestive infection, and lack of access to medical facilities results in thousands of Indian babies dying each year from dehydration caused by untreated diarrhea. Finally, 44.8 percent of the Indians in these rural communities over the age of 15 cannot read or write, a percentage that is also above both the national average and the average for the eleven-state region.

Unfortunately, the Mexican census does not permit us to develop a statistical profile of that part of the Indian population that has left the *municipios*. There are most likely significant differences between the Mexican Indians who continue to live in the traditional communities and those who have migrated out; and among the latter there may well be significant differences between the living conditions of those who continue to maintain their distinct cultural identities through language and styles of dress and those who have become more fully integrated into the national culture. Most likely, the material living conditions of those Indians who have migrated out of the tradition *municipios* are better.

Most anthropologists who have studied the Indian communities in the Mexican countryside have been struck by how their economies are both structurally different from and interrelated with the national economy. They have embraced one or another variation of what we can call a dual-economy interpretation of the rural Indian communities.[14] According to that interpretation, the national money economy penetrates but does not fully determine the economies of these communities. The rural Indian communities have particular economic characteristics that are not shared with other rural communities. In the most general terms, what distinguishes the Indian from non-Indian rural communities is that the former straddle the money economy to a much greater extent. In the Indian communities, one foot is firmly planted outside of the money economy in autarkic subsistence production for primarily household needs. In the non-Indian rural communities, most economic activity is integrated into the national money economy. The Indian household is both a reproduction unit, as are all households in the sense that it is there that labor force members receive sustenance, and a production unit in the sense that all members above an early age work to produce goods. In Max Weber's sense, the Indian household economy conforms to a premodern stage of development because the great historical shift of our time has been precisely the physical separation between where people live and where they work for income, and that separation has yet to develop fully in the Indian communities.

The resistance of Indians to being completely integrated into the national economy, in part, has pre-Hispanic origins. Horticulture before the Conquest was practiced primarily to fulfill household needs and secondarily to meet tribute obligations. Thousands of micro farms in the Indian *municipios* continue to orient their production toward meeting household needs first and only secondarily toward market sale. This type of production is also in part a reflection of many Indians' lack of willingness and resistance to being completely integrated into Mexican national identity. By having their own land, however small it may be and however meager a living it may afford, they have an economic basis to preserve their independence. These Indians, thus, if possible prefer to have land and be self-employed as a way to preserve their independence and particular cultural identities. The non-Indian rural population certainly prefers to have land rather than be landless, but it does not have the same cultural motives. If it does have land, it is more likely to orient all of its production to market sales. It is more likely to sell its land if the price is right. It is more likely to leave the area in search of income as migrant laborers. It can be more easily lured off the land by the perception of higher-paying employee positions in cities. It follows, therefore, that the structure of the labor force of the non-Indian rural population will more quickly be transformed according to the general tendencies of accumulation of capital and economic development in general in the countryside, tendencies which result in concentration of landownership and the consequent decline in self-employed farming. In brief, the Indian rural population has particular cultural motives that result in holding on to self-employed farming as a way of life and that are stronger than those of the non-Indian rural population. Aguirre Beltrán, therefore argues that the Indian communities cannot be seen simply as underdeveloped peasant communities. They represent more than that because they are "ethnic groups with a different internally cohesive culture that strongly resists integration [to the nation]."[15]

Capitalist development has therefore proceeded more rapidly in the non-Indian than the Indian areas of the Mexican countryside. This conclusion is reminiscent of Max Weber's classic *The Protestant Ethic and the Spirit of Capitalism* in which he argued that capitalist development proceeded more rapidly in the Protestant than in the Catholic regions of Europe. In both cases, specifically cultural factors hindered introduction and development of a particularly capitalistic way of life.

THE UNITED STATES

As described in Chapters 2 and 3, European-origin colonists achieved a farming toehold on the continent by pushing the indigenous peoples back from the shore lands. This push immediately triggered resistance, touching off a series of coastal wars during the colonial period. By the eve of the War of Independence, Indian resistance in the thirteen colonies had been reduced but not eliminated. But with more land-hungry settlers continually arriving and with the most fertile lands already claimed, pressure mounted for further expansion westward. The British colonial authorities, though, had negotiated a series of treaties with Indian tribes that limited further westward expansion of the colonies. This policy greatly irritated the new colonists and was one of the background grievances responsible for provoking the War of Independence.[16]

The British policy of limiting westward expansion of the colonies would have a number of consequences for the subsequent history of white-Indian relations in the United States. The policy won the support of most of the East Coast Indian tribes, who sided with the loyalist cause in the War of Independence. (This British-Indian alliance would carry over to the War of 1812.) The subsequent victory of the revolutionary army had disastrous consequences for Indians. The policy of the newly independent United States would be to remove all barriers to further westward expansion. Because of having sided with the British in the War of Independence, the East Coast tribes could not expect favorable policies from the new United States government or treatment from its military.

After the War of Independence the U.S. military was mainly preoccupied for the next eight decades, apart from the Mexican and Civil wars, with pushing Indians westward in order to free up their lands for European settlement. It is significant that from the beginning of its existence, the U.S. military generally fought alone as an institution against various Indian enemies. Unlike the French and English, who formed military alliances with whole *tribes*, the United States military generally only fought alongside of *individual* Indians, who had either betrayed their own tribes in time of war or were mercenaries.

The Indian thus was always marginalized in U.S. history. Unlike in Mexico, where the original Spanish colonists had encountered relatively dense populations whose labor they sought to exploit, in the United States virtually no attempt was made to exploit Indian labor. The only thing that the colonists wanted from the Indians was their land. The expropriation of that land, as described in Chapter 4, was the original condition for the continuing economic development of the United States.

In the first decade of the nineteenth century, Tecumseh, a Shawnee chief, formed the largest organized resistance to the policy of driving Indians westward. His confederacy of tribes carried out raids against the expanding white settlements, especially in the border areas of Ohio, Kentucky, and Tennessee. Many in the United States accused Britain of financially backing Tecumseh's campaigns. This British backing, coupled with incidents caused by the British policy of boarding U.S. vessels in the high seas in search of deserters, led President James Madison, on July 1, 1812, to declare war on Great Britain.

There were two objectives of the United States in the War of 1812. The first was to eliminate Indian military resistance in the East. The second was to drive Britain from the North American continent and take over its last holdings in the area that later became Canada. In pursuit of these objectives the U.S. military had to fight simultaneously against the British army, Indian armies, and Canadian civilian soldiers defending their border. The United States was able to accomplish the first objective of eliminating Indian military resistance in the East. In 1813, Tecumseh was killed in battle, and subsequently his confederacy and Indian military resistance in the East collapsed. The United States failed, however, to accomplish its second objective to expand its borders northward. The U.S. leaders had counted on Canadians joining with them to overthrow British control. But that expectation failed to materialize, as most Canadians remained loyal to the Crown. They were not won over by U.S. arguments that being annexed to their southern neighbors would be good for them. William Hull, the U.S. commander at Detroit, sought the support of the Canadians, proclaiming, "You will be emancipated from tyranny and oppression and restored to the dignified station of freedom."[17] Hull's proclamation, though, fell on deaf ears. No Canadians crossed over to his side, leading him to surrender without firing a shot to a superior British force significantly backed up by Indian allies. The successful defense of its territory in the War of 1812, which was significantly aided by Indian forces, was an important event in consolidating Canadian national identity. It also led to Indians generally faring better, though not without serious problems, in Canada than the United States.

With the last serious Indian resistance in the East ending with the War of 1812, the United States proceeded with its policy of pushing Indians westward. President Andrew Jackson's Indian Removal Act of 1830, which specified that all Indians should be moved west of the Mississippi River, consolidated the policy. Among the many atrocities touched off by this policy was the forced march in 1838 of 14,000 Cherokees from Georgia to Oklahoma, during which 4,000 died.[18] After the Indian Removal Act several thousand Indians escaped to Canada and took up permanent residence.[19]

By the 1840s the location of Indian resistance and wars had thus shifted from the East to west of the Mississippi. According to McWilliams, at the time of the signing of the Treaty of Guadalupe Hidalgo in 1848, which ended the Mexican-American War, the population of the Southwest was made up of 180,000 Indians, 60,000 Mexicans, and very few Anglos.[20] After the war, thousands of Anglos streamed in, some on their way to the California gold rush, others simply in search of land and other opportunities. This invasion provoked an increase in Indian hostilities.

The U.S. military in 1848 took over the job of pacifying the southwestern Indians, which had been initiated 300 years earlier by the Spanish, and succeeded in less than four decades. It fought, at one time or another, against all of the major band societies—Apaches, Navajos, Comanches, and Utes.[21] Seasoned Mexican and Indian recruits joined in its campaigns, significantly contributing to its successes.[22] In 1886, Geronimo, the last of the Apaches' warrior chieftains, was captured and, along with his followers, imprisoned, ending the Indian wars of the United States. The last of the imprisoned Apaches was not released from Fort Sill, near Lawton, Oklahoma, until 1912. A number of other Apaches, who escaped imprisonment, took to the hills, made their way to Sonora, and integrated themselves into the Yaquis—the origin of Apache names among a number of Yaquis today.

Although 1886 marked the end of the Indian wars per se, it was not the end of military repression. In the northern plains the Sioux had militarily resisted white encroachment on their lands up through the 1870s, culminating in the 1876 Battle of the Little Bighorn, in which they defeated General George Custer's army. After that, their warriors dispersed into smaller bands that the army systematically tracked down and defeated. In December 1890, a cavalry division of the U.S. Army entered the Pine Ridge, South Dakota, reservation and massacred 300 Sioux men, women, and children at Wounded Knee Creek. The Wounded Knee massacre drove home the final military defeat of Indians in the United States.

Once Indians were no longer a military threat, various attempts were made to integrate them into the evolving social structure of the United States. Policies shifted back and forth between treating Indians as peoples and placing them on reservations, and treating them purely as individuals to be integrated into the society of the United States. Among the most ambitious and disastrous of the latter integrationist policies was the Dawes General Allotment Act of 1887, which sought to turn Indians into family farmers by subdividing reservation lands, a policy which was somewhat similar to what had just occurred in Mexico with Indian communal lands. Some 150 million acres of reservation land were subdivided and turned into the private property of individual Indian families. But most of the families, who came from hunting and gathering backgrounds, were ill-prepared or unwilling to become farmers. Many quickly fell into debt and were forced to sell their land in order to raise funds for repayment. Other land, which had not been distributed to Indian families, was declared to be surplus and distributed to whites. By 1934, when the Dawes Act expired, Indians had lost 90 million of the original 150 million acres of reservation land.[23]

Of indigenous peoples living in the United States today, there are 1,878,285 Indians, 57,152 Eskimos, and 23,797 Aleuts.[24] Indians make up a scant 0.8 percent of the total national population. The greatest concentration of Indians begins at the Arkansas-Oklahoma border and then stretches westward to the Pacific across Oklahoma, New Mexico, Arizona, and California. A little over 44 percent of all Indians live in those four states. Oklahoma contains the largest number of Indians of any state.[25] Its Indian population was made up of indigenous Plains Indians and Indian tribes forcibly removed from the eastern states during the first decades of the nineteenth century. Up until 1907, the year of statehood, it was labeled on maps as "Indian Territory." New Mexico and Arizona's Indians are indigenous to the area. California contains a large number of Indian migrants from other states. Major urban areas containing large Indian populations are Los Angeles, Tulsa, Oklahoma City, San Francisco, Phoenix, and New York City.

There are dramatic differences between the living conditions of Indians who continue to live on reservations and those who do not. While overall Indians are significantly poorer than the average in the United States, their poverty rate compares favorably with those of Puerto Ricans, Mexicans, and blacks. However, the poverty rates of many of the reservations are exceedingly high. The poverty rates of the ten largest reservations in 1990 varied between 49 and 67 percent. About one Indian in four continues to live on a reservation, a proportion that has been steadily falling in the last few decades. The largest of the reservations, with 123,935 persons, is the Navajo, which spans parts of Arizona, New Mexico, and Utah. The second largest, the Pine Ridge in South Dakota, with 11,180 persons, belongs to the Sioux.[26] Thus, as in Mexico, the most significant indicator of Indian material living conditions is location: whether they remain in areas that are only loosely tied to the national economy or in areas that are well integrated.

As in Mexico and Canada, Indians in the United States are divided between traditionalists and integrationalists. The former seek to cultivate traditional cultural values (such as the stress on communal relations and respect for the land) as sources of cultural preservation and survival, while the latter are more interested in integrating into the larger society of the United States in as favorable a manner as possible. The former question the value of material improvements in living conditions if they are at the expense of cultural integrity. Traditionalist-oriented Indian militancy reached a high point during the late 1960s and 1970s, roughly the same period that blacks, Chicanos, Puerto Ricans, Chinese, Filipinos, and Japanese were active over civil rights issues. Traditionalist Indian political activism included an occupation of Wounded Knee, legal challenges to reclaim fraudulently expropriated land, and organization of cultural survival schools. As with other minority groups, militancy declined greatly in the 1980s. In a strange irony, gambling joined alcohol as a great enemy of traditional Indian values. In the 1980s gambling interests discovered a loophole in state antigambling laws: they did not apply on reservations because these were only under federal jurisdiction. As a result, a multimillion-dollar gambling business sprang up rapidly on a number of reservations, threatening to seduce and sweep away all but the most hardened of traditionalist values.

CANADA

Once the British Crown had secured control of all of the areas that would become Canada, its policies dictated how the Indian question was handled. As discussed earlier, the most important of those policies was established on October 7, 1763, when the British Crown by royal proclamation established the principle that would govern all future expropriations of Indian lands. All attempts to open up Indian lands for settlement would have to be through Crown purchase.[27] The lands could not simply be taken as they would be later in the United States.

Between 1871 and 1910 the Canadian government, continuing the principle of the Proclamation of 1763, opened up the country to westward expansion by negotiating ten major treaties with Indians in what were to become the prairie provinces of Manitoba, Saskatchewan, and Alberta. The Indians relinquished rights to certain areas and in return received guaranteed rights to reserves. According to Brown and Maguire, all of the treaties had provisions for "reserve lands; monetary payments, and occasionally medals and flags, at the treaty signing; suits of clothing every three years to chiefs and headmen; yearly ammunition and twine payments; and some allowance for schooling."[28] The experience in British Columbia was slightly different. There, in 1861, three years after it had become a crown colony, the governor simply identified Indian lands to be held in trust by the Crown as reserves. Unlike in the prairie provinces, no treaty negotiations were involved.[29]

The settling of European-background peoples in the western provinces of Canada proceeded, as described in Chapter 4, with significantly less Indian resistance and violence than occurred in either Mexico or the United States. In contrast to the experience on the U.S. frontier, where Indians were forcibly conquered and then had land-relinquishing treaties imposed upon them—as also happened in the Mexican-American War—the English Crown initiated the later Canadian policy of purchasing Indian lands *before* they were opened up to white settlement. This allowed European-descent settlers to enter the frontier in a relatively orderly and peaceful manner. Seymour Martin Lipset emphasizes that Canada had a strong cultural tradition of respect for law and order and little tolerance for outright individualism. Hence, as Canadians moved westward, the government bought land from Indians for orderly settlement, and the Royal Mounted Police, formed in 1873, set up operations to keep order, enforcing Indian as well as settler rights in the relinquished territories. Thus, in Lipset's analysis, the law arrived before individuals on the Canadian frontier, while individuals, embracing a strong cultural preference for individualism, arrived before the law on the U.S. frontier. The lynch mobs, vigilantism, and Indian massacres that were so much a part of the U.S. frontier experience were virtually absent during the settling of the Canadian frontier. In the United States the military was almost always on the side of the settler. In Canada, the state militia, in the form of the North-West Mounted Police, was much more neutral in enforcing law and order. Indians knew the difference between the two countries. The Sioux, for example, took refuge in Canada during their wars with the U.S. cavalry. This is not to argue that there were no problems between whites and Indians on the Canadian frontier or that the Canadian frontier was inhabited by European-background peoples without severe injustices being done to the indigenous peoples.[30] In all three countries, the indigenous peoples have suffered severe injustices, but they have suffered the least in Canadian history.

The long-term goal of British and Canadian policy was to transform Indians so that they could be assimilated into the dominant society. Toward that end, they pressured Indians to take up farming and abandon their hunting and gathering economies. In time, large numbers of boarding schools for Indian children were established. Many of the schools were entrusted to religious groups that were more interested in teaching the dominant society's language, values, and religious beliefs than the skills necessary to compete in the labor force. The assimilationist emphasis of early-twentieth-century Canadian policy was similar to that of the United States, where boarding schools were also used to break adherence to Indian languages and cultural values.

Canada today recognizes three groups of indigenous peoples: Indians, Inuits (Eskimos), and métis, who are of mixed European and Indian descent. What concerns us here will be Indians and Inuits. Discussion of the métis is reserved for Chapter 11. Canada makes a further distinction between status and nonstatus Indians. The former are registered with the federal government's Department of Indian Affairs. The latter are all others. Most of the status Indians are members of some 550 bands. The term "band" is a political label used by the federal government to designate groups of Indians that have common recognized interests in land. The average-size band contains approximately 500 persons. These bands have rights to 2,200 reserves. The total reserve area in Canada contains 6 million acres, or about 27 acres for each reserve resident.[31] Indian languages continue to be spoken by some 138,000 persons.[32]

In 1991, there were 365,375 people, 1.4 percent of the total Canadian population, who identified themselves as Indians and 30,085 who identified themselves as Inuits.[33] All surveys indicate that Indians, compared to the national averages, have significantly lower incomes, are more likely to be unemployed, and are less likely to be professionals or managers. On average, Indians occupy the lowest positions within the labor force of all racial groups, earn less income from employment, and are more likely to gain significant proportions of their income from government transfer payments.[34] About 40 percent of Canada's indigenous population lives on reserves, where economic and living conditions are severely depressed. Frideres notes that "less than one-half of the houses (44 percent) have running water, 30 percent have indoor toilets, 33 percent have telephones, and 82 percent have electricity."[35] The infant mortality rate of Indians is twice as high as that for all Canadians.

Nevertheless, Canadian government programs have succeeded in dramatically lowering the infant mortality rate for registered Indian children living on-reserve from 82 per thousand in 1960 to 15.9 per thousand in 1986.[36]

CONCLUSIONS

The end of the eighteenth century found European-descent peoples concentrated in the eastern areas of the United States and Canada and the central areas of Mexico. From the east of the United States and Canada they moved progressively westward as they moved northward from the central areas of Mexico. The northern states and territories—Sonora, Chihuahua, Sinaloa, Nuevo México, California—were the Mexican frontier, while the provinces west of Ontario were the Canadian frontier and the area west of the Mississippi the U.S. frontier. Overall two geographic frontiers existed in North America. The first spanned the northern parts of Mexico and the southwestern parts of the United States. The second spanned the north-central parts of the United States and the western parts of Canada. Both frontiers stretched across national borders, which nomadic Indians crossed back and forth. The settling of the U.S. and Mexican frontiers was exceptionally violent, marked by bloody confrontations with the indigenous peoples. In contrast, the settling of the Canadian frontier was relatively peaceful.

Once land had been expropriated or relinquished, the three countries of North America attempted through various means to assimilate Indians into their nation-building and economic-development projects. But, of all of North America's racial groups, Indians have been the most resistant to becoming fully integrated culturally and economically, especially into money economies with their competitive rules of conduct. The historical legacy of this resistance is found today in many of the Indian *municipios* of Mexico, the reservations of the United States, and the reserves of Canada.

CHAPTER 9

Afro–North Americans

The current distribution of blacks in North America—98 percent in the United States and 1 percent each in Mexico and Canada—largely follows from the distribution of slaves in the sixteenth through nineteenth centuries. The South of the United States was one of the three major locations of New World slavery—the other two were the Caribbean and Brazil. There was considerably less slavery in Mexico and very little in Canada. Each country's history thus has a black component, but with differing significances (see Table 9–1).

THE UNITED STATES

The development of the contemporary position of blacks in the United States can be divided into five historical stages: slavery (1620–1865), Reconstruction (1865–1877), segregation (1877–1964), the post–World War II civil rights movement (1945–1965), and the contemporary period.

Black history and the development of black inequality in the United States originated in the southern states with the slave system, which lasted more than two hundred years. For that reason, virtually all blacks in the United States today have ancestors from the South. As late as 1900 over 95 percent of all blacks in the United States lived in the southern states. Today outmigrations have reduced that figure to 50 percent, but the South still contains proportionately more blacks than any other region in the country. It was during slavery that black economic inequality was institutionalized and rationalized by the development of the racist notion of black biological inferiority.

The abolition of slavery was a by-product of the Civil War, which was fought primarily over the issue of the secession of the Confederacy. The

TABLE 9–1   Distribution of African-Americans in North America

	NUMBER[a]	PERCENT	PERCENT OF OWN COUNTRY
United States	29,986	98.0	12.2
Canada	314	1.0	1.2
Mexico	300	1.0	0.4
Total	30,600	100.0	

[a]In thousands.

Sources: Census of Population and Housing: Summary Population and Housing Characteristics (Washington, DC: U.S. Government Printing Office, 1992), Table 2; and Statistics Canada, *Ethnic Origin,* 1991 Census (Ottawa: Minister of Industry, Science and Technology, 1993), Table 1A; size of African-Mexican population based on estimate.

Emancipation Proclamation, which President Abraham Lincoln signed on January 1, 1863, was designed to create a fifth column in the South. The proclamation specifically did not abolish slavery in those areas that had remained loyal to the North. Nevertheless, the Emancipation Proclamation was soon followed by other measures, culminating in the Thirteenth Amendment to the Constitution, ratified in 1865, which completely abolished slavery.

The northern victory insured the end of slavery, but many questions still remained about the future political and economic fate of blacks. There was considerable disagreement among the victors over the exact political and legal status of ex-slaves, or freedmen as they came to be called. There was resistance even in the North to granting them the same legal status as whites or allowing them to vote. By 1870, though, the resistance had been overcome, and the states had ratified the Fourteenth and Fifteenth amendments to the Constitution, which guaranteed, respectively, black legal equality and the right to vote.

Reconstruction (1863–1877) is the period during which the northern victors militarily occupied the South and attempted to directly restructure its political life and economy. The period began in 1863, before the end of the war, in those areas of the South already under northern military control and ended with the withdrawal of northern troops in 1877. Generations of historians have offered sharply different appraisals of Reconstruction. For decades southern and many northern historians interpreted it as period in which misguided northern policies resulted in great harm and tragedy. This interpretation prevailed largely unchallenged until the 1930s, when W.E.B. Du Bois published his massive defense of Reconstruction's progressive features.[1] Du Bois recounts having been asked earlier by the editors of the *Encyclopaedia Britannica* to submit an article on the history of the American Negro for the fourteenth edition. The editors accepted the article but only after cutting out all of his references to the progressive features of Reconstruction because they contradicted the orthodox view. Du Bois then refused to allow publication of the article.[2] In the 1930s a number of historians associated in the Communist Party in the United States also argued that Reconstruction had been an important period of progressive and democratic change.[3]

The northern occupying armies insured that blacks could vote as mandated by the Fifteenth Amendment. As a result, in areas where the former slaves were a majority, they were able to elect mayors, governors, congresspersons, and senators. On the state level they elected more than six hundred legislators and eighteen major officials, including one governor and six lieutenant governors. On the federal level they elected sixteen members of Congress and one senator. The Forty-third Congress alone counted seven black members.[4] During Reconstruction there was more black democratic political participation than in any period before, obviously, or after until the gains of the civil rights movement restored democratic participation for blacks in the South, some ninety years after the end of Reconstruction.

During Reconstruction blacks and a number of white northern allies sought to match the democratic political gains with economic gains, advocating breaking up the plantations and distributing the land to the former slaves under the slogan "Forty acres and a mule." Had such a radical land reform been carried out, the subsequent history of blacks and the South would have been substantially different. But the northern elites never embraced land reform as a solution to the problems of the ex-slaves. During the war, large amounts of planter land had been seized by the occupying northern armies. In a number of cases, after the white owners fled, the land was turned over to blacks, with the ownership status of the land remaining ambiguous as the blacks worked it. The issue was settled at the end of the war, in September 1865, when President Andrew Johnson, who had succeeded the assassinated President Lincoln, ordered that land be restored to all pardoned owners in the South. Blacks living on that land were then required to either work for wages or leave. From 1865 to 1867 the northern occupying army evicted thousands of blacks from land that was being restored to its former owners.

The reluctance of northern elites to push through a radical land reform for ex-slaves was in part based on what they feared blacks would do with the land. In Haiti and the British Caribbean after abolition of slavery in 1791 and the 1830s, respectively, the ex-slave populations gained their own land and retreated into subsistence rather than market production. Consequently, sugar production plummeted. The same tendency to retreat into subsistence farming occurred in the South during and after the Civil War in those areas where blacks were able to control land. Blacks were more interested in becoming independent peasants than agricultural wage laborers, to the consternation of white elites in both the North and the South.

Many blacks saw the end of slavery as giving them more autonomous control if not over land then at least over time for personal development. As a result, an actual shortage of black labor developed, according to Foner, "largely because all former slaves were determined to work fewer hours than under slavery, and many women and children withdrew altogether from the fields." Black families were determined "to use the rights resulting from emancipation to establish the conditions, rhythms, and compensation of their work, and to create time to pursue . . . personal and community goals."[5] The black quest for increased autonomy clashed with the planters' need for a disciplined labor force, and, through one means or another, white owners sought to drive blacks back "into their places." White violence against the black population broke out immediately after the war in 1865 with many beatings and murders. In 1866 the Ku Klux Klan, the largest and most violent of the terrorist organizations that sought to restore white domination, formed in Tennessee and quickly spread to other areas of the South. Plantation owners and their supporters made it violently clear that, although now legally free, blacks would still be subjected to their rule and domination. Those blacks who thought emancipation meant equality would be publicly repressed to teach others a lesson. At the same time that blacks were making enormous political gains during Reconstruction, a white counterrevolution was gathering steam.

Reconstruction and northern military occupation of the South ended as a result of the Hayes-Tilden Compromise of 1876. Rutherford B. Hayes was the presidential candidate of the Republican Party, and Samuel Tilden the Democratic Party candidate. The election was fiercely contested, and there were many acts of violence. Tilden undoubtedly held the lead in the popular vote, but Hayes most likely had a decisive lead in the electoral college vote. There were large numbers of disputed returns, with rival vote counts being sent to Washington to be decided in the House of Representatives. There was even talk of a new civil war. The crisis was resolved through political maneuvering and compromises that ultimately ended Reconstruction. First, an electoral commission was established to rule on the disputed elections. The Republicans outmaneuvered the Democrats in the establishment of the commission, which then awarded all of the disputed elections to Hayes, giving him enough electoral votes for the presidency. But then the Democrats threatened to filibuster in the House of Representatives to block the tally of the electoral vote. It was at this point that Hayes' supporters negotiated an agreement with key southern Democrats: as president, Hayes would recognize the right of the southern states to govern themselves without northern interference in return for the southern Democrats ceasing to obstruct the count of the electoral vote. One Republican commented, "The policy of the new administration will be to conciliate the white men of the South . . . and niggers take care of yourselves."[6]

After assuming office, President Hayes quickly began to withdraw most of the northern troops that were still occupying the South. With that action, Reconstruction ended, and the fate of the ex-slaves was sealed for the next ninety years of U.S. history. Northern elites had forged a new tacit agreement with their southern counterparts. In return for the national loyalty of the southern elites, the northern elites allowed the legal edifice of segregation to be consolidated. Instead of backing reforms that would have enabled the ex-slaves to compete with some modicum of equality in the postwar South, the northern elites abandoned the initial aims of Reconstruction and gave tacit approval to allowing the old plantation owners to reassert control and resubordinate blacks in the class structure. With the northern troops withdrawn, the ex-slaves were left defenseless as the white counterrevolution triumphed, dismantled the institutions of Reconstruction, and restored white supremacy. All ex-slave claims to the land became moot. Whites rapidly reestablished control over local and state governments and disenfranchised blacks. They established segregation of the races in education, eating establishments, hotels, and public transportation as a legal principle.

White vigilante groups, such as the Ku Klux Klan, employed terrorist means, including lynchings of blacks, to significantly aid the reestablishment of white control. The terrorism had a number of classic sociological elements. It took place mostly in small rural towns whose traditional code of class and racial relations was being threatened. It was employed by a ruling class to intimidate and drive back into a subordinate position a rural lower class that had sought and temporarily enjoyed limited upward mobility. It was employed in an exemplary fashion in the sense that lynchings were carried out publicly with the victim left hanging as an example to other blacks of what could happen to them if they too stepped out of line. Local law officials often took part unofficially in the white vigilante actions. The use of lynch law to establish the Jim Crow South in the 1870s and 1880s was similar to the use of death squads to terrorize the Salvadoran peasantry in the 1980s. In both cases a rural lower class was threatening a traditional order, and in both cases the rural upper classes used terrorist means to intimidate into submission their challengers. In both cases members of the state apparatus took part unofficially in the terrorist repression. In both cases the state was an accomplice to the terrorism. Its agents—the local sheriff and his deputies in the case of the South, military officials in the case of El Salvador—unofficially took part in the terrorism. As a result, the respective state apparatuses took little or no action against the perpetrators of the violence.

What would have happened if the North had pushed Reconstruction to a more radical restructuring of the South rather than allowing the white counterrevolution to succeed? A more radical restructuring would have meant confiscating the property of the planter class and redistributing it to poor blacks and whites alike. If that had happened, then the old southern ruling class would not have been able to reestablish domination as it did. Poor whites would have had common cause with poor blacks, setting a basis for an interracial political alliance. Certainly the North would have had to continue military occupation for decades, and there would have been constant resistance from large numbers of whites. But if Northern elites had been willing to completely restructure the southern political economy, they could have avoided much of the racial tension that later plagued and continues to plague the United States. But they did not, choosing the easier course of allowing the old southern ruling class to resume control. Rather than struggle at all costs to establish the basis for interracial harmony, they tacitly allowed segregation of the races to be institutionally consolidated.

The legal basis of segregation in education was confirmed by the 1896 *Plessy* v. *Ferguson* decision, which established that education could be separate for the races so long as it was equal. A type of domestic apartheid thus existed from the end of Reconstruction in 1877 until the 1950s and 1960s when its legal structure was dismantled. It would be a mistake to believe that this segregation existed only in the South. Northern establishments generally followed the southern lead. In the 1920s in New York City it was common for fashionable midtown restaurants to refuse service to blacks. It was a segregated U.S. military, with separate white and black companies, that fought in World Wars I and II. The principle of segregation even applied to blood, with blood drawn from blacks and whites being kept in separate banks.

The legal basis of segregation began to be dismantled in the United States by a 1954 Supreme Court decision, *Brown* v. *Board of Education* (of Topeka, Kansas), which mandated integration of public education and therefore reversed the 1896 *Plessy* v. *Ferguson* decision. The Civil Rights Act of 1964 outlawed segregation in public facilities, removing the final legal basis of segregation. Ending the legal basis of segregation was a necessary but not sufficient step for ending segregation itself. Large parts of education, housing, and social life in general continue to be substantively segregated in the United States.

Most interpretations of the end of legally sanctioned segregation in the United States have focused on the role of the civil rights movement and its leaders, such as Martin Luther King, Jr. The major organizations of the civil rights movement—the Southern Christian Leadership Conference, the National Association for the Advancement of Colored People, the Congress of Racial Equality, and the Student Nonviolent Coordinating Committee—used lawsuits, lunch counter sit-ins, boycotts, marches, and other tactics to protest and eventually bring down the legal edifice of segregation. But there is an additional, often overlooked, reason why overt segregation ended in the United States. After World War II, as large parts of Africa and Asia became decolonized, newly independent third world countries entered and began voting in the newly formed United Nations. At the same time, the United States and the Soviet Union were competing for cold war allies in the third world. The existence of overt segregation became an increasing liability for U.S. foreign policy objectives. A number of embarrassing incidents occurred in the late 1940s and 1950s involving African diplomats stationed in the United States who were refused service and even arrested as vagrants when they traveled between Washington and New York. It was obviously difficult to enlist their support for the U.S. campaign against communism when they knew from personal experience that the "free world" was not as free as it purported to be. Elites in the United States thus began to see segregation as an increasing liability in the cold war and joined in the efforts to end it. The tacit allowance of segregation by northern elites, which began with the end of Reconstruction in 1877, thus ended partly, and ironically, as a result of the cold war in the 1950s.

With the main goals of the civil rights movement having been accomplished with the passage of the 1964 Civil Rights Act, nonviolent civil rights protest actions declined rapidly after 1965. At the same time, though, riots and rebellions began to break out in black northern ghettos outside of the South. Between 1965 and 1970, such major cities as New York, Philadelphia, Detroit, Cleveland, Newark, Los Angeles, Chicago, and Washington, DC, experienced serious breakdowns of law and order in black areas. During 1967 alone eighty-seven people lost their lives in racial disturbances.[7] The largest violent outbreaks occurred during the week after the assassination of Martin Luther King, Jr., in 1968. During that week more than 50,000 U.S. troops were deployed in black ghettos, more than the number then stationed in Vietnam. For the most part the riots were spontaneous outbreaks that could easily be ignited because of the charged atmosphere that existed in those years.

The traditional divide between integrationist and nationalist orientations was present in the 1960s black social movement. In many ways the Civil Rights Act of 1964 was the triumph of the integrationist organizations, which believed that the solution to racial injustice in the United States lay in removing the barriers to full and equal participation of blacks *within* the institutions of the society, including schooling, housing, electoral politics, and the workforce. These organizations, the oldest of which was the National Association for the Advancement of Colored People, had fought a long battle since the nineteenth century for blacks to be accepted and recognized as equal citizens of the United States. Not everyone in the black activist and intellectual community, though, agreed with the underlying assumptions of the integrationist-oriented organizations. Many questioned whether blacks should want to become a part of the fundamentally white-defined institutions of the United States. Many believed that the United States was in a period of decadence as anticolonial revolutions of nonwhite peoples were redefining the world order. The novelist James Baldwin questioned whether blacks wanted to be integrated into "a burning house." The separatist-oriented organizations, such as the Nation of Islam, believed that the racial division within the United States could not be reconciled within the near or medium future. Given the irreconcilability of the racial division, blacks should develop their own institutions until they achieved substantively equal standards of living. At that point, perhaps, the question of racial integration could be reopened but on the solid basis of an agreement between races that had substantively equal economic and social living conditions.

Throughout the late 1960s and 1970s the federal government was actively engaged in both implementing the mandates of the Civil Rights Act and attempting to ameliorate the conditions of economic deprivation in the ghettos. But, in the 1980s, during the administration of President Ronald Reagan, the federal government began to decrease its involvement in redressing the problems of African-Americans. The Reagan administration's stance followed from its conservative Republican philosophy of reducing governmental regulation of the economy and attempts at redressing social problems. During the 1980s, therefore, the gap between African-Americans and whites in the United States, which had been narrowing in the previous decade, began to increase again.

Throughout the 1980s there were sporadic violent outbreaks in some black communities, the most notable being Liberty City in Miami, but these did not come close to the scale of violence that occurred in the late 1960s. However, on April 29, 1992, a jury that contained no blacks acquitted four white Los Angeles police officers who had savagely beaten Rodney King, a black. The beating had been secretly videotaped, and millions around the world had seen the irrefutable proof of police brutality. The acquittal touched off nights of pent-up rage among mostly blacks in South Central Los Angeles, causing deaths, injuries, and millions of dollars in damage. The disturbance was not suppressed until after 6,000 National Guard troops were called in to patrol the mostly black areas of Los Angeles.

The most conventional way to interpret these events is to see the violence as a tragic and self-defeating response to injustice. There is, though, another interpretation. Piven and Cloward have noted that social-welfare spending in the United States generally expands after periods of threatened or real violence by the poor and contracts during periods when the poor are quiescent. In this respect, the New Deal social programs of Franklin Delano Roosevelt developed as a response to mass mobilizations of the unemployed, some of which were led by the Communist Party, during the early part of the depression. After the depression and the mobilizations associated with it ended, the scale of social-welfare programs decreased until the urban black eruptions of the late 1960s. The federal government then expanded old programs and developed new programs in an attempt to ameliorate desperate living conditions in the black ghettos.[8] By the 1980s, when the federal government began to cut back social-welfare programs, black activism was at a low point. If this line of interpretation is valid, then the most important consequence of urban riots, which few political leaders want to acknowledge, may well be the forcing of politicians to increase governmental social spending in the communities where the rioters live.

In class terms, it is clear that since 1964, as many discriminatory barriers have been significantly lowered, proportionately more blacks have been able to achieve middle-class standards of living. This important accomplishment in racial equality in the United States has had an unintended consequence. As families in general move up the class scale, they move out of poor areas and into neighborhoods befitting their new class positions. In the case of blacks, this tendency has resulted in ghettos being drained of professional role models for youth, resulting in class polarization within what was once a much more united black community in the face of common social oppression.

Politically, blacks vote significantly to the left of the national pattern, with the black vote being firmly in the Democratic Party. In each of the presidential elections between 1976 and 1992, 85 percent of blacks on average cast their votes for the candidate of the Democratic Party. Only 12 percent on average voted for Republican Party candidates.[9] Part of the reason why blacks vote as they do is that they have disproportionately low incomes and, like other low-income classes, believe that the Democratic more than the Republican Party will support social programs, such as subsidized housing and welfare, that will directly benefit them. In addition, blacks perceive the Democratic Party to be more willing than the Republican Party to use the powers of the federal government to remove discriminatory barriers in jobs, education, housing, and the like.

The black voting pattern responds to the basic differences between the Democratic and Republican parties. The Democratic Party is philosophically based in a liberal view of the relationship between the state and the economy and society, while the Republican Party is based in a conservative view. Twentieth-century liberalism views state action, through spending and programs, as necessary both to correct the problems that emerge from the normal functioning of a market-based economy—monopoly pricing, unemployment, and poverty—and to redress specific social concerns such as discrimination. Conservatives believe that the economy should be, as much as possible, self-regulating. For that reason the Democratic Party during the twentieth century has been much more willing than the Republican Party to use the federal government to redress specific grievances and problems of blacks and other low-income groups and consequently has won their votes.

MEXICO

Mexico's small contemporary black population is made up of the descendants of colonial slaves, escaped slaves from the United States, and Caribbean laborers imported for railroad, agricultural, and mining work. Like African-Americans in the United States, Mexico's African-origin population has called itself and been called a number of different names during its history. These have included *negros* (blacks), *prietos* and *morenos* (dark skinned), and *mulatos*. The name that is used most by researchers today is *Afromestizo*, a designation that incorporates recognition that most of this population combines indigenous or European as well as African origins. Because there has been considerable integration of African-origin individuals into the Mexican population through intermarriage and interbreeding with Indians, mestizos, and whites, today there are very few Mexicans, far less than 1 percent, of predominantly African descent. A much larger proportion, perhaps as high as half, of the population carries some traces of African ancestry.

   Only 0.1 percent of New Spain's population in 1810, at the beginning of the War of Independence, was made up of fully African-origin people. But a much larger and more significant 10.1 percent was made up of mulattoes.[10] Because slavery was practiced to greater and lesser extents in all of the areas of New Spain, it follows that the African-ancestry population exists to greater and smaller degrees in all parts of Mexico today. The greatest number of slaves were concentrated in and around Mexico City. Most of the descendants of these slaves in time interbred with the large Indian, mestizo, and white population that surrounded them. The proportion of slaves to the total population was higher in the tropical flatlands near Veracruz on the Gulf of Mexico coast, where sugar plantations could be established. For that reason, today there are more people who appear as blacks in Veracruz than any other part of the country.

   The second-largest concentrations of black-appearing people are in the mountainous coastal areas of Guerrero and Oaxaca on the Pacific Coast. These are mostly the mulatto descendants of escaped slaves who made their way to remote areas of these mountains and managed to resist capture. Within fifty years of the conquest, the Guerrero mountains were becoming known as a refuge of escaped slaves. The seriousness of the problem for owners was indicated by the 1579 Spanish policy of mutilating the genitals of recaptured slaves as punishment.[11]

In 1948, Mexican anthropologist Gonzalo Aguirre Beltrán studied the town of Cuajinicuilapa, which is located on the mountainous coast between Guerrero and Oaxaca. Cuijla, as the town was called for short, had been established by escaped slaves in the late 1500s. They had chosen the location because it was isolated and could be easily defended. Over the next two hundred years the inhabitants of Cuijla had pushed the indigenous population out of the area and resisted all attempts to recapture them. They were thus on hostile terms with both the Spanish authorities and the surrounding indigenous population. At the same time, over the centuries they progressively interbred with the indigenous population.

By 1948, when Aguirre Beltrán studied the town, the African origins of most of the mulatto inhabitants were clearly visible not only in negroid somatic features but also in cultural practices that were clearly different from those of the indigenous peoples of the region. The Spanish spoken by the town's inhabitants contained African-origin terms. Women went bare breasted in public and carried jugs on their heads. The town and surrounding area contained African-origin round huts with conical roofs.[12]

From 1829, when Mexico abolished slavery, to the end of the U.S. Civil War, Mexico was a destination for escaped slaves. While much more is known about the Underground Railroad traveled north to Canada by runaway slaves, there was also an Underground Railroad traveled south and west to freedom in Mexico.[13] There was a strong antislavery sentiment and considerable sympathy for the plight of escaped slaves in Mexico. During the thirty-six year period from 1829 to 1865, Mexico's receptiveness to escaped slaves from the United States was one of the major problems in the relations between the two countries.

Texas was the key link in the escape of U.S. slaves to Mexico. Before 1822, when the first Texas colony of Anglos was established by Stephen Austin, a number of runaway slaves crossed from Louisiana into the area and established themselves as free persons. After the migration of mainly southern whites into Texas, the area became not so much a destination as a transition point for escaped slaves. During the 1836 Texas War of Independence a number of slaves fled to the Mexican armies combating the Texans, where they were immediately freed and sent further south in Mexico for their safety.

The proximity of Mexico to the slave South was a consistent problem for the owners. A runaway slave simply had to make it to the border, and then she or he was free. Even the Texas Republic's first president, Sam Houston, suffered the misfortune of having two of his personal slaves escape to Matamoros, which was just across the Rio Grande.[14] The seriousness of the problem prompted the slave owners to pressure the federal government to seek a treaty with the Mexican government for the return of runaway slaves. From 1826 to the late 1850s the U.S. government unsuccessfully attempted to get Mexico to sign a treaty with a provision for the return of fugitive slaves. Because most Mexican politicians and the balance of public opinion favored the abolitionist cause, the government never agreed to return fugitive slaves to the United States. To the contrary, the Mexican government, by its antislavery attitude, encouraged an increase in runaway slaves to the country. During the 1850s the Mexican government granted land in Veracruz and Coahuila to runaways who wanted to establish themselves.[15]

In 1858 a slave ship destined for the United States ran aground on the Gulf coast near the Mexican town of Cabo Rojo. The captain was obliged to unload his human cargo as he sought repairs in the town. The authorities seized and formally freed the slaves under a provision of the constitution that all persons who step on Mexican soil are free.[16] Estimates of the total number of fugitive slaves who escaped to Mexico during this period vary widely— from several hundred to hundreds of thousands. Schwartz, who has done the most extensive research on the subject, believes that there were probably several thousand.[17] Some undoubtedly returned after the Civil War and emancipation in the United States. The majority remained. Their descendants are to be found today in the states of Tamaulipas and Coahuila, which border Texas, and Veracruz, which borders Tamaulipas to the south.

While there is no doubt that the majority of descendants of the Africans who arrived in Mexico have been dispersed into the country's larger genetic pool, there is considerable disagreement over whether the small black population that remains is fully integrated ethnically. Aguirre Beltrán, for example, in the study cited earlier, maintained that the people of Cuijla were not an ethnic minority living in segregated conditions as were, for example, blacks in the United States. They freely interacted and intermarried with the surrounding population. Blacks in Cuijla, according to Aguirre Beltrán, were more likely to identify themselves as Mexicans than the Indian population who chose instead to identify themselves either as Indians or according to their particular group.

Some researchers, such as Moedano Navarro, maintain that a separate ethnic identity exists today among Mexican blacks,[18] but Aguirre Beltrán, the classic researcher of Mexico's black population, goes so far as to state that "blacks do not exist now as a separate group."[19] Aguirre Beltrán argues that blacks have integrated much more rapidly than Indians into Mexican society in large part because they have had less cultural resistance to integration. "What is important," he notes, "is that the Negro, unlike the Indian, does not view the *Ladino* as his superior and, when the communications media break his secular isolation, he integrates himself spontaneously and without compulsion into the national society." He further maintains that, as in British North America, "the Negroes brought to New Spain came from different regions, each with its own language. Upon arrival, they were dispersed often as a deliberate means to prevent contact among speakers from the same linguistic group." This policy, which was also common in the areas that became the United States, facilitated their eventual integration into the national culture. Indians, on the other hand, continued to speak their own languages.[20] One of the indications of lack of a separate identity is that, unlike with Indians, there are no regional or national organizations of blacks as blacks. In this respect, if the African cultural roots are much less observable in the music, dance, and religions of U.S. blacks than Caribbean ones (especially Haitians, Cubans, and Puerto Ricans), they are even less observable among Mexican blacks. Put differently, compared to the Caribbean and the United States, the African origins of Mexico's black population were the most erased though their historical experience and are therefore the least observable in their contemporary cultural lives.

CANADA

There are about 314,000 blacks in Canada today, constituting 1.2 percent of the total national population (see Table 9–1).

The first blacks were brought in as slaves in the 1600s, with slavery lasting more than two hundred years until 1834, when by Imperial Act the British Parliament abolished it in all of the colonies. But it was never practiced on a large scale because the area was unsuitable for plantation agriculture. The slave population most likely never exceeded 5,000 at any one time.

The War of Independence in the United States and the War of 1812 led to an increase in both the free and unfree black populations of Canada. During the War of Independence the British promised freedom and land to slaves who deserted their rebel masters. Following the war, a number of loyalist slave owners fled to Canada with about 2,000 of their slaves.[21] During the War of 1812, the British repeated the policy of offering freedom and land to escaping slaves, resulting in an additional 2,000 blacks entering the country.[22]

By 1834, the year of abolition, there were perhaps 20,000 blacks in

British North America. Of these, no more than 50 were slaves.[23] Although Canada allowed slavery to exist until 1834, it considered runaway slaves from the United States to be free as soon as they touched Canadian soil. As a result, at least 10,000 southern slave runaways traveled the Underground Railroad to freedom in Canada. Estimates of the size of the Canadian black population at the time of the U.S. Civil War range between 20,000 and 75,000.[24] Winks considers 62,000 to be the most reasonable estimate, with about two-thirds of these having arrived as either fugitives or free migrants from the United States.[25] Many fugitive slaves only stayed in Canada temporarily, returning to the United States after the abolition of slavery. As a result, Canada's black population went into a century-long period of demographic decline, with the 1961 census reporting only 32,127 blacks in the country, probably barely half the number in 1861. Several thousand blacks from Caribbean British Commonwealth countries entered the country before 1961. About half came to be employed as domestics.[26] But their numbers were not enough to significantly offset the demographic decline of the black population overall.

The majority of blacks in the country today are first-generation Canadians who came after 1967, when Canada significantly altered its immigration policies to remove any restrictions on race or nationality. The Immigration Act of 1967 grants legal entry on the basis of a point system in which education level and skill are of prime consideration. The reforms have enabled large numbers of Caribbean blacks, particularly from Jamaica, to enter. A disproportionate number of these hold university degrees, with the proportion of all blacks in the Canadian labor force who hold university degrees now being higher than that for the labor force as a whole. As a result, black immigrants receive incomes that are close to the Canadian average. However, as reported by Lautard and Guppy, the overall Canadian black population, which includes native-born as well as immigrant members, occupies positions of lower than average status in the labor force.[27]

✳ CHAPTER 10

Original and New Asian Communities

More than 80 percent of North America's people of Asian origin live in the United States, less than a fifth live in Canada, and a bare trace live in Mexico (Table 10–1). Proportionately the greatest Asian presence is in Canada, where Asians are the largest minority, constituting 6 percent of the national population. As in the case of Latinos north of Mexico, it is erroneous to consider Asians to be a homogeneous minority. There are clear economic and cultural differences between Chinese, Japanese, Filipinos, and other Asian-Americans. In numerical terms, Chinese, Filipino, and Indians are now the largest Asian-origin minorities on the continent (Table 10–2).

The Asian–North American experience falls into two great periods: from the late 1840s until the 1930s, when immigrant Chinese, Japanese, and Filipino laborers formed the first communities of their respective nationalities on the North American mainland; and from the 1950s until the present, when the aftermath of the Korean and Indochinese Wars and liberalization of immigration laws in the United States and Canada produced surges in Asian immigration. Three out of every four Asians in North America today entered since the 1950s. Most of what we consider to be basic Asian–North American history concerns the former period, when the original communities were established and suffered great racial discrimination, but only a minority of Asians who live in North America today are descendants of those original immigrants.

TABLE 10–1   Distribution of Asian-origin Population in North America

	NUMBER[a]	PERCENT	PERCENT IN OWN COUNTRY
United States	7,273	80.6	2.9
Canada	1,607	17.8	6.0
Mexico	140	1.6	0.3
Total	9,020	100.0	

[a]In thousands.

Sources: U.S. Bureau of the Census, *Census of Population and Housing: Summary Population and Housing Characteristics* (Washington, DC: U.S. Government Printing Office, 1992), Table 2; Statistics Canada, *Ethnic Origin,* 1991 Census (Ottawa: Minister of Science, Industry and Technology, 1993), Table 1A; for Mexico, based on estimate.

ORIGINS OF THE ASIAN–NORTH AMERICAN COMMUNITIES

Chinese-North Americans

Chinese laborers first entered North America in the mid-nineteenth century through Pacific Coast ports in California, British Columbia, and Baja California. In all three countries they faced similar economic conditions and social experiences, working originally in mining, railroad construction, and agriculture and then later moving on to service employment as owners of small restaurants, laundries, stores, and the like. In all three countries, they encountered sharp racism and discrimination.

The first wave of immigrants came to California, beginning in 1849, just after the area had been taken from Mexico by the United States. By 1852 at least 20,000 had arrived. Warfare, poverty, and natural disasters pushed them out of China, and the gold rush lured them to California. Most were too poor to pay for their passage. Some obtained the tickets on credit, agreeing to pay off the loan on the California side. It usually took five years of labor, once in California, to accumulate enough to retire the debt. Others voluntarily entered into contract labor arrangements—a form of indentured servitude. They signed contracts to work for a specified number of years in return for the passage. These contracts were then sold to employers, mainly gold-mining companies, in California.

Throughout the 1850s mining absorbed the largest number of Chinese contract laborers in California. But by the end of the decade the mines had been played out. Simultaneously the discovery of gold in British Columbia in 1858 drew a number of laborers northward, producing the origins of Canada's

TABLE 10–2 National and Regional Origins of Asian–North American Populations

	UNITED STATES		CANADA		MEXICO		TOTAL NORTH AMERICA	
	Number[a]	Percent	Number[a]	Percent	Number[a]	Percent	Number[a]	Percent
China	1,645	22.6	587	36.5	100	71.4	2,332	25.9
Philippines	1,407	19.3	157	9.8			1,564	17.3
India	815	11.2	420	26.1			1,235	13.7
Indochina	1,001	13.8	117	7.3			1,118	12.4
Japan	848	11.7	49	3.0	30	21.4	927	10.3
Korea	799	11.0	44	2.7			843	9.3
Other or unknown	758	10.4	233	14.5	10	7.1	1,001	11.1
Total[b]	7,273	100.0	1,607	99.9	140	99.9	9,020	100.0

[a]In thousands.
[b]Because of rounding, percentages may not total 100.

Sources: U.S. Bureau of the Census, *Census of Population and Housing: Summary Population and Housing Characteristics* (Washington, DC: U.S. Government Printing Office, 1992), Table 2; Statistics Canada, *Ethnic Origin*, 1991 Census (Ottawa: Minister of Industry, Science and Technology, 1993), Table 1A; for Mexico, based on estimate.

Chinese population. Later, emigrants would leave directly from China for British Columbia. With white labor in short supply, employers sought Chinese labor both because it was cheap and because it was available. As in the United States, significant numbers of the Chinese originally came as contract laborers, having to pay off the cost of their passage before they were able to keep the full amount of wages.

In California by the late 1860s, after the mines were played out, the Central Pacific Railroad became the largest employer of Chinese labor. At one point 90 percent of Central Pacific workers were Chinese.[1] Canadian employers similarly used Chinese labor to construct the Canadian Pacific Railroad from 1881 to 1885, as would Mexican employers in later decades to construct their country's railroad infrastructure.

In the early 1860s a small number of Chinese laborers found their way to the Baja California peninsula of Mexico. Most came from Chinese communities already established in California. Many made livings fishing for abalone, which they sent to San Francisco for export back to China. In October 1871, Cuba expelled a small number of formerly indentured Chinese workers who then entered Mexico through Veracruz, touching off a national debate often couched in racial stereotypes over the desirability of Chinese immigration. From the time of independence forward in the nineteenth century, Mexico's leaders sought immigrants—but European immigrants—to populate and bring progress to the country. They did not have Asian immigrants in mind.

In the 1870s in California, after the completion of the railroads, Chinese labor was employed in land reclamation. In that decade Chinese laborers made up 75 percent of seasonal farm workers in California and 14 percent of the state's overall labor force.[2] McWilliams notes that it was the availability of cheap Chinese labor that made the development of California fruit production possible.[3] In British Columbia, Chinese laborers were significantly employed in salmon canneries and vegetable cultivation.

By the end of the 1870s, with the mines having given out, railroad construction over, and land reclamation finished, Chinese labor left the countryside for the Chinatowns of San Francisco and other cities. There the labor force would reform around small businesses—laundries, restaurants, shops, and the like. At the same time, because of the completion of the primary infrastructure of agriculture and railroads, whose construction had sustained high labor demand, massive unemployment descended upon the California economy.

California's whites, themselves immigrants, saw the Chinese as outsiders who threatened their economic interests. They saw themselves as being entitled to the state by virtue of the victory over Mexico, and they were willing to make good their claim with acts of violence against Chinese immigrants as well as the original Indian and Mexican inhabitants. In 1862 alone, 88 Chinese were murdered in the state.[4] In the 1870s, with unemployment on the rise, the Chinese immigrant worker became the scapegoat for the ills of the economy, and anti-Chinese agitation accelerated. In 1882 the U.S. government responded to the anti-Chinese sentiment in California by passing the Chinese Exclusion Act, which barred laborers, but not merchants, from entry into the country.

Because of the Chinese Exclusion Act, Chinese emigrants now entered Mexico for the first time in significant numbers. Some only used Mexico as a point of entry into North America and later crossed the U.S. border illegally to rejoin family and other contacts who had established themselves earlier in California.[5] The majority, though, stayed in Mexico, with many moving on from Baja California to Sonora, Chihuahua, Mexico City, Chiapas, and the Yucatán. They worked at first in fishing; coffee, cotton, and henequen farming; mining; and the building of the railroads. Later they opened laundries and specialized in the production and sale of ice cream. They entered for the most part during the thirty-year rule of President Porfirio Díaz, who had a policy of encouraging immigration. Díaz preferred European immigrants in order to increase the white population, but was willing to accept Chinese.

By the 1880s enough white laborers had arrived in British Columbia to cause a significant decrease in the area's labor shortage. The labor market advantage then passed to employers, and laborers had to compete among themselves for existing jobs. It was in those conditions, as in California, that anti-Chinese sentiment and racism began to build among whites. In 1875, Chinese were specifically banned from voting in British Columbia. By 1885, Canada passed the first specifically anti-Chinese federal legislation, requiring that all Chinese—but not Europeans—entering the country pay a $50 tax.

The balance of Mexican public opinion found the Chinese to be undesirable immigrants. Most Mexicans viewed the Chinese, in addition to being non-Christian, as depraved, plagued with sicknesses, and addicted to innumerable vices. In addition, they viewed Chinese culture as being completely foreign and unadaptable to their own. They especially viewed with alarm and horror the prospect of intermarriage between Chinese and Mexicans, which they thought would surely produce racial degeneration.[6] Nevertheless, contracting Chinese immigrants solved the problems of employers who needed labor that they considered to be cheap and docile. Thus the Chinese kept arriving, never in large numbers, but enough to be noticed. Early Chinese labor was concentrated in railroad construction projects, mines, and export crop plantations. The Chinese, once their contracted periods had expired, quickly

moved away from laboring positions and into commercial activities as owners of small restaurants, laundries, hotels, tailoring shops, ice cream stores,
and the like. But still their numbers were slight.

In 1895 there were only 1,026 Chinese in all of Mexico. Immigration increased significantly in the next fifteen years, most of it coming directly from
China rather than California. Because of the 1882 Chinese Exclusion Act in
the United States, Mexico became the destination of emigrants. Estimates of
the 1910 Chinese population in Mexico range widely between 13,000 and
40,000 out of a total Mexican population of 15,160,369. About a third of these
resided in the northern border state of Sonora, which would become the center of anti-Chinese sentiment.[7]

One of the outstanding demographic features of the original Chinese
communities in all three countries was that males heavily outnumbered females. In 1911 there were twenty-eight Chinese males for every Chinese female in Canada.[8] Mainly single men migrated, and the costs and other difficulties of the long trip from China discouraged married men from bringing
family members. Many in this generation assumed that they would make
money in North America and then return home to China to start or rejoin their
families, an assumption that generally did not work out. The lack of a family unit for most of the early Chinese males encouraged the growth of gambling, drug use, and prostitution in the early Chinatowns of North America.
In all three countries a common theme of anti-Chinese sentiment was the association of the population with vice. The 1882 Chinese Exclusion Act sealed
the gender imbalance by blocking the entry of family members to join males
who had already established themselves in North America. Antimiscegenation laws in the United States and Mexico further restricted the possibilities
for male Chinese to establish families. As a result, the rates of natural increase of the North American Chinese populations were much lower than average.

The 1910–17 Mexican revolution awakened a deep nationalism, which
was directed against all foreigners including the Chinese. This was in large
part because the Porfirio Díaz government, against which the revolution was
initially fought, had given favored treatment to foreign capital and foreigners,
especially those from the United States, for whom the best jobs were reserved
in the areas of the economy, such as in the railroads, that they controlled. The
belief that foreigners were benefiting economically at the expense of Mexicans was one of the indignities that fired the ire of revolutionaries. Much of
this nationalistic antiforeigner resentment, which was mostly targeted at U.S.
citizens, spilled over onto the Chinese, who had been modestly successful in
their commercial enterprises. Women were often at the forefront of the anti-

Chinese campaign during the revolution because they viewed the Chinese as taking away their traditional source of income from washing clothes, sewing, and cooking.[9]

During the revolution, there were outbreaks across northern Mexico, usually by local revolutionary forces, against Chinese residents. The worst incident took place during the first stage of the Revolution in Torreón, where in 1911 the Chinese community numbered some seven hundred persons and contained laundries, shoe repair stores, restaurants, hotels, farms, and a bank. On May 15, 1911, revolutionary troops, led by Emilio Madero, brother of Francisco, the future president, took Torreón. A detachment surrounded a Chinese-owned bank. When two of the bank's employees tried to keep the troops at bay by firing arms into the air, the troops opened fire. The two defenders were immediately killed, and the troops then went on a rampage against the whole Chinese community. By the end of the massacre 303 Chinese and five Japanese lay dead.[10]

In Sonora the anti-Chinese movement was the most pronounced. There, the Nationalist Anti-Chinese League was founded; and by 1916 under Governor and later President Plutarco Elías Calles further Chinese immigration into the state was prohibited, and two laws were passed to require Chinese already living there to stay in segregated residential districts. By 1916, one hundred Chinese had already lost their lives as a result of anti-Chinese violence.[11] In 1919 the mayor of Cananea, Sonora, ordered that all Chinese businesses close and that all Chinese residents, about one thousand, leave the town. However, the president of the country, Venustiano Carranza, countermanded the order on the grounds that it would harm diplomatic relations with China. In general Plutarco Elías Calles and Adolfo de la Huerta, both future presidents of Mexico, supported the anti-Chinese campaign in Sonora.

The decade of the 1920s saw a consolidation of anti-Chinese legal measures in all three countries. Canada in 1923 banned further immigration of Chinese and required all Chinese living in the country to register with the government. The next year the United States passed the Immigration Act of 1924, which banned all Chinese from entry as immigrants. In the 1920s every Mexican city with any significant Chinese population also had an anti-Chinese organization. Anti-Chinese committees were especially active in Sonora, Sinaloa, Baja California Norte, Chihuahua, Coahuila, Veracruz, Chiapas, and Yucatán. The legislature of Sonora in 1923 approved laws that required Chinese in the state to live in segregated districts, prohibited them from having businesses outside of those districts, and prohibited marriages between Chinese and Mexicans. In 1930 the Sonora government prohibited anyone from sleeping on the premises of a business, a measure aimed specifically at Chinese owners, who kept their operating costs to a frugal minimum by living above or behind the place of business. Throughout this period Chinese government leaders, including Sun Yat-sen, repeatedly protested through diplomatic channels to the Mexican government about the treatment of its emigrants.

In 1929 the leaders of postrevolutionary Mexico founded the Partido Nacional Revolucionario (PNR), the precursor of the present-day ruling Partido Revolucionario Institucional (PRI). The PNR participated in the anti-Chinese movement, including being actively involved in creating an anti-Chinese committee in the House of Deputies.[12]

In 1931 the government of Sonora enacted a series of measures to close down Chinese businesses. Vigilante groups called *guardias verdes* (green guards) stationed themselves outside of Chinese stores to keep customers out. That same year a number of towns in Sonora, including Hermosillo, Guaymas, and Nogales, began physically expelling Chinese residents, some to neighboring states and others to the United States. On August 2, 1932, police in the border city of Nogales took fifty-eight Chinese to a hole in the fence that marked the frontier with the United States and ordered them to cross to the other side or be shot. The U.S. government then deported them to China.[13] In November 1932 the U.S. government formally requested that Mexico stop forcibly expelling Chinese into Arizona, and the practice ceased. One of the consequences of the expulsions was that a number of Chinese males returned to China with their Mexican wives and children. As a result of the return of these families, according to Hu-DeHart, there continue to be definable Mexican barrios in certain south China villages.[14]

By the end of the 1920s the Directorate of the Nationalist Anti-Chinese Campaign in Mexico claimed that it had 215 affiliated organizations that counted two million members.[15] The claim was undoubtedly exaggerated, but it nonetheless indicated that anti-Chinese sentiment was both widespread and organized. However, the campaign never achieved its main goal of having federal anti-Chinese legislation enacted. It did, though, influence considerable anti-Chinese legislation on the local and state levels, and the virulent anti-Chinese campaign succeeded in driving three out of every four Chinese out of Mexico. The 1927 census found 24,218 Chinese-born residents in the country. The 1940 Census found only 5,848, less than a quarter, remaining.

During and after World War II the legal situations of Chinese in the United States and Canada improved considerably. The United States in 1943 repealed its Chinese Exclusion Act and in 1945 allowed Chinese to become naturalized citizens for the first time. After the war Asian antimiscegenation laws were repealed by the states. In Canada, Parliament in 1947 repealed the Immigration Act of 1923. By the 1950s, British Columbia and other provinces had repealed legislation banning Chinese from voting.

Japanese–North Americans

Japanese immigrants first started arriving in California in small numbers, about a thousand a year, in the 1890s. Hawaii had had a large Japanese-descent population for years. At the time of its annexation by the United States in 1898, some 40 percent of its residents were of Japanese descent. Most of Canada's early Japanese immigrants only used the country as a jumping-off point for getting to the United States. The advantage of using Canada as a stepping-stone was that if the immigrants were subsequently deported from the United States, they would be returned to Canada rather than Japan.[16] The same dynamic occurred among Mexico's early Japanese immigrants. Some 14,000 migrated to Mexico during the first part of the twentieth century. Of these, though, nearly 10,000 only stayed in Mexico briefly and then went on to the United States.

In California, the Japanese took laboring positions, mainly in agriculture; in 1909 they made up 41.9 percent of the agricultural labor force.[17] In California the Japanese encountered the same hostility from whites as had Chinese immigrants. E. A. Ross, a prominent sociologist, argued that the Japanese were unassimilable, worked for lower wages, had a lower standard of life, and were not prepared for democratic values. In 1900 the San Francisco Labor Council sponsored a meeting which urged that the 1882 Chinese Exclusion Act be extended to the Japanese as well.[18] Anti-Japanese riots broke out in San Francisco in 1906. That was the same year that the San Francisco School Board attempted to segregate Japanese with Chinese students in Chinatown. There was tension not only between whites and Japanese in California but also between the United States and Japan. The Japanese government protested the school board's decision. President Theodore Roosevelt, fearing that the incident was serious enough that it could even lead to war, convinced the school board to reverse its decision in return for halting some immigration.[19]

Tensions also grew between permanent Japanese and white settlers in Vancouver. In 1895, British Columbia extended its disenfranchisement of Chinese to Japanese residents. Because of the tensions, Japanese immigrants were one of the targets of an anti-Asian riot in 1907.[20]

In the United States, Japanese immigrants quickly moved out of laboring positions and into small business ownership, excelling at making marginal enterprises in agriculture and commerce prosper. They were especially good at making small farms thrive, in large part because they brought with them from Japan knowledge of intensive cultivation, fertilizers, land reclamation, and drainage. In part they were also able to succeed by running the businesses in an exceptionally thrifty manner. Shopkeepers kept living costs down by living on the premises and labor costs down by using the labor of family members.[21] By 1941, the Japanese controlled 42 percent of commercial truck crops in California and produced between 50 and 90 percent of such crops as celery, strawberries, cucumbers, artichokes, cauliflower, spinach, peppers, and tomatoes. They were the original developers of West Coast berry production.[22]

As in the United States, the Japanese-Canadian community gradually developed unusually successful small businesses in fishing and farming by the 1930s despite continually having to overcome discriminatory laws. Canadian whites viewed the Japanese as threatening their economic interests up through the beginning of the war. In Mexico, also by the 1930s, the Japanese immigrants who remained in the country had generally established successful businesses in farming and the professions.

Following the December 7, 1941, Japanese attack on Pearl Harbor, all three North American governments interned their Japanese-descent residents, ostensibly for security reasons. On February 13, 1942, President Franklin Delano Roosevelt signed Executive Order 9066, which required that anyone of one-eighth or more Japanese descent be removed from the West Coast to a relocation center. In all, some 113,000 Japanese-descent residents on the West Coast, two-thirds of whom were U.S. citizens, were then gathered at assembly centers for transport to the relocation centers in California, Arizona, Idaho, Wyoming, Colorado, and Arkansas. The authorities gave the future internees little time to arrange their affairs before being relocated. Many saw little alternative but to liquidate their small businesses at bargain basement prices. A total of 120,000 Japanese-descent residents served time in these centers.[23] Public opinion largely supported the internment because of identification of the Japanese-descent residents with a wartime enemy, decades of racist hostility, and resentment over the success of Japanese-owned small businesses.

The U.S. government called the camps relocation centers. Their harshest critics called them concentration camps. The connotation of a relocation center is that it is a place to which people are moved, usually after a natural disaster such as a flood or hurricane. The connotation of a concentration camp is that it is a place where prisoners are kept under the most repressive of conditions, as in the Nazi camps for Jews. The camps where the Japanese were interned were neither. To classify where they were kept as relocation centers obscures the fact that their residents came involuntarily. To call them concentration camps is an exaggeration. The camp residents were there involuntarily, but they were not routinely abused or harshly treated as were the Jews in the Nazi concentration camps. Essentially, these were internment camps— places where Japanese-descent individuals were interned involuntarily and unjustly for the duration of the war.

German- and Italian-descent residents and citizens were interned as well in Canada and Mexico but not in the United States, where only slight surveillance measures were taken against recent immigrants from those countries. Recent German immigrants, for example, could be forbidden to leave their city of residence for the duration of the war. Schaefer suggests that the Japanese were interned in camps whereas German and Italian-descent residents were not because many of the people involved in designing the internment policy had German and Italian ancestors.[24] The difference between the treatment of Asian and European-descent residents, who both originated in countries that the United States was at war with, has often been taken as proof of a fundamental racism, paralleling, in this respect, the U.S. decision in 1945 to drop the atomic bomb on an Asian but not a European enemy.

After the attack on Pearl Harbor, the Canadian government immediately took action against its Japanese-descent citizens and residents. It impounded some 1,200 Japanese fishing boats, closed down Japanese-language newspapers and schools, and initiated removal of Japanese living on the Pacific Coast to the interior. The removal process began in spring 1942, and altogether some 21,000 Japanese Canadians were removed to towns, internment camps, farms, and work projects, most of which were in British Columbia. The government took over custody of the properties, including land, that the internees had to leave behind. Later, it disposed of them in a compulsory sale.[25]

On December 11, 1941, four days after the Japanese attack on Pearl Harbor, the Mexican government ordered the removal of Japanese residents from its northern border and coastal areas, and their internment in the center of the country. The internment order was issued by Secretary of the Interior, later President, Miguel Alemán, after a meeting with U.S. Undersecretary of State Sumner Welles, who expressed fears that Japan would invade Baja California.[26] Some eight hundred families, including Mexican citizens, were interned at centers and camps within cities, such as Mexico City and Guadalajara, and in rural areas in the center of the country. These locations were guarded, though the inmates could leave with permission for short periods of time. Though the Japanese-Mexicans were involuntarily kept in internment camps, their conditions of incarceration was not as severe as those in the United States. The same fate was shared by German and Italian nationals in the country. Mexico thus differed in this respect from the United States.

Once the war ended, in all three countries the ex-internees found that the lands and businesses that had cost them so much intensive labor to develop had been taken over by others. In the United States, many who has worked and developed rented lands found that the lands had been rented to whites. Because of their age, these ex-internees were not able to redevelop farming operations on different marginal lands. In Canada, when the internees were released after the war, many returned to find that because their lands, which they had taken years to develop, had been sold to others, they were unable to restart their businesses. In 1947 a special commission was established by the Canadian government to settle claims of these resulting property losses. Property disputes continued in the Canadian courts until the late 1960s. In Mexico, after the war ended, the internees' rights were restored, and they were allowed to return to the northern areas. Many, however, found that their lands had been taken over by others or that irrigation arrangements for them had been diverted.[27]

Following the war, many of the children of the ex-internees entered universities in all three countries, presaging a postwar shift in the distribution of the Japanese labor force away from agricultural employment toward urban-based professional and managerial occupations.

In the 1980s ex-internees in the United States and Canada successfully completed long legal struggles to receive reparations for their unjust treatment during the war. In 1988 the U.S. government passed legislation to allocate $1.2 billion in reparations to 60,000 surviving internees. Each received $20,000. In Mexico, however, there has been no attempt on the part of the Japanese community to petition for reparations. In part the lack of a similar reparations movement reflects the lack of a tradition and basis in Mexican civil law for victims of injustice to receive financial compensation. But, more importantly, it reflects the cultural reality that Mexico generally does not recognize non-Indian ethnic minorities as having identifiable rights. Members of these minorities rarely confront their society as pluralist pressure groups seeking redress for harms suffered.

Filipino–North Americans

The first Filipino immigrants to North America may have arrived in Mexico as slaves through the port of Acapulco in the 1600s.[28] Because both Mexico and the Philippines were colonial possessions of Spain with regular shipping contact between them, inevitably there was some Filipino voluntary and involuntary migration. But the numbers were so slight as to have left no noticeable Filipino presence in Mexico.

Filipino immigration to the United States began in 1903, shortly after the United States took the Philippines from Spain. Up until 1935 some 150,000 migrants arrived. From 1906 to the 1920s most went to Hawaii. Sugar and plantation owners in Hawaii sent recruiters to the Philippines in search of cheap labor, for which they were willing to pay transportation costs. Most of the early Filipino migrants, therefore, were poor peasants, who were recruited for their agricultural labor abilities and who were willing to leave their home-land because of crushing poverty. In 1925, after the 1924 Immigration Act banned other Asians from entry, some 45,000 Filipinos moved to California and other western states to fill the consequent agricultural labor shortage.[29] As with Chinese immigrant laborers, males heavily outnumbered females, by fourteen to one, among these Filipino laborers. By 1930 there were 20,000 Filipino West Coast farmworkers, 11,000 service workers in hotels and restaurants, and 4,200 workers in Alaska salmon canaries.[30] There were also a number of kitchen workers in the merchant marines and on U.S. Navy ships. By the 1960s California replaced Hawaii as the state with the most Filipino residents.

The early Filipino population faced the same discrimination as other Asian immigrants. There were anti-Filipino riots in California farm areas in the 1920s and 1930s. In 1937, Oregon enacted a law that specifically forbade marriages between whites and Filipinos.[31]

This first generation of Filipinos continued to play a significant role in the agricultural labor force of California down through the 1960s, alongside Mexican migrant laborers. Filipinos played an active role alongside Mexicans and Chicanos in the formation of Cesar Chavez's United Farm Workers Association. In the 1960s a small number of the children of this first wave of Filipino immigrants entered universities. There were then no specifically Filipino student organizations in existence. But because of a sense of common identity that came from being the offspring of farmworker families, many participated in and socialized with Chicano student organizations.

During World War II a number of Filipinos served in the U.S. Army. In return they were granted citizenship, benefits for ex-soldiers (the GI Bill) and the right to migrate to the United States. Between 1946 and 1956, some 30,000 Filipinos entered the United States in this fashion to augment the original Filipino-American community.

RECENT IMMIGRANTS

Three historically overlapping events produced surges in Asian emigration to the United States and Canada. The United States has had a large number of troops stationed in Korea since the 1950–53 war. The first Koreans to enter the United States were brides of these troops, who were later able to send for family members. Today, there are close to 800,000 Koreans living in the United States. There are 28,000 in Canada, which has also had troops stationed on the Korean peninsula.

In 1965 and 1967, respectively, the United States and Canada liberalized their immigration laws. The new law in the United States, which took effect in 1968, allowed large numbers of Asians who had been previously blocked to enter by giving preference to relatives of people already in the country and to persons who had job skills that were needed. The Canadian law removed racial and geographical biases in its immigration quotas, thereby allowing large numbers of new Asian immigrants who qualified according to other criteria to enter the country. There was no comparable development in Mexico.

The demographic effects of the U.S. and Canadian changes of immigration policy on the Chinese and Filipino communities have been dramatic. In the United States, the Chinese population had grown at a rate proportionate to that of the population as a whole until 1968, when the 1965 law liberalizing immigration quotas took effect. Since then, the number of Chinese in the United States has doubled every ten years, from 436,000 in 1970, to 812,000 in 1980, to 1,645,000 in 1990.[32] Three out of every four Chinese in the United States today are new immigrants; only one in four is a descendent of the original nineteenth-century immigrant communities. In Canada, between 1971 and 1981 the number of Chinese more than doubled, as the proportion of Chinese in the total Canadian population shot up from 0.55 to 1.2 percent.[33] Between 1981 and 1986 it increased another 25 percent to make up 1.4 percent of the total Canadian population.[34] As of 1991, it had increased still further to make up 2.2 percent of the total Canadian population.[35] Over 90 percent of all Filipinos in the United States today came after the initiation of the immigration liberalization, as did most of the 157,000 currently in Canada.

Because there was no comparable development in Mexico, the number of Chinese-Mexicans remains very small, far less than 1 percent of the population, and they are dispersed throughout the country. We cannot assume that the Chinese population has had the same rate of increase as the Mexican population, because of the sexual imbalance whereby more than 90 percent of immigrants were males. There seems to be little doubt that the Chinese-descent population does not exceed 100,000 today. There are no Chinatowns that at all approximate in size those that exist in a number of U.S. and Canadian cities. There had been some small Chinatowns in the early part of the twentieth century, but these were abandoned as the Chinese population dispersed, leaving only traces to indicate their original identity. Along the Calle Alvaro Obregon of the Colonia Roma in Mexico City, for example, there are a number of buildings with clear oriental architectural features, indicating that they had once been the heart of a small Chinatown in the 1920s. By the 1950s, though, the Chinese had sold out and left. Large numbers of Chinese Hispanicized their names in the same way that immigrants from southern and eastern Europe to the United States were pressured into Anglicizing their names.

The period of immigration reforms also has had little effect on the Japanese–North American population. With Japan rapidly moving to the top rank of first world countries in the 1960s, there has been little incentive for its citizens to migrate. There are today approximately 920,000 Japanese-descent residents in North America. Over 90 percent live in the United States, and over two-thirds of these live in just two states, Hawaii and California. In Canada, Japanese-descent residents are a small percent not only of the total population but also of the Asian population. The 40,000 Japanese-descent Canadians make up less than 5 percent of Asian-descent Canadians. Four other Asian-descent populations—Chinese, Indians, Filipinos, and Vietnamese—are larger. In Mexico there are approximately 30,000 Japanese-descent residents. As in the United States, the Japanese communities in Canada and Mexico distinguish themselves according to generations since arrival—*issei, nisei, sansei,* and *yonsei.*

Since the 1960s, in addition to the original Asian–North American communities—the Chinese, Filipino, and Japanese—and the postwar Korean community, sizable Asian Indian and Indochinese communities have developed. Relatively few Indians migrated to the United States or Canada before the 1960s period of immigration reform.[36] Today there are 815,000 Asian Indians in the United States and 420,000 in Canada, disproportionate numbers of whom have entered already possessing university degrees. It was the U.S. losses in the Indochinese wars of the 1960s and 1970s, not the period of immigration reform, that have produced Vietnamese, Cambodian, and Laotian communities in North America, with slightly more than a million currently settled in the United States and some 73,000 in Canada.

Exit polls for the 1992 presidential election in the United States for the first time identified the voting preferences of Asian-descent citizens, and they revealed that they voted far more conservatively than the population as a whole. Bill Clinton, the Democratic Party candidate, received 43 percent of all votes cast but only 29 percent of the Asian vote. George Bush, the incumbent Republican Party candidate, received only 38 percent of all votes cast but 55 percent of the Asian vote. Independent candidate Ross Perot received 19 percent of all votes cast and 16 percent of the Asian vote.[37]

Most of the new generation of Asian immigrants vote conservatively in the United States for two general reasons. First, the immigration law favors for entry those with higher education and occupation skills. Second, those coming from Korea, Hong Kong, Taiwan, and Indochina bring anticommunist foreign policy views that find more resonance in the Republican than in the Democratic Party. In this respect, these Asians vote conservatively for largely the same reasons as do Cuban Americans, who have also entered the United States fleeing communism.

CONCLUSIONS

The United States is the country with the largest Asian presence in North America. There are, though, proportionately more Asian-descent residents in Canada, where they constitute 6 percent of the population and the largest racial minority. The presence of Asians in Mexico is considerably smaller, that is, unless one considers the indigenous population to have been originally constituted by migrations across the Bering Strait from Asia.

In the nineteenth and early twentieth centuries, generations of Chinese, Japanese, and Filipino immigrant laborers entered North America under the most adverse of racially discriminatory conditions. What is striking about Chinese and Japanese history in North America is how similar and interconnected the experiences have been in all three countries. The Chinese began coming immediately after the United States took California from Mexico and began developing its mining, railroads, and agriculture. In the nineteenth century, Chinese entered North America's Pacific ports from Baja California to British Columbia. In all three countries they met antagonism on the part of native-born citizens and suffered decades of discrimination. Japanese immigrants began entering about a half century after the Chinese. In all three countries they moved successively through laboring, small-business, and professional positions in the labor forces, eventually achieving relative economic success. But in all three countries they were also involuntarily interned during World War II as security risks and consequently lost much of their prewar gains. Much of the early Asian experience in North America was dictated by the particular development of California agriculture and its need for large supplies of cheap labor, which was supplied by Filipino, as well as Chinese and Japanese immigrants. Carey McWilliams thus concluded in summary form that "the history of farm labor in California has revolved around the cleverly manipulated exploitations, by the large growers, of a number of suppressed racial minority groups which were imported to work in the fields." In particular, "the growers, at an early date, began to look eastward, to the Orient, and south, to Mexico, for coolie and peon labor."[38]

But if the original Chinese and Filipino communities were forged by these early immigrants, they and their descendants are now minorities in their respective communities, having been displaced by a new wave of immigrants since the 1960s. More Asians in general have entered North America since 1968 than in the entire previous history combined; and alongside the traditional nationalities, new and sizable Asian Indian and Indochinese communities have developed. This new Asian–North American reality contains significantly new class and political dynamics. Because disproportionate numbers of the new immigrants already possess university degrees, they have entered the U.S. and Canadian labor forces in higher positions than did the originators of their communities. Although they have had to bear unequal and discriminatory treatment, these immigrants have not suffered the degree of social inequality that was suffered by the earlier generations of Asian immigrants. Because of both their higher class positions and the large proportion of Chinese and Indochinese, who were fleeing communist societies, in their ranks, they tend to be politically more conservative.

✸ CHAPTER 11

The Fifth Race

The four races—Indians, Europeans, Africans, Asians—that have coinhabited the North American continent for the last half millennium have inevitably produced mixed descendants, the pioneers of a new synthesis fifth race in world history. These mixed-race individuals now make up over a quarter of the contemporary population of North America. They have become the second-largest racial category and, in a continental sense, the largest racial minority.

Contact between European conquerors and indigenous peoples produced the first mestizos, North America's largest type of mixed-race individuals. Contact between whites—slave owners and indentured servants—and African slaves produced the first mulattoes. Contacts between Asians and whites as well as between blacks and indigenous peoples have produced numerically smaller types of race mixture.[1]

Mexico contains the largest number of mixed-race individuals, followed, in order, by the United States and Canada. But beyond national differences in the proportions of mixed-race individuals, there are dramatic differences in cultural perceptions, even the very recognition, of these individuals.

MÉXICO MESTIZO

Mestizos are the largest number of people of color in North America, making them the continent's largest racial minority (see Table 11–1). But only north of Mexico are they a minority, because in Mexico itself they are the majority—some 79 percent of the population. *El mestizaje*, for which there is no fully equivalent term in English, means the historical process of combining

TABLE 11–1   Multi- and Uniracial Identities of North America

	MEXICO	CANADA	UNITED STATES	TOTAL NORTH AMERICA
Multiracial				
Mestizo	79	2	5	21
Mulatto			10	7
Other				1
Uniracial	21	98	85	71
Total	100	100	100	100

Notes: Based on a biological, as opposed to social, definition of race. "Other" includes Eurasians, Afromestizos, and persons with ancestors from three or more races.

Sources: Estimates based on census data (see sources for Tables 6–1, 7–1, 8–1, 9–1, and 10–1) and the assumption that the majority of the people who define themselves as blacks or African-Americans in the United States also have at least some European ancestors and therefore are technically mulattoes (see James F. Davis, *Who Is Black? One Nation's Definition* (University Park: Pennsylvania State University Press, 1991).

of two or more racial groupings. That process has been and continues to be the driving force of Mexico's racial identity. All Mexican third graders read in the social sciences textbook provided by the Department of Public Education that during the colonial period, "indigenous people and Spaniards interrelated and from them mestizos were born, from whom we Mexicans are descendants today."[2]

The origins of race mixture in Mexico thus go back to the epoch of the conquest when Spanish males outnumbered Spanish females ten to one. For most Spanish males to be able to fulfill their sexual instincts as well as reproduce they had little choice but to find mates, willing or otherwise, in the Indian population. At first, the mixed race products of these unions were accepted on equal terms in New Spain. Prejudice and discrimination by the Spanish colonial population against mixed-race individuals only began to develop when the number of Spanish female immigrants began to equal the number of Spanish males.[3] Male black slaves faced the same sexual imbalance in the early colonial period. They outnumbered female slaves at least three to one.[4] This demographic situation led them to find mates among the indigenous population that resulted in the birth of mixed African and indigenous children. Early colonial society generally accepted legitimate offspring of Spanish-Indian matings as occupying the same social status as *criollos,* that is, American-born Spaniards. Illegitimate offspring of Spanish-Indian sexual relations and encounters occupied a distinctly lower status. The term "mestizo" in large part became a synonym for these latter mixed-race individuals and, at least during a good part of colonial society, was used as a pejorative. The stigma attached to the term "mestizo" disappeared only after the 1910

Revolution.[5] Mörner argues that although colonial society developed an elaborate list of categories to represent the infinite fractional possibilities of race mixture, in practice it separated people into five groups: whites, mestizos, mulattoes, blacks, and Indians.[6]

Colonial policy tolerated marriages much more between Spaniards, *criollos,* mestizos, and Indians than it did between anyone of those groups and Africans or mulattoes. Quite clearly, the crown considered African-descent people to be inferior to Europeans and Indians in this respect. It went to some lengths to discourage intermarriage of African-descent people with people of either European or Indian descent. In part the crown wished to avoid having the slave stock depleted, since the products of such unions would not be born in bondage as would the products of pure unions among slaves. At various times such mixed-race marriages required special permission from the authorities, whereas mixed-race marriages involving Europeans, mestizos, and Indians did not.[7]

In the nineteenth century many, mainly white, Mexican intellectuals viewed the country's growing *mestizaje* both in nationalist and racist terms. They believed that the country was divided between whites and Indians and so long as it was divided it could not develop a unitary national identity. In that respect, *mestizaje* would merge the two races into a unique hybrid race that would underpin the country's national identity. At the same time it would serve to eliminate Indian cultures, which they saw as holding back progress. The ideal mestizo, in their view, would imbue European cultural values. To further insure the country's cultural and racial Europeanization, they advocated large-scale European immigration. Not only did they hope that what they perceived to be Indian cultural backwardness would be eliminated, one intellectual, Francisco Pimentel, went so far as to predict that "the mixed race would be a transitional race; after a little time everyone would become white."[8]

During the Porfiriato (1876–1911) various estimates placed the mestizo proportion of the population at 44 percent.[9] By the 1921 census, 60 percent of the population was identifying itself as mestizo.

Throughout the twentieth century a number of Mexican intellectuals have continued to link *mestizaje* to the country's national identity. The interpretations of *mestizaje* as an antidote to Indian cultural backwardness or as a strategy for whitening the country have disappeared. Instead, intellectuals in the postrevolutionary era of the 1920s and 1930s saw *mestizaje* in positive terms as a source of national strength and pride.

José Vasconcelos (1882–1959) is the best known of the Mexican intellectuals who promoted the notion of *mestizaje* as underpinning the country's unique identity and revolutionary nationalism.[10] Vasconcelos wrote *La Raza*

Cósmica (The Cosmic Race), which celebrates *mestizaje* as a positive development in world history, originally as an essay in 1925. For most of world history, according to his account, the four races—whites, blacks, Asians, and Indians—developed separately because they lived in geographic isolation from each other. But with the colonization of the Americas they came together and began to combine through *mestizaje*. In Vasconcelos's words, the Americas were predestined in world history to "construct the nest of a fifth race founded from all of the peoples to replace the four that in isolation have been forging history." In even more Hegelian prose he maintained that "the hidden (ulterior) end of history is to achieve the fusion of all peoples and cultures."[11] Vasconcelos, a sharp critic of the cultural values of Anglo-America, noted acerbically that Anglo-Saxons in the Americas had been the reactionaries in this inevitable development by abhorring *mestizaje* and seeking to preserve the so-called purity of their race. Latinos on the other hand had been in the world-historical vanguard by embracing *mestizaje*. It was no accident, therefore, that Vasconcelos as rector of the Universidad Nacional Autónoma de México inaugurated as its slogan, which continues to appear on all official documents today: *"Por mi raza hablará el espiritu"* ("Through my race the spirit will speak").

Nevertheless, during the same period that Vasconcelos was promoting race mixture and Mexican revolutionary nationalists were celebrating *el mestizaje*, anti-Chinese sentiment was high, and it included, as mentioned in Chapter 10, pressure to ban marriages between Mexicans and Chinese. After the state legislature of Sonora in 1923 outlawed intermarriage between Mexicans and Chinese, a Chinese man who was found with a Mexican woman was jailed; in 1926 a Chinese man was prohibited from marrying a Mexican woman; and in 1928 the authorities, citing the 1923 law, annulled the six-year marriage of a Chinese man and Mexican woman. The town council of Fronteras, Sonora, lamented that "it is positively distressing to see walking through the streets children with yellow skin and oval eyes, products of marriages of Mexican women with Asians. These children appear in a sickly state, an evident demonstration of the degeneracy of the race."[12]

The horror with which some Mexicans viewed *mestizaje* with Asians notwithstanding, the *mestizaje* between Spanish and Indians is a reality with which the country identifies itself. But not everyone has seen it, like Vasconcelos, as necessarily being a source of strength, racial or otherwise. Other Mexican intellectuals have seen *mestizaje* as contributing to a sense of inferiority, divided psychological complexes, and self-denigration, with mestizos feeling ashamed of the Indian part of their identity. According to Ramos, the birth of Mexico was a traumatic encounter—the Conquest—in which a small minority of Spaniards set out without success to Europeanize a much larger indigenous population. By continually holding the unachievable goal of Europeanizing Mexico, they insured that the people would always feel a sense of failure and inferiority. In part the Spaniards were racially absorbed through *mestizaje*; in part they lost their identity as Spaniards; in part they destroyed the value of the indigenous cultures. The result was to create a national character that could never be satisfied with what it was. Ramos suggests that the driving force to create a Europeanized Mexico, which was impossible, has left a legacy of feeling inferior to the task. Ramos thus implied that the exaltation of European and depreciation of indigenous cultures created, in individuals who biologically incorporated genes from both, a sense of inferiority and self-denigration that was based on autoracism, that is, racism turned inward.[13]

Octavio Paz, in his exceptionally influential *The Labyrinth of Solitude*, argued that a deep-seated conflict related to *mestizaje* rests at the base of the Mexican national character. In the minds of most Mexicans the original *mestizaje* resulted from Spanish conquerors raping indigenous women. Mexico's *mestizaje* thus descends from an act of violence about which mestizos have mixed feelings. Hernán Cortes and doña Marina, La Malinche, represent the symbolic father and mother of Mexico. Their son, Martín Cortés, was the first mestizo. If Hernán Cortés represents strength, *el machismo*, and violent imposition, La Malinche, in contrast, represents the victim and, more importantly, betrayal, since she aided the Spanish in the conquest. Neither the symbolic father nor the mother is a positive figure, one representing foreign domination and the other betrayal. To their symbolic descendants, according to Paz, the two thus "are symbols of a secret conflict that we have still not resolved." That conflict is that "the Mexican does not want to be either an Indian or a Spaniard. Nor does he want to be descended from them. He denies them. And he does not affirm himself as a mixture."[14] Whatever the truth of Paz's interpretation as a characterization of all or even most Mexicans, which Bartra and others dispute,[15] it is widely believed to be true and hence forms a part of the national culture. That Paz's account may have contributed to the formation of the stereotypes of the Mexican male as having a *macho* exterior that masks an inferiority complex and of the Mexican female as being long-suffering does not mean that it was necessarily totally invalid. For it to be as widely accepted as it has been indicates that it struck a reality. Stereotypes, as implied by Emile Durkheim, are by definition exaggerations and falsifications, but they are nonetheless real if they enter into the collective consciousness of a people as social facts.[16]

Today, the living conditions of the Mexico's mestizo majority are on the average in between those of whites and Indians. In class terms, many see the mestizo as the urban proletariat in between the rural Indian peasantry and the white middle and upper classes. This view is probably valid, but only in proportional terms. That is, proportionately more mestizos than whites or Indians are urban workers and fewer are peasant-, middle-, or upper-class members. But mestizos are represented in all of the country's economic and social classes. Many maintain that there is also stratification within the mestizo population, with lighter-skinned mestizos being more privileged on the average than darker mestizos.

THE CANADIAN MÉTIS

Canada contains approximately 300,000 people, 1.2 percent of the population, who identify themselves as having mixed, that is, mestizo, European and Indian ancestry. Other estimates of the size of the mestizo population are higher, ranging between 500,000 and one million, or between 2 and 4 percent of the population.[17]

The major part of this population is an integrated part of the white population. A smaller minority, however, sees itself as métis, a separate people who are neither Indian nor white. Most are French and Indian descendants; a smaller number descend from English and Indian ancestors. The 1991 census found 75,150 people who identified themselves as métis.[18] Another 239,395 people identify themselves as having mixed European and Indian ancestry but not culturally as métis.[19]

The roots of métis identity go back to the period of French rule and the frontier fur trade. French men took Indian wives or were otherwise involved in sexual relationships. By 1760, when French rule ended, the mestizo offspring of these encounters were numerous enough to have established noticeable communities in the Upper Great Lakes region. By the 1800s there were other large métis communities in what are now Manitoba and Saskatchewan on the western prairies. It was in the 1800s, particularly at the Red River colony (where Winnipeg, Manitoba, is now) that the métis began to see themselves as a people with a distinct national identity. That identity was formed first from the mestizo offspring of French and Indian encounters and thus had a strong French component, but later it embraced the mestizo offspring of English and Indian encounters as well.[20]

The development of a separate métis identity reached its high point in the nineteenth century. At that time métis dominated the buffalo hunt, were fur trappers, transported goods, and acted as interpreters between whites and Indians on the western Canadian prairies. On different occasions the métis fought against Sioux Indians and Canadian government troops, proving that they truly occupied a separate position from either one. The development of the métis as a separate racial and cultural group reached its zenith in the last half of the nineteenth century with an attempt at national secession. Increasing white settlement, the end of the buffalo hunt, and the development of railroad links to the east were undermining the métis economy. Métis leaders, including Louis Riel, concluded that wealth produced by them in their area was being expropriated by eastern Canada and Great Britain. To end the expropriation, Riel advocated overthrowing the territory's colonial powers and establishing an independent republic that would be able to maintain control over its economy.

There were two open métis rebellions, in 1870 and 1884, to achieve sovereignty. In 1869 the British government arranged without consulting the métis for the Hudson's Bay Company, which controlled the Red River colony, to transfer control of the region to the dominion government of Canada. Under the leadership of Louis Riel, the métis organized and demanded representation in the transfer of power. In October 1869 they set up barricades and successfully blocked the entry of the designated governor into the territory, forcing him to withdraw into U.S. territory. The dominion government chose to negotiate with the National Métis Committee. As a result, Riel and the métis insured redress for their grievances in the Manitoba Act of 1870, which created Manitoba as a province in the confederation. The dominion government also set aside a 1,400,000-acre land grant for the métis in which each family was alloted 160 acres.[21]

In the 1880s, conflict between the métis and the Canadian government emerged again, this time to the west in the North-West Territories, where Saskatchewan is today. Many métis had moved there from Manitoba. A number had sold their interests in the land grant to retire debts and were landless. Others simply sought to escape the advance of eastern settlers. Declining economic conditions, which they blamed on increasing nonmétis settlement and competition to their freight business from the railroad, had squeezed métis living conditions. They enlisted the aid of Riel, who returned from Montana, where he had been living. Riel believed that the solution to their problems lay in métis self-determination, which could only be fully achieved through secession from Canada. Riel's program of national independence attracted some Indian and white as well as métis support. In order to secure independence, which the dominion government was not willing to grant, Riel and Gabriel Dumont formed a métis military force. But the North-West Mounted Police easily put down the rebellion after a brief clash. Riel was captured, tried, convicted of treason, and hanged in 1885.

The thorough defeat of the 1884 rebellion sent the surviving métis scattering throughout western Canada, never again to pose a serious threat to national authority. In historical retrospect, the métis-led rebellion of 1884 represented the last obstacle to Canada's expansion to the Pacific as a unified national territory and was disastrous for any further development of métis national self-determination and autonomy. By the 1950s over 80 percent of métis descendants had fully integrated into white Canadian society.[22] A smaller number have assimilated into Indian bands and live in their reserves. A separate métis identity still survives in Canada, but as Davis depressingly concludes, these métis "remain a broken, desperately poor people with little hope and extremely high rates of unemployment, welfare dependency, crime, school dropout, and alcoholism."[23]

RACIALLY MULATTO AND SOCIALLY BLACK
IN THE UNITED STATES

At least three-quarters of the population in the United States that is socially perceived to be black is in reality composed of mulattoes. Some, such as Davis, estimate that the proportion of mulattoes may be as high as 90 percent.[24] The vast majority of all African-Americans thus have at least one white somewhere in their family trees and therefore carry at least some caucasoid as well as negroid genes. Another implication of this biological reality is that a substantial number of whites, perhaps the majority, in the United States are distantly related to blacks. Since most cross-racial encounters took place in the slave South, it follows that most southern Ku Klux Klan members today share common ancestors with and are technically cousins to southern blacks. In a similar sense, many of the Jim Crow South's most racist politicians fathered black children.

The history of mulattoes in the United States begins with the seventeenth-century founding of the Chesapeake colonies, Virginia and Maryland. The first mulattoes were probably offspring of encounters between black slaves and white indentured servants, who initially outnumbered slaves in the colonies three to one.[25] Soon after, the more known pattern of relations between slave owners and slaves developed. The physical structure of the plantation economy encouraged close daily contact between slave owners, their sons, and slave women. In such conditions chance and longer-term cross-racial sexual relations developed. In addition, the patriarchal structure of plantation households favored cross-sexual relationships. The owner almost always maintained a relationship with a white legal wife who bore legitimate heirs to the property. But if that relationship was not sufficient to satisfy his sexual or emotional needs, there was little to stop him from also maintaining a compensatory relationship with a female slave. A substantial number of cross-racial sexual encounters also occurred between poor whites and slaves. But, as Joel Williamson concluded, "by far the most dramatic and the most significant portion [of miscegenation] was between upper-class white men of the slave holding class and mulatto slave women engaged in domestic service."[26]

The plantation household was similar in this respect to feudal landlord households of medieval Europe and parts of Latin America. In each it was assumed that the owner and his sons had as a right of property sexual access to the dependent population, be it serfs or slaves. In Mexico, the landlord had the "right of the first night." When peasants on his estate married, he, rather than the husband, had the right to sleep with the bride for the first night. For that reason, in many cases the first child of the peasant couple was often the offspring of the landlord. In the South, there was no traditional recognition of a "right of the first night," but a kind of right of any night. The result was the same, with many of the children of slave couples being the offspring of owners.

Cross-racial sexual encounters and offspring also occurred in the British, Spanish, and French Caribbean colonies, but they were viewed differently. There during the early stages of the development of plantation economies both white males and imported female slaves heavily outnumbered white females. For that demographic reason white plantation owners frequently engaged in cross-racial sexual relations and encounters that led to the birth of mixed-race children. Mulattoes and cross-racial sexual relations from the beginning thus became an accepted part of Caribbean society. It was also an accepted cultural pattern for planters to recognize, free, and provide for the education of their mixed-race offspring. The situation though was different in the South, where this marked imbalance between white males and females in the planter class did not exist. Cross-racial sexual encounters between plantation owners and slave women certainly occurred, but their existence was frowned upon from the beginning. Thus in the Caribbean race mixing occurred openly; in the South it was always an underground phenomenon. In the South no cultural pattern developed for plantation owners to accept responsibility for the products of their underground contacts with slave women. These would tend to be considered as undifferentiated members of the slave class.[27] White males from the southern planter classes could, more easily than those from similar Caribbean classes, take an irresponsible attitude that they were simply spreading wild oats among the slave class.[28]

By the end of the seventeenth century a substantial mulatto population had developed in a number of areas of the South. The majority were slaves. In a minority of cases plantation owners manumitted their mulatto offspring; these manumissions provided most of the populations of the early freed slave communities. In 1860, on the eve of the Civil War, the census found that over three-quarters of free persons who had been or were descended from slaves were mulattoes. At the same time though, 88 percent of the people who the census takers thought had visible evidence of being mulattoes were still slaves.[29] Thus, throughout the period of Southern slavery, although mulattoes were more likely to be free, the vast majority were still enslaved.

For the most part the mulattoes who were free viewed themselves as having an identity that was neither black nor white. It was only later in U.S. history that their identity would be merged with that of blacks. Separate mulatto identities developed the most in South Carolina and Louisiana, areas that had been more related culturally to the Caribbean and Latin America than the rest of the South.

South Carolina was settled by planters from the British West Indies who brought with them their cultural values regarding race mixing. In 1850 about a quarter of the population of South Carolina's capital, Charleston, was composed of free mulattoes that included a small elite of educated, rich slave owners. Whites in South Carolina tended to view mulatto society more as a kind of shadow of their own society than as being attached to slave society. They accepted mulattoes as having an in-between status that was closer to their own than to that of black slaves. The mulattoes occupied a position that was dramatically better than that of black slaves and almost as privileged as that of whites. It is not surprising that these mulattoes were in general allies of whites rather than blacks.

Louisiana before becoming a part of the United States in 1807 had been a possession alternately of Spain and France. The proof that a separate legal identity existed in Louisiana was that in 1808 its Civil Code prohibited "free people of color," that is, mulattoes, from marrying either whites or blacks.[30] There were 14,083 free mulattoes in Louisiana in 1850. A small number of these were slave owners themselves, with some owning as many as a hundred slaves. The New Orleans mulatto community operated its own schools and churches. Mulattoes "monopolized the building trades, catering, the cigar industry, and service positions like barbering and tailoring."[31]

In addition to being culturally linked to the Caribbean and Latin America, South Carolina and Louisiana were also located in the black belt South where the slave population was densest. In those demographic conditions, the development of an in-between identity for free mulattoes, as a buffer group between whites and blacks, helped to protect the slave system. In the 1820s a legislative committee that had investigated the Vessey insurrection in South Carolina concluded that mulattoes were "a barrier between our own color and that of the black—and, in cases of insurrection, are most likely to enlist themselves under the banners of the whites."[32]

At first mulattoes had a unique social identity that was different from those of either whites or blacks—the term "mulatto" appears in many writings in the United States up through the nineteenth century. But by the end of the nineteenth century mulattoes would be considered undifferentiated members of the black population. Part of the reason for the shift was the erasing of the distinction between free and slave mulattoes. The separate mulatto in between had been most pronounced among the small minority of mulattoes who had lived in free conditions before abolition. The end of the slave system ended their special position as well.

Part of the shift in perception, though, began in the 1850s before the Civil War for a more directly economic reason. In the early nineteenth century the importance of slavery to the southern economy grew with the industrial revolution and its need for cotton as a raw material. Mills in England and New England, employing free workers, spun the cotton planted and picked by slaves in the South. The industrial revolution enabled textiles to become a mass industry, thereby dramatically increasing the demand for southern cotton. The southern slave economy thus rode of the crest of the industrial revolution with an increasing need for slaves. At the same time slavery spread westward into Texas, which had been seized from Mexico. The increasing demand for slaves, who could no longer be legally imported after 1808, drove many plantation owners to blur the distinction between mulattoes and blacks. If mulattoes were not different from blacks, then there was no legal, moral, or other reason for them to be freed. They could, without qualms, simply be considered undifferentiated members of the slave labor force whose economic importance grew with the demand for cotton.

The mulatto elites in Charleston and New Orleans maintained their alliances with whites at the beginning of the war, even to the point of offering to serve in the Confederate Army and raising funds for the families of its active soldiers. But by the end of the war, all had shifted their allegiances to the Union cause.[33] Other free mulattoes had moved to the North and served in its army during the war. At the end of the war many of these decided to return to the South either to pursue economic opportunities or for more altruistic motives to give professional aid to the ex-slave population as teachers, ministers, doctors, and the like. In a sense this movement of mulattoes from the North to the South obeyed the same altruistic motives of the earlier abolitionist and later civil rights movements. In both, an ethic of antiracist idealism moved large numbers of young people to attempt to rectify through their actions the horrendous treatment that blacks have received in U.S. history. The same attitude prevailed among the educated elite of southern-based mulattoes. It was thus during Reconstruction that mulattoes, largely out of disgust with white racist attitudes, fused their identities with the black population. Williamson argues that they provided much of the leadership of the ex-slave movement during Reconstruction. "It was precisely where Negro numbers were high [South Carolina, Louisiana, and Florida] and mulatto leadership most concentrated and aggressive that Reconstruction had its longest and most significant life."[34]

After the defeat of Reconstruction, the inauguration of segregation added additional pressure to dissolve the in-between social identity of mulattoes. During slavery, whether a particular mulatto or black was free or a slave could be easily determined because the condition was legally registered. The goal of segregation legislation, though, was to maintain the so-called purity of the white race by socially separating it from all people of color, mulatto or black. Segregation thus established the Manichean definition that people were either black or white with no space left for in-between possibilities. In pursuit of their primary goal of protecting the so-called purity of the white race, the southern states, building on prewar precedents, carefully demarcated whites from mulattoes and blacks according to what came to be known as the one-drop rule: a person was black who had any amount, no matter how slight, of African blood. For different reasons the one-drop rule became increasingly accepted by mulattoes and blacks, so that today there is virtually no separate mulatto identity in the United States. By the early decades of the twentieth century mulattoes had all but completely dissolved their separate identities and merged with the larger black community, and after 1920 the U.S. census stopped distinguishing mulattoes from blacks.

But they did not merge as undifferentiated members of that community. Instead, a distinct tendency for them to move into the top economic, social, and political positions of the black community was already evident during Reconstruction. In class terms they tended to merge upward. As segregation set in, the upper rungs of the black community became increasingly occupied by lighter-skinned individuals and families. In this sense, skin color corresponded to class position to some extent within the black community,[35] paralleling the same phenomenon among Mexican mestizos.

In the eyes of many in the early part of the twentieth century, the merger of mulatto and black identities produced a new synthesis identity that was neither black nor mulatto. Thus, in the 1930s and 1940s many of the products of this new identity called themselves brown Americans. Joe Louis, the boxer, for example, was known as "the Brown Bomber." "Brown" indicated that they were neither black nor white, since race mixing had produced a new type.[36] It was only in the 1960s as a consequence of the black nationalist and black power movements that "black" definitively replaced "brown" as the color adjective. There is, though, no reason to assume that "black" or the more recent "African-American" will remain as permanent labels because, as post–Civil

War history as shown, the self-identity of that community evolves and shifts according to a number of internal and external conditions.

There is also no reason to assume that the children of black and white parents will necessarily always be identified as parts of the black community. Since 1967, when the Supreme Court ruled all antimiscegenation laws to be discriminatory and therefore unconstitutional, the number of black-white married couples has quadrupled, and they now make up one out of every fifty married couples. With the number of resulting first-generation cross-racial persons increasing, there could well be a questioning of the cultural legacy of the one-drop rule, which is unique in the hemisphere.

LATINOS IN THE UNITED STATES AND CANADA

The racial identities of Latin American–origin people in the United States are ambiguous. Unlike being white, black, Asian, or Indian, being Latino or Hispanic does not imply a single racial origin. There are white, black, mestizo, and mulatto Latinos. The U.S. census found 22 million Latinos, 9 percent of the national population. Of these, 60.4 percent are Mexican, 12.2 percent Puerto Rican, and 4.7 percent Cuban. In racial terms, a slight majority (51.7 percent) identify themselves as white, 3.4 percent as black, and 0.7 percent as Indian. What is highly indicative is that a full 42.7 percent identified themselves as "other" (see Table 11–2). In other words, they did not identify with any of the census's basic racial categories of white, black, Indian, or Asian. What is still more indicative is that these Latinos were almost the only persons in the United States who could not identify with the census's basic racial categories. They were an overwhelming 97.5 percent of all the people in the United States who marked "other" for their racial identification. The dilemma of these Latinos when confronted by the census takers is that they saw themselves as mestizos or mulattoes—categories which are not recognized in the United States.

Because of its experience as a major area of slavery, the different countries in the Caribbean contain significant proportions of blacks and mulattoes in their populations. Because of its contiguity to the United States, the Caribbean is a staging area for large-scale travel and migration to the United States. About half of the Puerto Ricans who live on the mainland of the United States are mulattoes. Another 10 percent are blacks. In the case of the Dominican Republic, which has become an equally large source of migrants to the New York area, close to three-quarters are mulattoes.[37]

When mulatto Caribbeans travel or migrate to the United States they enter a different, racially Manichean world in which their traditional senses of

TABLE 11–2   Latin American–Origin Persons in the United States, 1990

	NUMBER	PERCENT	MEDIAN INCOME[a]	PERCENT BELOW POVERTY[b]
A. National Origin				
Mexican	13,495,938	60.4	$22,439	28.1
Puerto Rican	2,727,754	12.2	$16,169	40.6
Cuban	1,043,932	4.7	$25,900	16.9
Other	5,086,435	22.8		
Total[c]	22,354,059	100.1		
B. Racial Identification				
White	11,557,774	51.7		
Black	769,767	3.4		
Indian	165,461	0.7		
Asian	305,303	1.4		
Other	9,555,754	42.7		
Total[c]	22,354,059	99.9		

[a]For households.
[b]For persons.
[c]Percentages do not total 100 because of rounding.

Sources: U.S. Bureau of the Census, *The Hispanic Population in the United States,* pp. 13–17, and *Census of Population and Housing, 1990,* Summary Tape Files 1C, CD-ROM (Washington, DC: U.S. Government Printing Office, 1991 and 1992).

social interaction cease to function. A mulatta student from Puerto Rico recounts traveling by car through North Carolina and seeing distinctly white and black towns as well as neighborhoods within the larger cities. "In which do I go?" she asked ironically. Davis observes that "the same light mulatto defined as black in the United States might be classed as 'coloured' in Jamaica and white in Puerto Rico."[38]

Mexican-origin people make up one of the two sources of the mestizo population in the United States. The other is made up of the descendants of unions between Anglos and Indians. Mexican-origin people in the United States can suffer from the double oppression of being perceived to be racially inferior and culturally foreign. Most of the Mexican-origin people who live in the United States and Canada are mestizos. For that reason most whites perceive the Mexicans and Chicanos that they encounter as having darker skins and therefore being racially different. But most whites do not understand the mestizo origins of the Mexican majority. Most whites in the United States are not even aware that the vast majority of North America's Indians live in Mexico. Anglo-Indian mestizos in the United States are racially but not culturally parallel to mestizo Mexicans. They were a part of nineteenth-century frontier society looked down upon by whites, as in Canada, as "half-breeds." Today, predominantly European-descent and white-appearing individuals in the

United States will consider it a point of pride if they have some Indian background—but they will never refer to themselves as mestizos. They consider themselves to be white—not mestizo—with a trace of Indian descent. Davis thus maintains that mestizos and Eurasians with one-fourth or less nonwhite ancestry are perceived more as "assimilating Anglo-Americans" than as racial minorities in the United States.[39]

Like the black vote and generally for the same reasons, the Latino vote disproportionately goes to Democratic Party presidential candidates. In the presidential elections from 1976 to 1992, Latinos overall gave Democratic Party candidates 66 percent of their votes.[40] But it is not an undifferentiated vote. The great majorities of Mexican and Puerto Rican votes go to Democratic Party candidates; the great majority of Cuban-American votes though go to Republican Party candidates. Because Cuban migrants have disproportionately come from the middle and upper classes, their living conditions are much higher than those of Mexicans or Puerto Ricans in the United States (see Table 11–2). They are therefore not as likely to respond to the nature of the Democratic Party's class appeal as are Mexicans and Puerto Ricans. In addition, the vast majority of Cubans in the United States, who are fiercely anti-communist and anti-Castro, find more support for their foreign policy views in the Republican than in the Democratic party.

There are very few Latin American–origin persons living in Canada. Altogether they make up just 0.6 percent of the labor force. More than half of that population comes from South American countries, with smaller numbers coming from Haiti and other parts of the Latin Caribbean, Mexico, and Central America.[41] Latin Americans thus continue to have only a marginal presence in the Canadian population.

CONCLUSIONS

The largest racial minority in North America is made up of the mixed descendants of two or more of the four races—Indians, Europeans, Africans, and Asians—that came together in North America beginning in the sixteenth century. These persons have alternately been despised as "half-breeds" and praised as precursors of the new synthesis fifth race of the future.

At this point in North American history halfway steps have been taken toward the creation of the fifth race with the formations of mestizos, mulattoes, and Eurasians. Mexico has the greatest experience in this direction, since 79 percent of its citizens are mestizos. In the United States the largest proportion of mestizos are of Mexican origin—both descendants of Mexican inhabitants of the Southwest before 1848 and subsequent migrants. There is a smaller number of Anglo-Indian mestizos. In Canada, the métis are a mestizo population that has carved out a separate identity and that was at the center of the 1884 rebellion, one of the central conflicts in Canadian history.

Canadian métis are virtually identical racially to Mexican mestizos. Both populations are the products of encounters between Europeans and Indians; the European origins of all of the Mexican mestizo population and the majority of the Canadian mestizo population were the contiguous Latin countries of Spain and France. There are, though, sharp cultural differences between these populations despite their common racial background. In Mexico, mestizos are the majority; in Canada, they are a small minority. In Mexico, the majority position of the mestizo population resulted from Spanish settlers entering the region of North America that was the most densely populated by indigenous peoples. Spanish settlers and their *criollo* descendants would never gain numerical superiority over the indigenous population. Inevitably in time sexual encounters between the Spanish and Indians would produce a certain percentage of mestizo offspring. In time, mestizos would become the majority.

The same process occurred in Canada, but in different demographic conditions and with different results. French and English settlers entered areas that were sparsely populated by indigenous peoples. Sexual encounters and mestizo offspring resulted. But French and English migrants quickly outnumbered Indians. The European-origin population was eventually so much larger than the indigenous population that it had enough of a base to maintain its separate racial identity throughout succeeding generations. Unlike in Mexico, the mestizo population would become marginalized as a minority and much more subjected to cultural racist-tinged oppression. Although "métis" is the most acceptable term for this population today, until the early twentieth century it was common for the majority English-origin population and métis themselves to use the terms "half-breeds," as in the frontier United States, and "half-castes." In addition to the majority- versus minority-difference in the two North American mestizo populations, there are other cultural differences, with one people developing in the context of Spanish colonialism and then an independent Mexican nationalism and the other developing under French colonialism and then Anglo cultural identification. Latin American people in the United States are therefore mystified when they see Canadian-origin mestizos. They appear to be Latino but do not act Latino.

Mulatto identity has been contradictory in a double sense in North America. First, it has been contradictory because of the common experience of all people of mixed descent. They are often caught between conflicting senses of identity and loyalty. Second, it is contradictory because the United States, where the vast majority of the continent's mulattoes live, classifies mulattoes as blacks, thereby negating a separate identity. In reality, though, between three-quarters and 90 percent of those who are socially perceived as blacks in the United States also have some white ancestry. The question of mulatto identity in the United States is further complicated for mulatto Puerto Rican, Dominican, Jamaican, Cuban, and other immigrants from the Caribbean islands. Their separate mulatto identity is recognized as such in the Caribbean but not in the United States, where they are socially perceived to be blacks.

The United States' one-drop rule is unique in the hemisphere. Caribbeans distinguish race according to appearance rather than descent. Hence, they distinguish mulattoes—sometimes called coloured—who are light skinned, and blacks, who are dark skinned. A very light-skinned mulatto is considered to be white. There is nothing comparable to the U.S. practice of defining as black anyone who has any African ancestry.[42]

Presumably, in time, there will be significant numbers of individuals who combine ancestry from all races, and presumably at that time separate racial identification—and racism—will dissolve. This process would be somewhat like the history of English and Irish immigrants in the United States. At first, they were distinctly separate ethnic groups, with the former enjoying privileges over and despising the latter. Generations of intermarriage, though, produced large numbers of persons of combined both English and Irish ancestry. For this mixed ethnic group, their separate ethnic backgrounds have little contemporary importance as they internalize a synthesis "ethnic melting pot" identity as whites in the United States. Similarly, in the future, it seems logical that mixed racial identity will become so common that it will have little meaning as a badge of honor or stigma. In this sense it seems obvious that *mestizaje* is the future of the human race. With communications and international migration every day bringing all regions of the world into closer contact, it will become more and more impossible for the races to continue to develop separately. In this respect Mexico has been in the vanguard, since it is there, more than in the United States or Canada, that *mestizaje* has both been a reality and been embraced, though not wholly, as a positive development.

CHAPTER 12
The New North American Division of Labor

Since the 1960s, growing trading relations and investments have made North America's three economies increasingly interrelated. The two greatest steps in the direction of continental economic integration were taken in 1965 with the inauguration of the Border Industrialization Program, which allowed mainly U.S.-based multinational corporations to set up assembly plants in the Mexican border cities, and in 1990 with the beginning of negotiations for the North American Free Trade Agreement (NAFTA) to drop tariffs and thereby establish free trade relations between the United States, Canada, and Mexico. Growing economic integration of North America's first and third world countries portends significant long-range changes in the configuration of its class structures.

MAQUILADORAS AND THE EXPANSION OF THE BORDER ECONOMY

There are two literal borders in North America: between Mexico and the United States and between the United States and Canada. The 1,945-mile border that separates Mexico and the United States is the sharper dividing line of the two existing borders, for it separates, in addition to the two countries, Latin and Anglo America and North America's third and first worlds as well.

Definitions of this border zone vary. Some concentrate on the major twin cities (Brownsville-Matamoros, McAllen-Reynosa, Laredo–Nuevo Laredo, El Paso–Ciudad Juárez, Calexico-Mexicali, and San Diego–Tijuana), where more than half the population live. Others have a much broader definition that includes everything within two hundred miles of either side, including such major U.S. cities as Los Angeles, Phoenix, and San Antonio and the interior Mexican cities of Monterrey, Chihuahua, and Hermosillo. The majority of observers define the border zone as the twenty-six U.S. counties which touch it to the south and the thirty-five Mexican *municipios* which touch it to their north.

It is on the border that we can see in unusually sharp relief many of the particular manifestations of class and race in North America. The U.S.-border labor force has been traditionally divided along racial lines, for the most part between Anglos and Mexican-descent members, many of whose living conditions have been among the worst in the country. Average living conditions on the other side of the border are much more depressed, although they compare favorably with Mexican national averages. An impoverished and marginalized surplus population surrounds the Mexican border cities. Thousands live on illegally squatted land in shacks made of whatever is at hand. There are whole neighborhoods of houses made from packing cartons. Many survive only by scavenging what is left by the throwaway society on the U.S. side. Each dawn they search the U.S. parks for empty cans to sell, hunt for newspapers in alleys, and comb the city dumps for a piece of board, a broken chair, or perhaps a shirt that can be sewed again or even sold. In the blocks before the border, stores sell clothing *by the pound*—the absolute last stop of the U.S. cast-off and defective clothing markets.

The desert sun is crueler for the poor in Ciudad Juárez. Without air conditioners many cool off in the Rio Grande, whose muddy calm covers treacherous currents in the summer. Hardly a summer day passes without filler items in the El Paso newspapers announcing the washing up of another yet-to-be-identified body of a "Mexican national." Water service in Ciudad Juárez varies according to the prosperity of the neighborhood. The higher the income, the more likely it is that taps in the house will always work; the lower the income, the more likely it is that the water will come from a neighborhood communal pipe or open barrel. In the summer, water is scarce, and its availability slows to a drip in many of the poor *colonias*.

The poor in the Mexican border cities who turn to open begging are immediately evident. Others practice disguised forms of begging—offering to wash windshields (children) or to keep parking meters fed for a tip (adults). Still another indicator of the poverty is the large number of servants on both sides. There are probably many more servants per capita in the U.S. border cities than anywhere else in the country. The going rate in El Paso for a full-time live-in maid does not exceed $60 to $70 a week, a situation that the middle and upper classes as well as some employed workers eagerly exploit. However, the maids who cross the border back and forth daily or weekly to go to work can be pushed too far by the oppressiveness of their situation. In

March 1979, for example, the U.S. Immigration and Naturalization Service (INS) decided to crack down on maids who were going to work using border-crossing permits that were only valid for shopping trips. On a Friday morning, which is the normal payday, the INS stopped the majority of maids from going to work in El Paso and confiscated their crossing permits. The maids returned to Ciudad Juárez and then came back with large crowds that proceeded to close the international bridges for two days and, in the course of the demonstrations, throw the U.S. flag into the Rio Grande.

The border's traditional economic bases are divided between those which derive from the land and those which derive from the irrationalities and artificialities of its being a zone separating countries. In the first group are agriculture, ranching, and mining. Large stretches of the border zone are covered by desert, but irrigation practices that date back to pre-Hispanic times and the federally financed reclamation projects of this century make agriculture possible. Irrigation is especially important in the Rio Grande Valley (Texas) and the Imperial Valley (California), which are among North America's most productive fruit and vegetable sources. The center of the border, from west Texas to Arizona and from Chihuahua to Sonora, contains the foothills of the Rocky and Sierra Madre mountains, where copper veins run.

The copper economy produced the border's first industrial working class and unions. At the beginning of the twentieth century, U.S. corporations, including the American Smelting and Refining Company (ASARCO), owned by the Guggenheims, and the Cananea Consolidated Copper Company, owned by Colonel William Greene, developed mines and refineries on both sides. In 1906, during the regime of Porfirio Díaz, the workers at Cananea went out on strike. When violence broke out, Greene sent for 275 Arizona Rangers to protect his interests. The governor of Sonora, Rafael Izábal, gave permission for them to cross the border and patrol Cananea. Within days and after several dozen deaths, the strike was broken. The Cananea tragedy quickly became a leading issue fueling the Mexican Revolution, since it exemplified the Porfiriato's subservience to foreign U.S. interests.[1] On the U.S. side, mainly Mexican-descent miners and refinery workers organized through a progression of unions, which began with the Western Federation of Miners, an offshoot of the Industrial Workers of the World (IWW) that later reformed itself as the Mine, Mill, and Smelter Workers Union; and when the Mine, Mill, and Smelter Workers Union disbanded after being driven out of the Congress of Industrial Organizations (CIO) in the 1950s under the charge of being communist dominated, its locals affiliated with the United Steelworkers. They fought famous battles in, among other places, Bisbee, Arizona, and Silver City, New Mexico, the latter dramatically portrayed in the blacklisted 1951 classic labor movie *Salt of the Earth*.

Specifically because it is a zone separating two countries, a large part of the border economy is based on legal and illegal commercial activities and tourism. Trucking and freight-train routes converge at the border points of entry and exit. About 40 percent of the vegetables destined for the U.S. winter market pass through Nogales, Arizona. Though many of the goods pass through to interior markets, they still generate a quantity of economic activities to service the trade. Other goods remain on the border to be sold to citizens on the other side. Some large part of the economic prosperity of twin cities is dependent on the existence of each other as mutual export markets. In terms of relative importance, the U.S. merchants are more dependent on sales to foreigners. Whenever the Mexican peso devalues, Mexican buying power decreases, sending a number of stores on the U.S. side out of business. The merchandizing of tourism further inflates the border's artificial merchant character. For many in the United States, Mexico is the only foreign country that they will ever visit, their visits sustaining a service industry of hotels, restaurants, souvenir shops, and the like. Widespread smuggling is the illegal side of the border's merchant economy. The smuggling goes both ways. The highest profits come from smuggling marijuana, cocaine, and heroin into the United States. Lesser profits are made from smuggling more prosaic items such as automobiles, consumer durables, and machinery into Mexico. The large smugglers make prudent investments in the legal and political communities to insure immunity.

Through the 1960s the border cities were economic backwaters, known mainly for their tourist dives, smuggling, and the Border Patrol's perpetual war on undocumented workers. But since then the border has become a major world industrial center as multinational corporations have rushed in to take advantage of its cheap labor by building assembly plants, called *maquiladoras,* on the Mexican side. A *maquiladora* is essentially a factory where workers use imported materials to complete the assembly stage of a multinational corporation's production process. The completed product is then exported to the multinational corporation's home country from where it is marketed. Somewhere on the final product or its container can usually be found words such as "Assembled in Mexico of U.S. materials." A host of U.S. corporate giants—including General Electric, Zenith, RCA, and General Motors—as well as many smaller subcontractors, have set up shop along the border, dominating the economies of such border cities as Ciudad Juárez, Tijuana, and Mexicali.

The opening up of the border cities to *maquiladoras* began in 1965, when Mexican President Gustavo Díaz Ordaz inaugurated the Border Industrialization Program for the announced aims of attracting jobs and technological development to the region. The timing of the program was prompted by the ending a year earlier of the U.S. Bracero Program, which had allowed thousands of temporary agricultural workers into the country since the labor-shortage period of World War II. The Mexican government viewed the ending of the Bracero Program as potentially dangerous for the stability of the border cities, where many of the temporary workers lived.

Making the potential crisis more ominous was the 1964 outbreak of guerrilla warfare in Chihuahua. Concluding that the Mexican agrarian reform was a fraud, that the government was giving away rich forest and mineral concessions, and that the Tarahumara Indians were being subjected to increased exploitation, rural schoolteacher Arturo Gamiz retreated to the Sierra Madre mountains to create a guerrilla *foco,* as was occurring at the time in many other parts of Latin America. The Mexican army was quick to respond, and on September 23, 1965, Gamiz and most of his followers were killed in battle at Madera, Chihuahua. Though the Gamiz movement was a manifestation of mainly rural problems, it still worried government officials who were in charge of the border cities, which were the destinations for many of the peasants pushed off the land by impoverishment. By 1965, Mexico was fully committed to export-oriented agricultural policies that favored large growers at the expense of these peasants, causing out-migration to urban centers such as the border cities.

Meanwhile, in the board rooms of the multinational corporations to the north, the middle 1960s were being experienced as a period of transition from wide-open expansion to renewed competition. The United States had pursued policies during the last year of World War II to make the free movement of commodities and capital a cornerstone for the reconstruction of postwar international relations. Multinational corporations based in the United States were in a unique position to profit because their industrial plants had not been bombed out during the war. But by the 1960s, Japan, West Germany, and other economic powers had rebuilt themselves and were beginning to penetrate U.S. domestic and foreign markets. In the labor-intensive garment industry, as well as the labor-intensive electronics industry, which was just beginning to expand, labor costs became vital factors in the new world of international corporate competition. Taking advantage of greatly improved transportation networks, multinational corporations began to shift labor-intensive units of production outside of the home country to such cheap labor areas of the third world as South Korea, Taiwan, Singapore, and the Mexican border cities. If the logic of the first period of Western industrialization was to bring workers to capital, the new logic of the present period is to take capital to where cheap workers are.

In choosing among third world labor areas, U.S. multinational corporations generally considered three factors: labor cost, freedom, and stability. Labor cost in market economies is inversely related to unemployment: the higher the unemployment, the lower the labor cost, since when the supply of a commodity such as labor exceeds its demand, its price drops. High unemployment also acts to increase the productivity of those who are employed because the knowledge of how easily one is replaceable by others desperately seeking employment acts as a psychological whip to work harder. Without even counting the added unemployment caused by the ending of the Bracero Program, the border cities with 30 to 40 percent under- and unemployment rates easily met the multinationals' first requirement.

The multinationals' second requirement for foreign investments, freedom, necessitated government policy compliance on both sides. Ideally, multinational corporations want to be able to place their assembly plant in the host country as if it were only a department of a global factory from and to which capital, materials, and products can be moved without tax and customs restrictions. Mexico's Border Industrialization Program obligingly cooperated by designating the frontier area as a free trade zone and waiving special taxes on foreign corporations. On the border the *maquiladoras* have virtually all the privileges of Mexican-owned corporations. The U.S. government complied with the plan by establishing provisions 806.30 and 807 of the Tariff Code for *maquiladora* products. Upon reentry into the United States, those products are taxed at a customs duty according to the value of the labor added in Mexico. How the value added is defined makes a great deal of difference. It is not defined as the difference between the value of the raw materials and the market value of the assembled product, as one might think. Rather, it is defined as the value of the wages paid in Mexico, which is a lot less. In effect, the Tariff Code contained a loophole that allowed the free movement of above-average profits back into the United States.

The third requirement, stability, is also eminently a political question. Corporations prefer not to make risky investments. Like any business firm, they like to be able to calculate with reasonable accuracy their short- and long-term returns. Concretely, they want assurances that the government is not going to change from friendly to hostile, the leftist opposition is kept under control, the unions are cooperative, and the workers in general are disciplined. In Mexico there is both extraordinary government control and sharp rumblings under the surface. The governing PRI's practice has been to skillfully co-opt as much as possible the leadership of movements from below and leave the rest to be physically repressed by the state or right-wing terrorist organizations. That governmental control became a more attractive advertising feature after the 1968 Tet offensive in South Vietnam made it clear that stability in that part of Southeast Asia was crumbling. Not entirely coincidentally, 1968 saw the entrance of the first *maquiladora* in Ciudad Juárez, which became the largest center of these activities. There, Jaime Bermudez, the multimillionaire nephew of the first director of Mexico's national oil monopoly, PEMEX, financed the building of an industrial park specifically designed for *maquiladoras*. He rents out the buildings mainly to U.S. multinational corporations for their assembly plants.

The *maquiladora* operations on the border expanded greatly between 1965 and 1980, from 12 factories with 3,087 workers to close to 600 factories with 119,546 workers (see Table 12–1). By 1975, over three-quarters of all industrial jobs in the Mexican frontier were *maquiladora* jobs, and Mexico displaced Southeast Asia to become the largest assembler of U.S. components for reexport to the U.S. market. Employment prospects in the *maquiladoras* attracted peasants from the impoverished countryside, swelling the populations of the border cities. Over 70 percent of *maquiladora* work in the 1970s was in electronics and apparel, both of which required considerable labor for final assembly. The home factory farmed out, or in corporate terminology "outsourced," this work to save on labor costs. Most of the workers were young women first employed in their middle teens. The corporations believed them to be more dexterous, more patient for tedious work, easier to control, and thus better suited to assembly work than men. Thus, when *maquiladora* workers marched in the annual May Day parades behind the names of their companies, they looked like contingents from girls' high schools. RCA went so far as to dress its workers up in red and white U.S.-style miniskirted cheerleader outfits and march them behind "His Master's Voice" corporate insignia as male managers barked out marching orders through megaphones.

Since electronics assembly could only be done in clean, temperature-controlled areas to avoid deterioration of the parts, the new factories were air-conditioned—to protect the parts, not the workers—from the dry desert heat in most of the border cities, which can rise to 114 degrees. Apparel parts are not as vulnerable to the heat. Many of the sewing *maquiladoras* tended to be scattered about the border cities in older buildings without cooling equipment.

From the point of view of the companies, the *maquiladora* program was a tremendous success. Richard Michel, general manager of seven General Electric *maquiladoras* in Mexico during the 1970s, painted a glowing picture. With seven years of experience on the border, GE found the absentee rate to be only 2 percent compared to the 5 to 9 percent rate among its U.S. workers; and the productivity of the *maquiladora* workers was 10 to 15 percent above that of their U.S. counterparts at the time.[2]

A tenuous labor peace has generally reigned within the *maquiladoras*, but there have been isolated confrontations. In 1975 urban guerrillas from the Liga Comunista 23 de Septiembre, whose name was taken from the date on

TABLE 12–1   Growth and Location of *Maquiladora* Industry

	FACTORIES	EMPLOYEES
A. Growth		
1965	12	3,087
1970	120	20,327
1975	532	67,214
1980	600	119,546
1985	n.a.	211,986
1990	2,013	486,723
B. Principal Locations, 1991		
1. Border Cities		
Ciudad Juárez	255	123,514
Tijuana	466	60,797
Matamoros	94	37,195
Ciudad Reynosa	66	26,307
Mexicali	131	20,794
Nogales	65	18,479
Ciudad Acuña	45	16,504
Nuevo Laredo	62	16,128
Piedras Negras	42	7,756
Agua Prieta	26	5,973
Tecate	75	4,699
San Luís Rio Colorado	17	2,322
Rio Bravo	12	1,575
2. Interior Cities		
Ciudad Chihuahua	57	31,915
Guadalupe	19	5,146
Guadalajara	24	5,097
Hermosillo	17	3,702
Torreón	25	3,169
Mexico City	26	2,994
Ensenada	36	2,559
Monterrey	16	1,858

Sources: Instituto Nacional Estadística Geografía e Informática (INEGI), *Estadística de la Industria Maquiladora de Exportación, 1978–1988* and *Estadística de la Industria Maquiladora de Exportación, 1991* (Aguascalientes: INEGI, 1989, 1992). El Paso, Texas Chamber of Commerce twin plant publications, 1968–80.

which Chihuahua guerrilla leader Arturo Gamiz was killed by the Mexican army, entered a Sylvania *maquiladora* in Ciudad Juárez, killed a Mexican manager who tried to stop them, and distributed leaflets. The response of the *maquiladoras* was to beef up security. The Mexican government in turn speeded up its successful campaign to crush the Liga's presence in Ciudad Juárez and the rest of the country. In one incident in 1976, the army opened fire on and killed a number of guerrilla suspects in an outlying Ciudad Juárez neighborhood. The right-wing Brigada Blanca kidnapped and presumably murdered a number of others with suspected links to the Liga.

Although the pay of *maquiladora* workers is a pittance compared to the profits that are wrought out of them, it has still been enough to place their jobs among the better paying ones on the Mexican side of the border. A major complaint, though, has been that while the pay remains constant or increases in terms of its nominal peso value, it fluctuates greatly in terms of its real purchasing power and exchange rate with the dollar. The value of the pay in terms of its convertability to dollars is especially important on the border where *maquiladora* workers do a lot of shipping in the United States and U.S. prices influence the price of Mexican goods.

Mexican law requires that senior workers be assured job security, but there are many ways for multinational corporations to get around the requirement. Employers can slash hours or shut the plant down for a period, thereby forcing the employees to seek work elsewhere. Companies have also been known to swap workers, eliminating accrued seniority in the process. If a worker does not make production quotas, there is cause for firing that will be upheld by the government's Board of Arbitration, which exists to adjudicate labor disputes. Jorge Carillo studied 482 judgments concerning *maquiladora* workers made by the Board of Arbitration between 1971 and 1978 and found that only fourteen were favorable to the workers.[3]

Serious problems also exist off the job. The practice of hiring almost exclusively young women unbalanced employment patterns in the border cities. Not only were men left unemployed, but they were also stripped of whatever traditional identity they had as providers. Women were pulled out of the houses into the factories, and men were thrust back into the houses. This dramatic reversal of roles for which neither partner was prepared produced severe consequences. The idling of the married male working class produced increases of all the social problems traditionally associated with unemployment, including alcoholism, bar fights, and family tensions. In a typical development, a young married couple with children found that only the woman could get a job. She began to work, a grandmother took care of the children, and the husband increasingly felt worthless. He then became tempted to abandon his family and search for work as an undocumented worker in the United States. Both Ciudad Juárez and El Paso Spanish-language radio stations during the 1970s regularly broadcast appeals from wives searching for husbands. Unmarried teenage men, who looked forward to bleak employment prospects, in turn increasingly sank into gang membership, drug smuggling, and petty criminal activities in general.

Although the border zone competed with similar tax-break, cheap-labor havens in other parts of Latin America, it had a unique selling point: the "twin plant" concept. The multinational corporation can keep the capital-intensive part of its operation in the United States and the labor-intensive side a short distance away in Mexico. In apparel the cloth can be cut on the U.S. side (a relatively skilled job that requires expensive and often computerized capital equipment) and then sent less than a mile away to the Mexican part of the factory where it is sewn, a more labor-intensive exercise. It is then returned to the shipping department on the U.S. side for distribution. The corporation for a minimum investment can thus take advantage of Mexico's cheap labor without major risks to its capital equipment.

The decade of the 1980s saw a further expansion of the border *maquiladora* economy. Between 1980 and 1991 the total number of *maquiladora* employees in Mexico nearly quadrupled, rising from 119,546 to 467,454 (see Table 12–2). *Maquiladora* wages remain very low by U.S. standards but average by Mexican standards. In 1992 *maquiladora* workers received an average *daily* wage of $6.80.[4] There were two new developments in the 1980s. A number of *maquiladoras* were located in interior Mexican

TABLE 12–2   *Maquiladora* Industry, 1991

| | FACTORIES | EMPLOYEES[a] | | EMPLOYEES ON BORDER[b] (PERCENT) | FEMALE WORKERS[c] (PERCENT) |
		Number	Percent		
Electronics	389	112,540	24.1	84.9	67.1
Auto parts	158	111,956	24.0	72.2	51.1
Electric machines	107	49,267	10.5	88.1	63.3
Apparel	308	45,726	9.8	44.0	76.2
Furniture and other wood	254	26,528	5.7	92.0	28.7
Services	90	22,334	4.8	71.3	72.3
Food	47	7,789	1.7	50.6	59.8
Chemical	92	7,560	1.6	83.2	54.4
Toys	28	7,451	1.6	100.0	66.8
Shoes and other leather	51	7,289	1.6	79.4	53.3
Tools	36	4,894	1.0	100.0	33.4
Miscellaneous industry	365	64,120	13.7	53.3	62.6
Total[d]	1,925	467,454	100.1	73.8	60.4

[a]Total work force.
[b]In the border *municipios*.
[c]Assembly workers.
[d]Because of rounding, percentages may not total 100.

Source: Calculated from Instituto Nacional Estadística Geografía e Informática (INEGI), *Estadística de la Industria Maquiladora de Exportación, 1991* (Aguascalientes: INEGI, 1992).

cities, which now contain nearly a quarter of all *maquiladora* employees. However, most of these have not moved very far into Mexico because a full 92.4 percent of all maquiladora jobs are still located in the six border states of Baja California Norte, Sonora, Chihuahua, Coahuila, Nuevo León, and Tamaulipas. The second new development was that male *maquiladora* employment increased significantly from 22.7 to 39.6 percent of line workers. That increase occurred largely because auto parts became a new branch of *maquiladora* industry, displacing apparel as the second largest after electronics, and about half of its line workers are males. Electronics and most of the other *maquiladora* branches continue to depend disproportionately on young female labor.

The 1980s also saw the developing of service *maquiladoras*, that is, factories that provided a service as opposed to assembling a physical product. In one of the more notable cases, Ciudad Juárez became the destination for discount shopping coupons. In the United States, manufacturers of food and other household goods often promote their products by distributing discount coupons through newspapers and other means. Stores accumulate large numbers of these, which they need to redeem for credit from the manufacturers. In the 1980s most of these cashed coupons were sent to a service *maquiladora* in Ciudad Juárez, where they were sorted and counted with the information being entered on computer tapes for reexport to the U.S. manufacturers. In this case, the cashed coupons were the raw materials and the tabulated information about them the product for export.

The *maquiladora*-fueled population growth of the Mexican border cities was matched by equally impressive growth rates three to five times the national average of cities on the U.S. side. Part of the reason for the growth was related to the existence of the twin plants. But more important for the economy of the U.S. side of the border than the full-fledged twin plants, whose number was actually low, were parallel electronic and apparel assembly plants with predominantly "green card" Mexican commuter and Mexican-descent U.S. workers. A number of manufacturers choose to operate only on the U.S. side because customs duties and the legal complications of operating in Mexico nullify the labor cost savings when they can pay low wages or piece rates in the United States. The size of the strictly assembly operations on the U.S. side is growing and will grow further so long as wages keep it competitive with the Mexican side.

Class and racial relations have historically overlapped to a startling degree in these U.S. border cities. The main social divide, which is largely perceived in racial terms, is between Anglos and Mexican-descent citizens and residents, who have been variously called Chicanos, Mexicanos, and Mexican-Americans.[5] Numerous researchers have documented the extent to which

Mexican-descent members of the labor force are disproportionately concentrated in occupations of low status and pay.[6]

A key question was whether the population boom, which was fueled by the investment of multinational corporate capital on both sides of the border, resulted in any change in this correspondence between class and race or whether it simply accommodated itself to it and reproduced it on a larger scale. This question can be partially answered by examining what happened in El Paso, the twin city of the largest Mexican *maquiladora* location, Ciudad Juárez, and itself a major electronics and garment-manufacturing center. With such major manufacturers as Levi Strauss, Wrangler, Calvin Klein, Billy the Kid, and Farah, El Paso is called by *Forbes* "the blue jeans capital of the world."

The overall class structure of the El Paso labor force changed little between 1970 and 1990, with the working class remaining at roughly three-quarters of the labor force, the new middle class at about a fifth, and the combined capitalist and small business classes at 5 percent. If equality existed between Anglos and Chicano-Mexicanos on the border, then each would have the same proportions of its members in each class. That is, if 20 percent of the labor force was made up of new middle-class members, then 20 percent of both Anglos and Mexicano would hold new middle-class positions. But equality does not reign, as Table 12–3 indicates. Anglos began and ended the two decades greatly overrepresented in new middle-class positions, while Mexican-descent people began and ended them greatly overrepresented in working-class positions. What is more, an examination of 1970 and 1990 per capita incomes indicated that the gap between Anglo and Chicano-Mexicano living conditions widened. The ratio of Anglo to Chicano-Mexicano per capita income grew from 2.2 to 1 in 1970 to 2.6 to 1 in 1990.

There are further intraclass correspondences between class and race. Anglo capitalists own larger and more powerful businesses than do Mexican-descent capitalists. A survey, conducted by Gelernter and Sweeney, of the individuals who occupied the top positions of the city's major corporate and civic boards of directors found thirty-two individuals, not one of whom was of Mexican descent. Nor did any Mexican-descent person have a reputation for major power among the thirty-two.[7] A survey of the twenty-one highest-paid corporate executives also failed to find any Spanish surnames.[8] While the city includes some Mexican-American–owned businesses that are large enough to have employees, they are not among the city's largest or most powerful. The major Anglo bankers and industrialists in El Paso consulted by Gelernter and Sweeney were asked to name their Chicano-Mexicano counterparts. Many had trouble thinking of any.

There is a clear difference between Anglo and Chicano-Mexicano small

TABLE 12–3   Economic Classes in the El Paso Labor Force, 1970–1990

	MEXICAN-DESCENT		ANGLO		TOTAL	
1970						
Self-employed	2,451	4.2	3,191	6.7	5,642	5.3
New middle class	6,539	11.1	15,553	32.5	22,092	20.7
Working class	49,780	84.7	29,134	60.9	78,914	74.0
Total	58,770	100.0	47,878	100.1	106,648	100.0
1980						
Self-employed	3,939	4.0	4,657	6.8	8,596	5.2
New middle class	12,007	12.2	21,805	31.9	33,812	20.3
Working class	82,498	83.8	41,948	61.3	124,446	74.6
Total	98,444	100.0	68,410	100.0	166,854	100.1
1990						
Self-employed	5,424	3.8	7,620	11.8	13,044	6.3
New middle class	22,519	15.7	23,992	37.2	46,511	22.4
Working class	115,282	80.5	32,856	51.0	148,138	71.3
Total	143,225	100.0	64,468	100.0	207,693	100.0

Note: Because of rounding, percentages may not total 100.

Sources: Calculated from U.S. Bureau of the Census, *Census of Population, 1970,* Characteristics of the Population, Vol. 1, Part 45, Section 2, Table 173; *Census of the Population, 1980,* Characteristics of the Population, Vol. 1, Chapter D, Part 45, Table 220; Census of the Population and Housing 1990, El Paso, TX, USA, Tables 18, 29, and 31 (Washington, D.C.; U.S. Government Printing Office, 1972, 1982, and 1992); and 1977 and 1987 Economic Censuses, Survey of Minority-Owned Business Enterprises, Hispanic (Washington, D.C., U.S. Government Printing Office, 1980 and 1990).

businesses. The former tend to be in the more profitable white-collar occupations and the latter in blue-collar occupations, and this pattern did not change greatly in the period. Mexican-descent persons owned disproportionately more of El Paso blue-collar businesses (repair shops, construction contractors, plumbers, small restaurants and cafés, etc.) and disproportionately less of its white-collar businesses (stores, professional practices, real estate companies, etc.). Most Mexican-American small businesses are too small to form more than a lumpen bourgeoisie. Nearly three-quarters of all Chicano-Mexicano businesses in El Paso have no paid employees.[9] This figure is in sharp contrast to small businesses as a whole in the United States, 80 percent of whom are large enough to have at least one employee.[10] These Mexican-American small business owners in El Paso, are, in social-class terms, much more a part of the working class than the middle class. The greatest disproportion between Anglo and Mexican-American white-collar businesses is in the professions (physicians, lawyers, architects, engineers, etc.).

Within the working class, Anglos tend toward white-collar positions and Mexican-Americans toward blue-collar positions. Thus, most Anglo workers work in white-collar positions, while most Mexican-American workers work in blue-collar positions. In absolute numbers, Mexican-descent persons began the period holding a majority of the blue-collar positions and a minority of the white-collar positions. But by the end of the decade, they held the majority in both strata of the working class. The growing demand for Mexican-American white-collar workers in part reflects the increasing need of commercial establishments and offices that deal directly with the public to have Spanish-speaking workers. Increasingly dependent on business from Mexico and from newly arrived immigrants, many El Paso businesses find the employment of Spanish-speaking workers to be a necessity. Many of these new positions have been taken by women. Sixty-five percent of new working-class jobs filled by Mexican-Americans in El Paso in the 1970s went to women, and of those 54.6 percent were white-collar.

These layers of perceived social superiority built upon noticeable economic cleavages divide Anglo from Mexican-American workers and even Mexican-American from Mexican workers. Anglo workers feel superior to Mexican-Americans, and Mexican-American workers often resent undocumented Mexican workers on the U.S. side and look down upon Mexican workers on the other. The social division of the working class is reinforced by capital's ability to take advantage of surplus Mexican labor. Thirty to 50 percent un- and underemployment rates on the Mexican side of the border hold wages on both sides down. The impoverishment on the Mexican side also puts a damper on union militancy among Mexican-American workers, ever mindful that while worse off than the Anglos, they are much better off than their Mexican counterparts.

Thus, Mexican-descent persons did not greatly "rise" with the expansion of the border cities. Rather, they were reassigned to their traditional slots within an enlarged class structure. There were slight gains for Mexican-American white-collar employees in the new middle and working classes, but for the most part, the nationality/racial correlates of the border class structure remained intact during the population growth. The border class structure with its institutionalized Mexican-American subordination simply expanded proportionately.[11]

NAFTA

During the 1980 presidential campaign in the United States, Republican Party candidate Ronald Reagan announced his goal of creating a free trade zone "from the Yukon to the Yucatán." By 1988, his last year in office, he had succeeded in negotiating a free trade agreement with Canada. His Republican Party successor, George Bush, then carried the campaign forward and by the spring of 1990 began negotiating the North American Free Trade Agreement (NAFTA), which would cover Mexico as well as the United States and Canada.

In one sense, the NAFTA negotiations represented the capstone of the increasing tendency for the three countries to become economically interrelated, although the relationship is an asymmetrical one between two first and one third world countries. It was the seemingly logical and natural consolidation of tendencies that had long been under way, including, most importantly, the establishment of *maquiladora* industry in Mexico and the steady lowering of Mexican tariffs, begun by the administration of Miguel de la Madrid in 1983.

A free trade agreement is one in which the participants allow each other's commodities to enter their domestic markets duty free. As such, free trade policies are the opposite of protectionist policies. In the latter, countries shield their domestic industries from international competition by charging tariffs on imports, making them more expensive than domestically produced goods. During the late nineteenth century, the United States facilitated its industrialization in large part by establishing high tariff walls. These enabled its infant industries to grow by shielding them from the competition of already developed, more powerful foreign industrial corporations. Protectionist policies have been followed by other countries, most notably Japan, seeking to industrialize. Mexico for a number of decades up through the 1980s followed strict protectionist policies. Free trade policies have traditionally been advocated by the more industrially advanced and strongest of international competitors in order to give them access to larger markets.

Free trade policies also are consistent with conservative political philosophies, which take the form of Republicanism in the United States, neoliberalism in Mexico, and Toryism in Canada. From the point of view of conservatism, state interference with the laws of the market should be eliminated or minimized. In that respect, protectionist policies represented state interference with the laws of the international market, and NAFTA represented the international dimension of Republican Party, neoliberal, and Tory policies. NAFTA thus coincided with the ascendancy of conservative political philosophies in all three countries during the 1980s.

The emergence of the NAFTA project in 1990, though, was not entirely predictable. Mexico had maintained its traditional foreign policy, a correct but distant posture toward the United States, during the 1980s; and from 1981 to 1987 the U.S. government seriously objected to Mexico's Central America policies. At the same time that the Reagan administration was mounting its campaign to destroy the Sandinista revolution in Nicaragua and isolate the rebels in El Salvador, the Mexican government was sending aid to Nicaragua and tacitly recognizing the legitimacy of the political and military representatives of the Salvadoran revolution. The Mexican government was following two long-standing principles: independence (from the United States especially) in its foreign policy and active support of Latin American revolutionaries and revolutions. Mexico, for example, was the only Latin American country that did not bow to the pressure of the United States to break diplomatic relations with Cuba in the 1960s. Mexico had also been the location from where Fidel Castro and Ernesto "Che" Guevara, in exile, had planned the Cuban revolution.

The public perception of the Mexican government in the United States fell victim to the Reagan administration's determination to destroy leftist governments and movements in Central America. The Reagan administration never respected the right of Mexico to have an independent foreign policy and decided to punish the country for Central American policies that were interfering with U.S. goals. The punishment took the form of accusing the Mexican government of being corrupt and undemocratic and of abetting drug smuggling.

The U.S. government indirectly and the press directly accused the Mexican government of committing massive electoral fraud in the 1986 state elections. A number of television and print media in the United States predicted electoral fraud, concluding that the governing PRI would steal certain victories from the conservative Partido de Acción Nacional (PAN). This coverage was unusual. If the U.S. press has generally taken little interest in Mexican national elections, it has taken even less interest in Mexico's state elections. The only possible reason for this newfound interest was that the Reagan administration was orchestrating a campaign to punish Mexico for not joining its Central American campaign. Thus the U.S. government and press directed public attention to the necessity of democratizing Mexico during the period 1981–87 at the same time that they were hitting the Sandinistas hard for the supposed lack of democracy in Nicaragua. The perception promoted in the United States was that democracy did not exist in either Mexico or Nicaragua.

In 1988 two events, which occurred almost simultaneously, contributed to a change in perceptions and frames of reference in the U.S. press regarding Mexico. The first was the Free Trade Agreement that Canada and the United States signed. The second was the presidential election in Mexico. The probable victory of the candidate of the leftist opposition, Cuauhtémoc Cárdenas, sent shock waves through the U.S. embassy in Mexico City. Top embassy officials calculated that a Cárdenas victory would completely destabilize bilateral relations between Mexico and the United States. For that reason the embassy explicitly decided to not make any direct or indirect statement about the elections as it had in the 1986 state elections. Instead, it would let the Mexican authorities resolve the crisis. On this occasion, when doing so was useful to its interests, the United States adopted a policy of not interfering in Mexican politics.

The posture of the *New York Times* was curious. On the day after the election it reported that possibly the PRI had been defeated. It reported in detail that the computer responsible for tabulating the vote had suddenly and suspiciously broken down when it became clear that Cárdenas was leading the official candidate, Carlos Salinas de Gortari. The *Times* coverage for three days created the impression and perception that the PRI had lost the elections and was preparing a fraud to maintain presidential control. The *Times* reported with skepticism the official result that Carlos Salinas de Gortari had won with just over 50 percent of the votes. On the fourth day after the election, the *Times* coverage changed completely. It ceased interpreting the election as fraudulent and began to report the official results as accurate without commentary.

It is clear that maintaining the interpretive framework that the Mexican electoral process was fraudulent would not serve the national interests of the United States if it resulted in supporting a significant leftward shift in the Mexican government. For that reason, concern over democracy in Mexico began to disappear from the U.S. press in the fall of 1988.

During 1989, officials of the new Bush administration tried to convince their counterparts in the new Salinas de Gortari administration of the advantages of a free trade agreement. At first the Mexican government opposed the agreement on the grounds that the country was too weak economically to benefit from such an agreement and that it would open the door to greater penetration and control from its powerful neighbor. But then in spring 1990, the Mexican government did a complete about-face and announced that it was enthusiastically seeking a free trade agreement with the United States. NAFTA would indeed become the cornerstone of the Salinas de Gortari administration's modernization project.[12]

Why the Mexican government suddenly changed its economic policies is the subject of considerable debate and speculation. To some degree the prior de la Madrid administration had begun to lower tariffs in 1983, and, hence, acceptance of NAFTA was a logical consequence. However, it is not likely that by 1989 the Mexican government was ready to take as radical a step as entering into a full-fledged free trade agreement. What most likely pushed it over the last doubts was the collapse during that year of the governments in Eastern Europe that had relied on state-led economic policies—as had Mexico.

At the same time, there had from the beginning been significant opposition in Canada to its free trade agreement with the United States. When it was announced that the agreement would be extended to Mexico, opposition increased even further. Economic recession in 1988 and 1989, which was in large part blamed on the free trade agreement, fueled opposition. The economic recession hit earlier and harder in Canada than the United States. In Quebec, however, the bulk of public opinion has favored the country's free trade agreement with the United States and NAFTA. Free trade agreements allow Quebec's independent-minded merchants and producers to develop direct trading links with the United States without the approval of Ottawa.

In order to support the negotiations for NAFTA and win its subsequent approval in the United States Congress, the Bush administration and its allies in the press began to struggle to establish a new intepretive framework for stories about Mexico. Given the controversial 1988 elections, they could not sustain the thesis that Mexico was a model democracy. In its place, they emphasized a country that was struggling to modernize itself and was led by a young, able, and, most important, pro-American president. As part of this effort to spread a favorable image of Mexico in the United States, the highly successful art exhibition "Mexico: Splendor of Thirty Centuries" toured the country. At the same time, the Mexican government for the first time employed a public relations firm in Washington to design another campaign to create positive images and perceptions of the country. One of its most ironic conquests was nominating President Salinas de Gortari for an ecology award and obtaining it for him, when Mexico undoubtedly has the most polluted capital in the world. Although the award came from a minor environmental organization, it was widely reported in Mexico as being "the equivalent of the Nobel Prize for Ecology."

The campaign to change the image of Mexico and its government in the United States had great success by 1991. It is not coincidental that it was then that the U.S. Senate authorized the "fast track" process for negotiating NAFTA. That process would allow NAFTA to be negotiated within a defined period, signed, and approved without amendments by simple majorities in Congress within sixty days after enabling legislation was presented by the president.[13] During that period it was common in the United States to describe with good intentions the Mexican president as "the Mexican Gorbachev"—a problematic analogy given what subsequently occurred with the collapse and dismemberment of the Union of Soviet Socialist Republics.[14]

Very little opposition to NAFTA appeared in the Mexican press. The opposition Partido de la Revolución Democrática (PRD), headed by Cuauhtémoc Cárdenas, at first equivocated on NAFTA, only complaining that the negotiations were secretive and not carried out democratically. The PRD only later took a position of full opposition to NAFTA. The press, over which the government exerts indirect control, in general cheered the negotiating process on, seeing NAFTA as the solution to Mexico's economic problems. The common analysis was that the post–cold war world was dividing into three economic blocs—the European common market, an Asian bloc led by Japan, and now, a North American bloc led by the United States—and Mexico had the historic opportunity to link up with an economic superpower and be a player in the economic big leagues. If Mexico did not, so the taken-for-granted analysis ran, it would remain mired in the third world periphery. As NAFTA gathered steam, remarkably optimistic press headlines promised, "With NAFTA Mexico Will Leave the Third World for the First," and, "Five Years after the Inauguration of NAFTA Mexican Wages Will Equal Those of the United States."

In the fall of 1991 the campaign for approval of NAFTA was going very well. Its approval seemed inevitable. So too did the reelection of President Bush, who triumphantly emerged from the Persian Gulf War with a 90 percent public approval rating. But then the economic recession in the United States deepened, and, more important, the U.S. public began to perceive it as such. By the beginning of 1992 it was evident that neither the reelection of President Bush nor a rapid approval of NAFTA in the United States was inevitable.

In the United States the most reliable variable for predicting a standing president's reelection possibilities is the state of the economy. More than anything else, U.S. voters demand of their presidents that the economy be healthy. The perception that the economy is healthy gives a standing president a tremendous advantage in an election, as was the situation of Ronald Reagan in 1984. But, when voters perceive that the economy is not going well, as was the case of Jimmy Carter in 1980, the opposition candidate, whether Republican or Democrat, has possibilities to win.[15] With the economy in full recession in the summer of 1992, it was clear that President Bush would not win an easy reelection. Among the president's vulnerabilities was precisely his sponsorship of NAFTA. During the primary elections, many of the other candidates attacked, or at least questioned, NAFTA, arguing that with it the economy was going to suffer more because it would lead to the exportation of jobs to Mexico, where wage costs are dramatically lower.

In September 1992 the final draft of NAFTA was completed. President Bush delayed signing it until mid-December, well after the conclusion of the election in which he was defeated. The new Clinton administration then inherited the agreement, which still faced ratification by Congress. Bill Clinton, during the campaign, had walked a tightrope on support for NAFTA. He was caught between growing grassroots opposition to NAFTA in the electoral base of the Democratic Party and the counsel of his advisers that failure of the United States to ratify the agreement would likely provoke political and economic crises in Mexico that could pose a security threat to the United States. Not only was President Salinas de Gortari betting all of his and the PRI's political capital on passage of NAFTA, but Mexico had also greatly restructured its economy through privatization of state industry, lowering of tariffs, and other measures in anticipation of the agreement. The Mexican government had also maintained a policy of subsidizing the value of the peso vis-à-vis the dollar, a policy that resulted in overvaluation of the peso and a growing unfavorable trade imbalance with the United States. All of this was in anticipation of passage of NAFTA before the 1994 Mexican presidential elections.

If during the 1980s it was common to view the Soviet Union and Mexico as the greatest and next-greatest potential security threats, the collapse of the old Soviet system had now elevated Mexico into first place. Candidate Clinton resolved the problem by pledging support both for NAFTA and for the inclusion of new side agreements to address environmental and labor concerns. Once in office the Clinton administration negotiated the side agreements, but these agreements did little to diminish opposition to NAFTA among labor and environmental constituencies at the liberal base of the Democratic Party. Opposition to NAFTA then spread to some leading conservatives, including columnist Pat Buchanan. Making matters still more difficult for the Administration was that Ross Perot, the maverick, multimillionaire, presidential candidate in the 1992 election, joined the opposition to NAFTA and mounted a well-financed campaign against its passage. It appeared that the left and right of United States politics were uniting in opposition to the center. By early Fall 1993, many were predicting that Congress would not approve NAFTA. The possible collapse of NAFTA sent shock waves not only through Mexico but also through the United States State Department, which was facing its greatest potential crisis with Mexico since the 1988 disputed election.

The fight over the controversial trade agreement reached its critical phase in early November. The Clinton administration, with significant corporate backing, concentrated all of its energies on passage of NAFTA. In the final days before the crucial show-down in the House of Representatives, both sides took to the airwaves. Never before had a proposed *trade agreement* been so controversial in United States politics; much of the publically-aired debate was concerned with the specifically class-related issue of whether it would lead to an increase or decrease in jobs. On November 17, 1993, the pro-NAFTA forces prevailed by a small majority (234 to 200) in the House of Representatives. The last serious obstacle to NAFTA had been overcome. The Senate then passed NAFTA by a significantly larger margin.

THE NEW NORTH AMERICAN DIVISION OF LABOR

The economies of North America are facing significant changes and restructuring in the coming decades and, barring unforeseeable developments, will become more closely integrated. Capital will circulate more widely and freely on the continent as a whole, producing transformations in underdeveloped regions, especially in Mexico. The *maquiladora* transformation of the Mexican border cities is a preview of what will increasingly occur in other parts of the country. There will be a significant movement of industrial jobs from high-wage areas in Canada and the United States to low-wage areas in Mexico. In general terms, as Mexico industrializes, the United States and Canada will increase their deindustrialization, or put more optimistically, postindustrialization. The end effect will be a kind of continental economic rationalization.

But what is economically rational is not always socially or politically rational. Mexicans fear that their country will be turned into a giant *maquiladora* and their vibrant national culture drowned in an orgy of U.S.-style consumerism. People in the United States and Canada fear for their jobs, as once-proud communities like Flint, Michigan, a former center of General Motors, are turned into industrial ghost towns ravaged by crime, drugs, and despair.

At the same time, the existence of low wages is not a sufficient condition for corporations to change location. They also have infrastructural requirements. Assembly plants need to be connected by modern roads to their products' destinations. With large parts of Mexico unconnected by modern roads, the whole country's attractiveness to that type of investment remains limited. For that reason most *maquiladoras* have huddled near the border where they have relatively quick access to the modern U.S. interstate highway system, that is, after getting past the border bottleneck. There are also political and legal conditions that impinge upon the decision to change locations from one country to another. However attractive Mexico's cheap labor supply may be to U.S. corporations, most remain yet to be fully convinced that they will be able to operate a factory there as easily as they can at home. These obstacles will somewhat brake the tendency toward a wholesale shift of industrial jobs to Mexico.

Mexico faces the greatest restructuring in the next decades. As the weakest of the three economies, it faces the greatest social change. Integration with the economic giants to its north will inevitably alter its economic and class landscape. Economic development that is tied to increasing North American integration will go in the direction of greater concentration and centralization of capital and business ownership in Mexico, as it did in previous decades in the United States and Canada. Historically, this type of process has been propelled either by the state, as in the formerly socialist countries, or by large private capital. In the case of contemporary Mexico, it seems clear, at least for the foreseeable future, that large private capital will be the agency of greater concentration and centralization of capital.

The hidden hand behind NAFTA and similar free trade developments is that U.S. and (to a much lesser degree) Canadian large capital will increase their presence in the country, outcompete and eventually displace small- and medium-size domestic businesses, and thereby speed up the concentration process, accomplishing what their Mexican counterparts thus far have been unable to. Free market conditions favor powerful actors because unrestrained competition inevitably results in the stronger eliminating the weaker. The clearest effect of free trading arrangements in this respect will be to remove restraints on continental competition and thereby on the concentration of capital assets in the hands of the strongest competitors—U.S., Canadian, and Mexican multinational corporations.

A number of conditions have heretofore retarded capital concentration in Mexico. The Mexican state has traditionally pursued policies that have restrained capital concentration in a double sense. It has intervened in and regulated Mexican markets in favor of small competitors at the expense of larger ones. The *ejido* program, for example, restrained land concentration in agriculture. The Mexican state, through import substitution policies, also protected its domestic producers from more powerful foreign competitors. Therefore, NAFTA was part of an overall policy of the Salinas de Gortari government to remove these fetters on both domestic private initiative and foreign investment. As such, its inevitable effect was to accelerate the concentration of capital ownership.

Acceleration of concentration of capital ownership will greatly alter the economic class profile of Mexico. Concentration of greater amounts of capital in the hands of large businesses will give them more leverage to drive small businesses out of many different commodity markets and thereby decrease the possibilities of independent employment in the labor force.[16] As large businesses expand, they will open up new middle- and working-class positions. In short, in the coming years and decades, if present economic policies continue, there is likely to be a wholesale shift for a large part of the labor force from independent small-business positions to working-class positions. For a smaller part, there will be a shift into new middle-class professional and managerial positions. The capitalist, new middle, and working classes will thus expand as small-business possibilities decrease due to the strengthening of the positions of large businesses. In this respect, the Mexican economic class structure will move toward approximating that of the United States. In the long run, as the proportion of the labor force made up of self-employed or independent owners of businesses declines and the proportion of employees increases in Mexico, more income will be distributed in the forms of wages and salaries and less as profits. This process will have a long-term equalizing effect on income distribution because distributions of wages and salaries are less unequal than distributions of profits.

There are a number of reasons to believe that this process will lead to greater long-term economic growth, efficiency, productivity, and benefits for the country as a whole by sweeping away many anachronistic forms of economic organization. The legions of small and micro businesses may be colorful and folkloric, but they neither represent the most efficient forms of production or distribution nor afford decent incomes for their owners. The large number of nearly autarkic micro farms in the Mexican countryside do little to meet the country's food needs. The spread of cholera during the early 1990s in Mexico, along with other infectious diseases, occurred at least partially because so many small restaurants prepare food in precarious sanitary conditions that are virtually impossible to regulate.

The rationalization of the Mexican economy will be associated, however, with significant short-run and medium-run negative impacts. Social inequality will increase in a society that already has the continent's most unequal distribution of income. As Mexico replaces statist policies that provided some measure of security to lower income strata with more laissez-faire policies, income will inevitably be redistributed upward. Concentration of capital and business ownership will result in increased unemployment because of the displacement of large numbers of farm and nonfarm small-business owners; and massive new unemployment could easily be a recipe for increased social and political instability. In addition, some part of the new unemployed population will most certainly attempt to cross into the United States as undocumented workers in search of work, producing an unintended consequence of the free trade agreement. Already one out of every five Mexicans in the world lives in the United States. That proportion is likely to increase significantly over the next decades if capital concentration produces significant displacement.

The proponents of free trade argue that it will attract enough new foreign job-creating investments to offset the loss of small business employment. But, numerous cases in history have demonstrated that in periods when people are driven off the land or expropriated by the force of market competition from small-business ownership, the pace of new employment creation rarely keeps up, at least in the short run, with the destruction of traditional forms of independent employment, and rarely do such periods proceed peacefully. In the United States, the squeezing of family farmers off the land, which began in the last quarter of the nineteenth century and lasted through the depression, set off periods of turbulent and often violent political conflict.

If U.S. agricultural surpluses are dumped onto the Mexican market, as they were in Puerto Rico in the late 1940s and 1950s, hundreds of thousands of small farmers, as well as the town merchants who supply them, will find themselves driven out of business; and, like many Puerto Ricans before them, many will find migration to the United States as undocumented workers to be their best option for economic survival. The displaced Mexicans will be different from the Puerto Ricans in that they will not be allowed to move freely to the United States in search of incomes, since NAFTA does not encompass removing obstacles to the movement of labor.

Free trade and economic integration, therefore, will likely bring about a significant restructuring of the class profile of Mexico. As the rate of concentration of capital increases, many small-business owners will be displaced and face unemployment. In the medium and long runs, as the small-business class declines, some new middle-class positions will expand with the growth of new corporate bureaucracies. But what will expand the most will be working-class positions. In this sense, capital concentration and proletarianization are the twin dynamics of the coming decades. Whether these will accompany a peaceful period of economic growth and modernization, as is hoped by the proponents of *maquiladora* industrialization and free trade, or a period of increased class conflict and political instability, remains to be seen.

Notes

CHAPTER 1. INTRODUCTION

1. World Bank, *World Development Report* (New York: Oxford University Press, 1990).

2. Ibid.

3. The infant mortality rate of Mexico is the subject of considerable controversy, with widely different estimates from governmental and international agencies. A leader of the Centro Mexicano por los Derechos de la Infancia (the Mexican Center for Children's Rights) maintains that the government's main statistical agency neither has collected information to develop an accurate estimate nor has an interest in doing so because it would be politically embarrassing. See Andrea Bárcena, "El INEGI en el Cemedin." *La Jornada* (Mexico City), April 30, 1992, p. 39.

4. Calculated on the basis of data in World Bank, *World Development Report,* pp. 179 and 231.

5. Seymour Martin Lipset, *Continental Divide: The Values and Institutions of the United States and Canada* (London: Routledge, 1990).

6. Ibid., p. 92.

7. Samuel Ramos, *El Perfil del Hombre y la Cultura en México* (Mexico City: Colección Austral, 1990, originally published in 1934), p. 159. Surprisingly, it is my impression that there are relatively fewer accidents in Mexico City despite the seeming traffic disorder than in the orderly large cities of the United States and Canada. The reason may be that to survive in Mexican traffic full alertness at all times is required. Drivers learn to always expect the unexpected. The wide lanes and orderliness of U.S. and Canadian freeways, on the other hand, tend to have a lulling effect that can precipitate accidents. As one Mexican motorist admitted, "We drive very badly, but with a great deal of skill." This impressionistic hypothesis, though, cannot be empirically verified because of the lack of reliability of the comparative data. In all three countries, many motorists involved in accidents prefer to settle privately to avoid insurance rate hikes. Such accidents, therefore, are never recorded for statistical purposes. Many motorists in Mexico have an additional motive to

settle privately. They do not wish to get involved with the police, who often require the payment of a bribe.

8. For example, William Julius Wilson, *The Declining Significance of Race: Blacks and Changing American Institutions* (Chicago: University of Chicago Press, 1980).

9. I have discussed this particular methodology for the analysis of class positions more completely in *Modes of Production in World History* (London: Routledge, 1989) and *Introduction to Macrosociology* (Englewood Cliffs, NJ: Prentice Hall, 1992).

10. Robert Miles, *Racism* (London: Routledge, 1989).

11. Richard T. Schaefer, *Racial and Ethnic Groups*, 4th ed. (Glenview, IL: Scott, Foresman, 1990), p. 13.

CHAPTER 2. THE ENDING OF THE FIFTH SUN

1. Instituto Nacional de Estadística, Geografía e Informática (INEGI), *XI Censo General de Población y Vivienda, 1990* (Aguascalientes: INEGI, 1992).

2. Kenneth Hale and David Harris, "Historical Linguistics and Archaeology," *Handbook of North American Indians,* vol. 9 (Washington, DC: Smithsonian, 1979), pp. 170–177.

3. R. Douglas Francis, Richard Jones, and Donald B. Smith, *Origins: Canadian History to Confederation* (Toronto: Holt, Rinehart and Winston of Canada, 1988), p. 8.

4. Other writers use such terms as "Asiatic" and "tributary mode of production" for this type of society.

5. Thomas D. Hall, *Social Change in the Southwest, 1350–1880* (Lawrence: University Press of Kansas, 1989), p. 40.

6. Francis, Jones, and Smith, *Origins,* p. 15.

7. Roger Bartra, "Tributo y Tenencia en la Tierra en la Sociedad Azteca." In Roger Bartra, ed., *El Modo de Producción Asiático* (Mexico City: Ediciones Era, 1969), p. 215.

8. Michael Meyer and William L. Sherman, *The Course of Mexican History* (New York: Oxford University Press, 1979), p. 89.

9. Marc Bloch, "Feudalism, European." In *Encyclopedia of the Social Sciences* (New York: Macmillan, 1933) and *Feudal Society*, trans. L. A. Manyon (Chicago: University of Chicago Press, 1961, originally published in 1940).

10. Roger Bartra, *La Jaula de la Melancolía: Indentidad y Metamórfosis del Mexicano* (Mexico City: Grijalbo, 1987).

11. Alfred M. Crosby, *The Columbian Exchange: Biological and Cultural Consequences of 1492* (Westport, CT: Greenwood Press, 1972).

12. See Carey McWilliams, *North from Mexico* (Westport, CT: Greenwood Press, 1968, originally published in 1949).

13. George Brown and Ron Maguire, "Indian Treaties in Historical Perspective." In James S. Frideres, *Native People in Canada* (Scarborough, Ontario: Prentice-Hall Canada, 1983), p. 49.

14. Ibid., p. 40.

15. Francis, Jones, and Smith, *Origins,* p. 47.

CHAPTER 3. CLASS, RACE, AND COLONIAL RECONSTRUCTION

1. For a discussion of the similarities and differences, see James W. Russell, *Modes of Production in World History* (London: Routledge, 1989), pp. 50–51.

2. Max Weber, *The Protestant Ethic and the Spirit of Capitalism* (New York: Scribner's, 1948, originally published in 1905).

3. Karl Marx and Max Weber initiated the polar sides of this debate in classical social theory. Marx in *Capital*, vol. 1 (Moscow: Progress Publishers, n.d., originally published in 1867), p. 703, maintained that "the discovery of gold and silver in America, the extirpation, enslavement and entombment in mines of the aboriginal population, the beginning of the conquest and looting of the East Indies, the turning of Africa into a warren for the commercial hunting of black-skins, signaled the rosy dawn of the era of capitalist production. These idyllic proceedings are the chief momenta of primitive accumulation." Weber in *General Economic History*, trans. Frank H. Knight (New York: Collier Books edition, 1961, originally published in 1923), p. 223, in contrast, concluded that though "the profits of the slave labor were by no means small . . . this accumulation of wealth . . . has been of little significance for the development of modern capitalism."

4. Roger Bartra, "Tributo y Tenencia en la Tierra en la Sociedad Azteca." In Roger Bartra, ed., *El Modo de Producción Asiático* (Mexico City: Ediciones Era, 1969), p. 216.

5. Angel Palerm Vich, "Factores Históricos de la Clase Media en México." In Miguel Othon de Mendizabal et al., *Ensayos sobre las Clases Sociales en México* (Mexico City: Editorial Nuestro Tiempo, 1968), pp. 93–94.

6. Ibid.

7. Gonzalo Aguirre Beltrán, *Cuijla: Esbozo Etnográfico de un Pueblo Negro* (Mexico City: Fondo de Cultura Económica, 1958), p. 8.

8. Rolando Mellafe, *Negro Slavery in Latin America* (Berkeley: University of California Press, 1975), p. 69.

9. David M. Davidson, "El Control de los Esclavos Negros y su Resistencia en el México Colonial, 1519–1650." In Richard Price, ed., *Sociedades Cimarronas* (Mexico City: Siglo Veintiuno Editores, 1981), p. 87.

10. José L. Franco, "Rebeliones Cimmaronas y Esclavas en los Territorios Españoles." In Price, *Sociedades Cimarronas*, p. 43.

11. Mellafe, *Negro Slavery in Latin America*, p. 105.

12. See Aguirre Beltrán, *Cuijla*.

13. Ibid., p. 59.

14. Alexander von Humboldt, *Ensayo Político sobre el Reino de la Nueva España*, vol. 1 (Paris, 1822), p. 262, cited in Gonzalo Aguirre Beltrán, *La Población Negra de México* (Mexico City: Secretaria de la Reforma Agraria—Centro de Estudios Históricos del Agrarismo en México reprint, 1981, originally published in 1946).

15. Aguirre Beltrán, *La Población Negra de México*; Othon de Mendizabal et al., *Ensayos sobre las clases sociales en México*, p. 9.

16. For an introduction, see the excellent issue of *Artes de México* (Mexico City), number 8, summer 1990, which is devoted to paintings of the castes.

17. Edward J. Sullivan, "Un Fenómeno Visual de América." In *Artes de México*, pp. 60–71.

18. The etymological origin of the Spanish term *mulato* is based on the racist analogy of a mule, which is a cross between a horse and a donkey. Presumably the horse in the analogy is the European, who is superior to the donkey, who is the African. The mulatto product then is inferior to the horse, or European, and superior to the donkey, or African.

19. María Teresa Huerta Preciado, *Rebeliones Indígenas en el Noreste de México en la Epoca Colonial* (Mexico City: Instituto Nacional de Anthropología e Historia, 1966), p. 103.

20. R. Douglas Francis, Richard Jones, and Donald B. Smith, *Origins: Canadian History to Confederation* (Toronto: Holt, Rinehart and Winston of Canada, 1988), pp. 78–79.

21. Ibid.; also Robin W. Winks, *The Blacks in Canada* (New Haven, CT: Yale University Press, 1971).

22. Weber, *The Protestant Ethic and the Spirit of Capitalism.*

23. Herbert S. Klein, *African Slavery in Latin American and the Caribbean* (New York: Oxford University Press, 1986), p. 53.

CHAPTER 4. THREE SOCIETIES, TWO WORLDS OF DEVELOPMENT

1. Ronald Manzer, *Public Policies and Political Development in Canada* (Toronto: University of Toronto Press, 1985), p. 30.

2. Spurgeon Bell, "Productivity, Wages and National Income." In: Richard Edwards, Michael Reich, and Thomas Weisskopf, (eds.), *The Capitalist System,* 2nd ed. (Englewood Cliffs, N.J.: Prentice Hall), p. 180; U.S. Department of Labor, Bureau of Labor and Statistics, *Employment and Earnings,* vol. 38, no. 12, December 1991, Table A–24.

3. James O'Connor, *The Fiscal Crisis of the State* (New York: St. Martin's Press, 1973).

4. John Blair, *Economic Concentration* (New York: Harcourt Brace Jovanovich, 1972).

5. Roger Bartra, *Estructura Agraria y Clases Sociales en México* (Mexico City: Ediciones Era, 1974), p. 131.

6. For an analysis, see Wayne A. Cornelius, "The Politics and Economics of Reforming the *Ejido* Sector in Mexico," pp. 3–10 of *LASA Forum,* Latin American Studies Association, vol. 23, no. 3 (Fall 1992).

7. U.S. Bureau of the Census, *Historical Statistics of the United States,* Part 1 (Washington, DC: U.S. Government Printing Office, 1976), p. 139.

8. David J. Weber, *Myth and the History of the Hispanic Southwest* (Albuquerque: University of New Mexico Press, 1988), p. 141.

9. Rosalie Schwartz, "Across the Rio to Freedom: U.S. Negroes in Mexico," *Southwestern Studies* monograph 44 (University of Texas at El Paso, Texas Western Press), p. 11.

10. Weber, *Myth and the History of the Hispanic Southwest,* p. 141.

11. Twentieth-century examples of this tendency include the following: The Soviet Union, after the Bolshevik Revolution, was obliged to give up border areas to Germany; Ethiopia, after its 1970s revolution, faced a series of border wars with Somalia; and Iran, after the 1979 Islamic revolution, fought a long border war with Iraq.

12. Schwartz, "Across the Rio to Freedom," p. 32.

13. Quoted in Weber, *Myth and the History of the Hispanic Southwest,* p. 139.

14. U.S. Bureau of the Census, *Statistical Abstract of the United States* (Washington, DC: U.S. Government Printing Office, 1989), p. 193.

15. Ibid.: calculated from data in Table 698, p. 430.

16. Seymour Martin Lipset, *Continental Divide: The Values and Institutions of the United States and Canada* (London: Routledge, 1990), pp. 91–92.

17. See Engels' September 12, 1888, letter to Sorge in Karl Marx and Friedrich Engels, *Letters to Americans* (New York: International Publishers, 1963).

18. For a description, see Guillermo Bonfil Batalla, *México Profundo* (Mexico City: Grijalbo, 1990).

19. U.S. Bureau of the Census, *Statistical Abstract of the United States* (Washington, DC: U.S. Government Printing Office, 1990).

20. U.S. Department of Labor, Bureau of Labor Statistics, *Employment and Earnings* vol. 38, no. 3 (March 1991), pp. 6, 40.

21. See Bartra, *Estructura Agraria y Clases Sociales en México*, chap. 3.

22. Instituto Nacional de Estadística, Geografía e Informática (INEGI), *VI Censos Agrícola-Granjero y Ejidal, 1981* (Aguascalientes: INEGI, 1988), p. 3.

23. U.S. Bureau of the Census, *Statistical Abstract of the United States, 1989*, p. 629.

24. INEGI, *Encuesta Nacional de Ingresos y Gastos de los Hogares, Cuarto Trimestre de 1984* (Aguascalientes: INEGI, 1989).

25. Examinations of distributions of income and wealth differ according to the unit of analysis, that is, whether the distribution being examined is between individuals, families, households, or some other unit. Individuals can refer either to direct income recipients in the labor force only or to all population members, which include both income recipients and their dependents, such as children. Families, as defined in censuses, are groups of two or more people related by blood or marriage who live together in a separate living quarter. Households are made up of any individual or group of one or more who live in a separate living quarter. In general, distributions are presented in terms of percentiles: how much of total national income or wealth is received by, for example, each 20 percent of the population, from the poorest to the richest.

26. For more explanation of the Gini coefficient, including instructions on its calculation, see Morley Gunderson, *Economics of Poverty and Income Distribution* (Toronto: Butterworths, 1983). These findings are consistent with the results of Raj K. Chawla's study of distributions of wealth in the United States and Canada in 1984 ("The Distribution of Wealth in Canada and the United States," *Perspectives on Labour and Income* [Statistics Canada], vol. 2, no. 1 [Spring, 1990]). Chawla studied the actual ownership—as opposed to the distribution of income derived from that ownership, which is reported here—and concluded that the Gini coefficients for total wealth less equity in the home were 0.71 for Canada and 0.78 for the United States. According to Chawla, "Whether calculated on the basis of total wealth, total wealth less equity in home, or total wealth less equity in business interests, all Gini coefficients for Canada were lower than for U.S. households. . . . Only 1 percent of all Canadian households held wealth of $500,000 and over and they controlled 19 percent of the total household wealth. In the U.S. these households formed 2 percent of the total, and they held 26 percent of the wealth. At the other end of the wealth distribution, 34 percent of all Canadian households with wealth under $10,000 held about 2 percent of the total wealth compared with 33 percent of their American counterparts holding less than one percent of the total."

27. The distinction between those who are and those who are not engaged in the production of goods and services would seem to be clear enough. But closer examination reveals am-

biguities and controversies over whom to include. The role of unpaid laborers is ambiguous, for they work at the production of goods or services but do not directly receive forms of remuneration. The issue of whether to include them in the calculation of labor force sizes and compositions is important for comparative purposes because there are relatively large numbers of such laborers in Mexico and relatively few in the United States. Official estimates of the size of the unpaid Mexican labor force thus vary considerably, depending on whether farm family children who perform chores are included. If they are included, unpaid workers make up nearly a quarter of the entire labor force. If they are not included, unpaid workers make up 2.6 percent of the labor force, which is still proportionately more than five times as large as the unpaid portions of the U.S. and Canadian labor forces. Should housewives and mothers be included as members of labor forces? In conventional economics they are not. But they certainly provide valuable economic services. Household maintenance enables laborers to eat, sleep, relax, and otherwise recuperate their strength in order to be able to return to work each day. The raising of children, in cold economic terms, amounts to the production of that very important labor market commodity, labor itself. Thus there is considerable reason to question the convention of economics that considers household labor, the vast majority of which is performed by women, to be outside the economy. There is also the question of what to do with subsistence peasant laborers, that is, those who mainly produce goods for household consumption rather than market sale. The further back we go in economic history in all areas, the more labor of this type that we find. We can still find some of it in Mexico, especially among indigenous peoples, and perhaps in Canada. If our concept of a labor force requires that the laborer be producing a good or service that will eventually be sold, then we cannot include subsistence peasant laborers. But then we would miss a type of labor which, while statistically small in the 1990s, continues to have cultural importance (see Bonfil Batalla, *México Profundo*) as well as be, in the anthropological sense, an indicator of a past economic way of life. Thus a labor force is not synonymous with the population of that unit, since the latter also includes children, the aged, invalids, and others who are not actively engaged in the production of goods or services. Nor is a labor force synonymous with a labor market, since the latter only includes those members of a labor force who work for a wage or salary and thereby excludes those who are self-employed owners of businesses.

28. Labor forces are categorized in official statistics according to classes and sectors of activities. By "classes of activities" is meant that they are internally divided between self-employed owners of businesses and employees, with these in turn being divided between those who are paid and those who are not. By "sectors of activities" is meant that labor forces are structured horizontally according to how their members are distributed in agricultural, industrial, and service activities—or the more inclusive categories of primary, secondary, and tertiary activities.

29. INEGI, *Encuesta Nacional de Ingresos y Gastos de los Hogares*, p. 13.

30. U.S. Small Business Administration, *The State of Small Business* (Washington, DC: U.S. Government Printing Office, 1989), p. 78.

31. Much of what is being described here in terms of self-employed and unpaid workers is often included in the concept of the *informal economy*, which is widespread in Mexico and most of the rest of Latin America. If we consider the Mexican informal labor force to be made up of unpaid laborers and self-employed workers who have neither fixed places of businesses nor employees, then it constitutes at least one-third of the total labor force. To the extent that there is an informal labor force in the United States, it does not absorb reg-

ularly more than 1 or 2 percent of the total labor force at most. The size of the informal labor force reflects, once again, the lack in Mexico of capital formation that is capable of creating regular paying jobs.

32. INEGI, *XI Censo General de Población y Vivienda, 1990* (Aguascalientes: INEGI, 1992).

33. INEGI, *Encuesta Nacional de Ingresos de los Hogares, 1989* (Aguascalientes: INEGI, 1992).

34. U.S. Bureau of the Census, *Historical Statistics of the United States.*

35. The labor force participation rate of the United States and Canada is also higher than that of Mexico primarily for two reasons. There are proportionately more women working outside of the home and in the labor force in the United States than in Mexico, thereby accounting for part of the difference in overall adult labor force participation rates. There is also a purely demographic factor that accounts for a significant difference in labor force participation rates. The Mexican population contains significantly more members who are under 16 years of age and therefore by definition outside of the labor force than do those of the United States and Canada.

36. See Daniel Bell, *The Coming of Post-industrial Society* (New York: Basic Books, 1973).

CHAPTER 5. CONTEMPORARY CLASSES

1. Alan Riding, *Distant Neighbors: A Portrait of the Mexicans* (New York: Vintage, 1989, originally published, 1984), p. 190.

2. One percent—Dennis Gilbert and Joseph A. Kahl, *The American Class Structure*, 3rd ed. (Chicago: Dorsey Press, 1987) p. 332; 1.8 percent—Erik Olin Wright, Cynthia Costello, David Hachen, and Joey Sprague, "The American Class Structure," *American Sociological Review*, vol. 47 (1982), pp. 709–726; 2.1 percent—Albert Szymanski, *Class Structure: A Critical Perspective* (New York: Praeger, 1983), p. 93.

3. U.S. Internal Revenue Service, Statistics of Income Division, *Individual Income Tax Returns, 1987* (Washington, DC: U.S. Government Printing Office, 1990), pp. 28–32.

4. Calculated from U.S. Department of Labor, Bureau of Labor Statistics, *Employment and Earnings*, vol. 38, no. 3 (March 1991), pp. 6, 31, 40; and U.S. Bureau of the Census, *Statistical Abstract of the United States* (Washington, DC: U.S. Government Printing Office, 1990), p. 387.

5. Instituto Nacional de Estadística, Geografía e Informática (INEGI), *Encuesta Nacional de Ingresos de los Hogares, 1989* (Aguascalientes: INEGI, 1992).

6. Ibid. pp. 58–59.

7. INEGI, *VI Censos Agrícola-Granjero y Ejidal, 1981, Encuesta Nacional de Ingresos y Gastos de los Hogares, 1984, Resultados Oportunos* (Aguascalientes: INEGI, 1988, 1989, 1990).

8. For a description, see Guillermo Bonfil Batalla, *México Profundo* (Mexico City: Grijalbo, 1990).

9. Seymour Martin Lipset, *Continental Divide: The Values and Institutions of the United States and Canada* (London: Routledge, 1990), p. 207.

10. Max Weber, *The Protestant Ethic and the Spirit of Capitalism* (New York: Scribner's, 1948, originally published in 1905).

11. U.S. Bureau of the Census, *Statistical Abstract of the United States, 1989* (Washington, DC: U.S. Government Printing Office, 1989), Table 509. This estimate differs from those of W. Lloyd Warner, and Paul S. Lunt in *The Social Life of a Modern Community* (New Haven, CT: Yale University Press, 1941) and Richard P. Coleman and Lee Rainwater, with Kent A. McClelland, in *Social Standing in America: New Dimensions of Class* (New York: Basic Books, 1978), who estimated that the rich in the United States were the upper 3 percent of income recipients.

12. U.S. Bureau of the Census, *Statistical Abstract of the United States, 1989.*

13. U.S. Department of Labor, Bureau of Labor Statistics, *Handbook of Labor Statistics* (Washington, DC: U.S. Government Printing Office, 1989), pp. 189–193.

14. The Canadian government does not publish an official estimate of the extent of poverty in the country. Instead, it calculates the percentage of the population with low incomes. However, this figure is not comparable to a poverty estimate as used in the United States. Brigitte Buhmann, Lee Rainwater, Guenther Schmaus, and Timothy M. Smeeding ("Equivalence Scales, Well-being, Inequality, and Poverty: Sensitivity Estimates across Ten Countries Using the Luxembourg Income Study [LIS] Database," *The Review of Income and Wealth*, series 34, no. 2, June 1988, pp. 115–142) did calculate a poverty figure of 7.3 percent for Canada and 12.1 percent for the United States in 1983 using the same method that is used by the U.S. government. The poverty figure of 8.7 percent used here to estimate the size of the Canadian lower class assumes that poverty grew in Canada at the same rate as it did in the United States during the 1980s.

15. Statistics Canada, *Income after Tax, Distributions by Size in Canada, 1989* (Ottawa: Minister of Industry, Science and Technology, 1991), p. 16; U.S. Bureau of the Census, Current Population Reports, Series P–60, *Measuring the Effect of Benefits and Taxes on Income and Poverty, 1990* (Washington, DC: U.S. Government Printing Office, 1991), Table B.

16. Pedro Aspe and Javier Beristain, "Toward a First Estimate of the Evolution of Inequality in Mexico," pp. 31–57 in *The Political Economy of Income Distribution in Mexico*, edited by Pedro Aspe and Paul E. Sigmund (New York: Holmes & Meier, 1984), p. 4.

17. Programa Nacional de Solidaridad (PRONASOL), *El Combate a La Pobreza* (Mexico City: El Nacional, 1990), p. 20.

18. INEGI, *XI Censo General de Población y Vivienda, 1990* (Aguascalientes: INEGI, 1992).

19. INEGI, *Encuesta Nacional de Ingresos de los Hogares, 1989*, pp. 48–49.

20. James W. Wilkie and Paul D. Wilkins, "Quantifying the Class Structure of Mexico, 1895–1970," pp. 148–165 in *Statistical Abstract of Latin America*, vol. 21, edited by James W. Wilkie and Stephen Haber (Los Angeles: University of California Press, 1981), p. 582.

21. See, for example, Claudio Stern, "Notas para la Delimitación de las Clases Medias en México," pp. 19–28 in *Las Clases Medias en la Coyuntura Actual*, edited by Soledad Loaeza and Claudio Stern (Mexico City: El Colegio de México, 1990), p. 25.

22. The earlier estimates were larger in large part because their authors included within the middle class clerical and skilled workers whose incomes afford no more than a working-class standard of living. They applied an essentially three-class (upper, middle, lower) model patterned on the work of W. Lloyd Warner instead of the four-class (upper, middle, working, lower) model employed here. The three-class model inevitably inflates the size of the middle class by not considering the existence of a separate social working class in the middle ranges of the class structure.

23. Calculated from INEGI, *Encuesta Nacional de Ingresos de los Hogares, 1989*, p. 48.

24. Aspe and Baristain, "Toward a First Estimate of the Evolution of Inequality in Mexico."

25. Richard Weisskoff and Adolfo Figueroa, "Traversing the Social Pyramid: A Comparative Review of Income Distribution in Latin America," *Latin American Research Review,* vol. 11, no. 2 (1976), p. 88.

26. Calculated from INEGI, *Encuesta Nacional de Ingresos de los Hogares, 1989,* pp. 48, 60.

27. INEGI, *Encuesta Nacional de Ingresos de los Hogares, 1984*; INEGI, *Encuesta Nacional de Ingresos de los Hogares, 1989,* p. 39; U.S. Bureau of the Census, Current Population Reports, Series P–60, No. 180, *Money Income of Households, Families, and Persons in the United States, 1991* (Washington, DC: U.S. Government Printing Office, 1992), Table B-3; Statistics Canada, *Income Distributions by Size in Canada, 1990* (Ottawa: Minister of Industry, Science and Technology, 1991), Table 55.

28. See Ralph Miliband, *The State in Capitalist Society* (New York: Basic Books, 1969); and G. William Domhoff, *Who Rules America?* (Englewood Cliffs, NJ: Prentice Hall, 1967) and *Who Rules America Now?* (Englewood Cliffs, NJ: Prentice Hall, 1983).

29. John Porter, *The Vertical Mosaic* (Toronto: University of Toronto Press, 1965), p. 292.

30. Paul M. Sweezy, "Power Elite or Ruling Class?" Published as a pamphlet (New York: Monthly Review Press, 1956).

31. Nicos Poulantzas, "The Problem of the Capitalist State," *New Left Review* (November-December, 1969).

32. The *New York Times* (November 5, 1992, p. B9) compiled the results of exit polls from the five presidential elections between 1976 and 1992, dividing voters into five family income classes ranging from under $15,000 to over $75,000 yearly. In each of the elections the proportion of Republican votes directly rose with each step upward in income class. For a specialized study of the relationship between specifically middle-class position and political ideology, see Carolyn Howe, *Political Ideology and Class Formation: A Study of the Middle Class* (Westport, CT: Praeger, 1992).

33. Tomás Oropeza Berumen, "Entrevista con Salvador Castañeda," *La Jornada Semanal* (Mexico City), No. 139, February 9, 1992.

34. Carlos Montemayor, *Guerra en el Paraiso* (Mexico City: Editorial Diana, 1991).

CHAPTER 6. RACE AND PIGMENTOCRACY

1. William Julius Wilson, *The Declining Significance of Race: Blacks and Changing American Institutions* (Chicago: University of Chicago Press, 1980).

2. Reported in Luz María Valdés and María Teresa Menéndez, *Dinámica de la Población de Habla Indígena (1900–1980)* (Mexico City: Instituto Nacional de Antropología e Historia, 1987).

3. Mexico is not alone, though, among Latin American countries in not using racial categories in its census. The Cuban government also does not use racial categories on the grounds that all citizens are Cubans regardless of color. The reality that there are racial differences in Mexico, though, is indicated by passport applicants being required to identify their skin color from the following list: *morena oscura* (dark), *morena clara* (light), or *blanca* (white). The first two options generally correlate with Indian and mestizo.

4. Carlos Monsivais argues that there is a clash between the official denial of racial problems

and their latent reality: "In Mexico it is believed that the racial problem does not exist because ethnicity, it seems, is not a problem. This, while quantitatively true is culturally and economically false. Mexico lives today in a boom of psychological Criolloism (moderately racial) that hawks its Anglo-Saxon models on television (the nation prominently blond), and from the very nature of the situation wants to convince those submitted of their natural inferiority. Up until now this Criolloism seems well on top" ("La Raza: Fichas para un Diccionario," paper presented at the conference "Imagenes de la Frontera," May 4, 1992, at Tijuana, Baja California, Mexico, and reported by Arturo García Hernández in "Racismo Latente y Peligroso en México," *La Jornada* [Mexico City], May 6, 1992, p. 39).

5. Jorge Bustamante, "Imagenes Reales y Virtuales de la Frontera," paper presented at conference reported in note 5.

6. Samuel Ramos, *El Perfil del Hombre y la Cultura en México* (Mexico City: Colección Austral, 1990, originally published in 1934).

7. Octavio Paz, *El Laberinto de la Soledad* (Mexico City: Fondo de Cultura Popular, 1950).

8. Cf.: "The forms of discrimination are subtle. In large part they are based in the self-discrimination of the mestizos and Indians. . . . The main people who reinforce the ideas of separation and discrimination are the mestizos who deeply despise their own race" (José Agustin Ortiz Pinqueti, "El Festin de los Criollos," *La Jornada*, March 29, 1992). For a sustained critique of the interpretation of Ramos, Paz, and others that an inferiority complex is a deep-seated part of the Mexican national character, see Roger Bartra, *La Jaula de la Melancolía: Indentidad y Metamórfosis del Mexicano* (Mexico City: Grijalbo, 1987).

9. Ramos, *El Perfil del Hombre y la Cultura en México*; Paz, *El Laberinto de la Soledad*; Bartra, *La Jaula de la Melancolía*.

10. Ramos, *El Perfil del Hombre y la Cultura en México*, p. 58.

11. One newspaper columnist (Ortiz Pinqueti, see note 9) refers to Jardines del Pedregal along with San Angel, Coyoacán, Polanco, and Lomas de Chapultepec as being *ghettos blancos* (white ghettos) in Mexico City.

12. About 80 percent of those who attend the symphony in Mexico City are white. This fact, as expected, indicates that whites, more than mestizos or Indians, are drawn to the products of European culture. It indicates more, though, about cultural pluralism in the country than racial inequality as such. Students at the Colegio de México, one of Mexico City's major private universities, are more likely to have white faces and blond hair than students at the Universidad Nacional Autónoma de México, the major public university. This difference occurs because the cost of private education is much higher than that of public education and because white parents on the average have more income than mestizo or Indian parents. For the same reasons, the vast majority of Mexican students who go abroad for their education are white.

13. Paul W. Bennett and Cornelius J. Jaenen, *Emerging Identities: Selected Problems and Interpretations in Canadian History* (Scarborough, Ontario: Prentice Hall Canada, 1986), p. 201.

14. Agnes Calliste, "Canada's Immigration Policy and Domestics from the Caribbean: The Second Domestic Scheme." In Jesse Vorst, ed., *Race, Class, Gender: Bonds and Barriers* (Toronto: Between the Lines, 1989).

15. John Porter, *The Vertical Mosaic* (Toronto: University of Toronto Press, 1965).

16. Hugh Lautard and Neil Guppy, "The Vertical Mosaic Revisited: Occupational Differentials among Canadian Ethnic Groups." In Peter S. Li, ed., *Race and Ethnic Relations in Canada* (Toronto: Oxford University Press, 1990).

17. See Porter, *The Vertical Mosaic*, p. 71.

18. Carey McWilliams, *Prejudice—Japanese Americans: Symbol of Racial Intolerance* (Boston: Little, Brown, 1944), p. 26.

19. See Max Weber, "Structures of Power." In Hans H. Gerth and C. Wright Mills, trans. and ed., *From Max Weber: Essays in Sociology* (New York: Oxford University Press, 1958, originally published in 1921).

20. Carey McWilliams, *North from Mexico* (Westport, CT: Greenwood Press, 1968, originally published in 1949).

21. Magnus Mörner credits the Chilean Alejandro Lipschutz with the first use of the term "pigmentocracy" to describe Latin American race relations: *Race Mixture in the History of Latin America* (Boston: Little, Brown and Company, 1967), p. 54.

CHAPTER 7. EURO–NORTH AMERICANS

1. Stanley Feldstein and Lawrence Costello, eds., *The Ordeal of Assimilation: A Documentary History of the White Working Class* (Garden City, NY: Anchor Press, 1974), p. 4.

2. Information on the Saint Patrick's battalion was taken from Robert Ryal Miller's much-needed and well researched 1989 account, *Shamrock and Sword: The Saint Patrick's Battalion in the U.S.-Mexican War* (Norman: University of Oklahoma Press). His is the first extensive and well-documented study of the events. Prior to its publication, many of the existing accounts were largely based on legend and suffered accordingly in terms of their accuracy. In addition to establishing that the majority of the members of the battalion were not Irish, Miller casts doubt on whether persecution of Catholics in the United States and views of the U.S. invasion as unjust were the main motivations for the desertion of the *San Patricios*.

3. Among the German revolutionaries who arrived in 1853 was Friedrich Sorge (1827–1906), a friend of Marx and Engels. He organized many of the U.S. sections of the First International—Marx's attempt to develop an international organization of trade union and revolutionary organizations. Sorge was the grandfather of Richard Sorge, who was one of the two most prominent Soviet spies during World War II. (The other was Leopoldo Trepper—for information, see his memoir, *The Great Game: Memoirs of the Spy Hitler Couldn't Silence* [New York: McGraw-Hill, 1977]). Richard Sorge grew up in Germany. As a student revolutionary he established contacts with the new Soviet authorities in the aftermath of the 1917 Bolshevik revolution. By 1939 he had managed to install himself as the press officer of the German embassy in Tokyo. From there he was able to learn that the Japanese were not planning to attack the Soviet Union from the East. This strategic information allowed Stalin to divert troops from guarding the Asian border to the fight against the German invasion. Many believe that Sorge's information was the critical element that allowed the Soviets to successfully expel the German invaders. Sorge was discovered and imprisoned in 1944 and hanged in 1945. During his imprisonment he wrote his memoirs. These were seized during the postwar occupation by the U.S. authorities. They are included in Major General Charles A. Willoughby's ultraright-wing description

of Soviet Asian spy activity, *Shanghai Conspiracy: The Sorge Spy Ring* (New York: E. P. Dutton, 1952).

4. U.S. Bureau of the Census, *Statistical Abstract of the United States, 1989* (Washington, DC: U.S. Government Printing Office, 1989), p. 40.

5. For the classic study, see W. I. Thomas, and Florian Znaniecki, *The Polish Peasant in Europe and America*, 4 volumes (New York: Dover, 1958, originally published 1918–20).

6. Cf.: "Your great obstacle in America, it seems to me, lies in the exceptional position of the native-born workers. Up to 1848 one could speak of a permanent native-born working class only as an exception. The small beginnings of one in the cities in the East still could always hope to become farmers or bourgeois. Now such a class has developed and has also organized itself on trade-union lines to a great extent. But it still occupies an aristocratic position and wherever possible leaves the ordinary badly paid occupations to the immigrants, only a small portion of whom enter the aristocratic trade unions. But these immigrants are divided into different nationalities, which understand neither one another nor, for the most part, the language of the country. And your bourgeoisie knows much better even than the Austrian government how to play off one nationality against the other: Jews, Italians, Bohemians, etc., against Germans and Irish, and each one against the other, so that differences in workers' standards of living exist, I believe, in New York to an extent unheard of elsewhere" (Friedrich Engels, March 30, 1892, letter to Hermann Schuter in Karl Marx and Friedrich Engels, *Letters to Americans*, New York: International Publishers, 1963). Engels' observations regarding the internal stratification of the working class were at odds with his and Marx's earlier belief in the 1848 *Communist Manifesto* that "the various interests and conditions of life within the ranks of the proletariat are more and more equalized, in proportion as machinery obliterates all distinctions of labor, and nearly everywhere reduces wages to the same low level." Clearly, the opposite was occurring within the working class in the United States. In England, during the same period, Engels also perceived a growing stratification with the working class, though not for the same reasons of immigration and ethnic diversity as in the United States. Based on these observations Engels developed his concept of a labor aristocracy that occupied the most privileged positions within the working class and that tended to be conservative politically in order to protect that privilege. V. I. Lenin in *Imperialism, the Highest Stage of Capitalism* (in V. I. Lenin, *Selected Works in Three Volumes* [Moscow: Progress Publishers, 1970, originally published in 1916]) later inherited Engels' concept of the labor aristocracy, arguing that the labor aristocracy provided the main base of working-class support for imperialist policies. One can assume that if native-born whites constituted a labor aristocracy, they also constituted the aristocracy in a loose use of the term, as well.

7. Asian household income averages are equivalent to those of white households, largely because Asian households have, on average, more members working in the labor force than do white households. The average income of white members of the labor force in 1990 remained higher than that of Asian members. See U.S. Bureau of the Census, *Poverty in the United States, 1991* (Washington, DC: U.S. Government Printing Office, 1992), p. x.

8. For exit poll data on white voters in presidential elections, see the *New York Times*, November 5, 1992, p. B9.

9. John Porter, *The Vertical Mosaic* (Toronto: University of Toronto Press, 1965).

10. Statistics Canada, *Canada Year Book, 1989* (Ottawa: Statistics Canada, 1989), pp. 2–26.

11. Porter, *The Vertical Mosaic*, p. 91.

12. Hugh Lautard and Neil Guppy, "The Vertical Mosaic Revisited: Occupational Differentials among Canadian Ethnic Groups." In Peter S. Li, ed., *Race and Ethnic Relations in Canada* (Toronto: Oxford University Press, 1990).

13. Max Weber, *The Protestant Ethic and the Spirit of Capitalism* (New York: Scribner's, 1948, originally published in 1905).

14. Porter, *The Vertical Mosaic*, p. 95.

15. U.S. Bureau of the Census, *Migration between the United States and Canada* (Washington, DC: U.S. Government Printing Office, 1990), p. 7.

16. Porter, *The Vertical Mosaic*, p. 64.

17. Howard Palmer, "Reluctant Hosts: Anglo-Canadian Views of Multiculturalism in the Twentieth Century." In R. Douglas Francis and Donald B. Smith, *Readings in Canadian History: Post-Confederation*, 2nd ed. (Toronto: Holt, Rinehart and Winston of Canada, 1986).

18. Ibid., p. 185. There is some evidence though that, in contrast to policies prevailing in the United States, Canadian officials in the late nineteenth and early twentieth centuries unofficially assured non-English-speaking immigrants that they could retain their languages and cultures. See p. 157.

19. Ibid., pp. 185–186.

20. See Seymour Martin Lipset, *Continental Divide: The Values and Institutions of the United States and Canada* (London: Routledge, 1990).

21. Samuel Ramos, *El Perfil del Hombre y la Cultura en México* (Mexico City: Colección Austral, 1990, originally published in 1934); Guillermo Bonfil Batalla, *México Profundo* (Mexico City: Grijalbo, 1990).

22. Consejo Nacional de Población (CONAPO), *Población y Desarrollo en México y el Mundo*, vol. 4, Anexo Estadístico (Mexico City: CONAPO, 1988), p. 1099.

23. Instituto Nacional de Estadística, Geografía e Informática (INEGI), *XI Censo General de Población y Vivienda, 1990* (Aguascalientes: INEGI, 1992).

24. U.S. Bureau of the Census, *Statistical Abstract of the United States, 1989*, p. 40.

25. Statistics Canada, *Canada Year Book, 1989*, pp. 2–26.

26. CONAPO, *Población y Desarrollo en México y el Mundo*, p. 1101.

27. Seymour Martin Lipset (*Continental Divide*, p. 135) cites data that nine of the 32 richest families in Canada and one-fourth of the 400 richest in the United States are Jewish. While Jews in Mexico are also undoubtedly disproportionately rich, I know of no studies that document the extent to which that assumption is true.

28. Oral interview, March 15, 1992.

29. Estimates of the numbers of U.S. and Canadian citizens living in Mexico vary as widely as do estimates of the number of Mexican undocumented workers living in the United States. In 1980, according to official sources (see U.S. Bureau of the Census, *Migration between the United States and Canada*, Tables 5 and 6), there were 97,246 U.S.-born persons and 3,352 Canadians living in Mexico. The actual number of U.S. citizens living in Mexico may be much higher though. Officials of the U.S. embassy in Mexico City, whom I interviewed in 1992, believed that there could be as many as 250,000 U.S. citizens living in Mexico City and 40,000 more living in Guadalajara. Of those, approximately 50,000 are registered with the embassy.

30. José Agustin Ortiz Pinqueti, "El Festin de los Criollos," *La Jornada* (Mexico City), March 29, 1992.
31. Kenneth B. Clark and Mamie P. Clark, "Racial Identification and Preferences in Negro Children." In Theodore M. Newcomb and Eugene L. Hartley, eds., *Readings in Social Psychology* (New York: Holt, Rinehart and Winston, 1947).

CHAPTER 8. INDIANS AFTER THE FIFTH SUN

1. Gonzalo Aguirre Beltrán, *La Población Negra de México* (Mexico City: Secretaria de la Reforma Agraria, Centro de Estudios Históricos del Agrarismo en México, reprint, 1981, originally published in 1946), p. 234.
2. For descriptions and documents, see Leticia Reina, *Las Rebeliones Campesinas en México, 1819–1906* (Mexico City: Siglo Veintiuno Editores, 1980).
3. Thomas D. Hall, *Social Change in the Southwest, 1350–1880* (Lawrence: University Press of Kansas, 1989), pp. 160–163.
4. Cf.: "By the time of Mexican independence it was widely recognized that some Apaches and Comanches, and probably Wichita bands such as the Taovayas, stole horses and mules from Tejanos and exchanged them for guns and ammunition with traders in Louisiana." David J. Weber, *Myth and the History of the Hispanic Southwest* (Albuquerque: University of New Mexico Press, 1988), p. 122.
5. Guillermo Bonfil Batalla, *México Profundo* (Mexico City: Grijalbo, 1990), p. 151; Hall, *Social Change in the Southwest, 1350–1880*, p. 161; James E. Officer, *Hispanic Arizona, 1536–1856* (Tucson: University of Arizona Press, 1987), p. 150.
6. For a description, see James E. Officer, *Hispanic Arizona, 1536–1856 (Tucson, AZ: University of Arizona Press, 1987).*
7. Hall, *Social Change in the Southwest, 1350–1880*, p. 104.
8. The Yaquis also inhabited land that is now a part of the United States. There is a small Pascua Yaqui reservation in Pima County, Arizona.
9. Ramon Eduardo Ruiz, *The People of Sonora and Yankee Capitalists* (Tucson: University of Arizona Press, 1988), p. 180.
10. Samuel Ramos, *El Perfil del Hombre y la Cultura en México* (Mexico City: Colección Austral, 1990, originally published in 1934).
11. Bonfil Batalla, *México Profundo*.
12. Luz María Valdés, *El Perfil Demográfico de los Indios Mexicanos*, 2nd ed. (Mexico City: Siglo Veintiuno Editores, 1989), p. 137.
13. Max Weber, *Economy and Society*, 2 volumes (New York: Bedminster Press, 1968, originally published in 1922).
14. For example, see Ricardo Pozas and Isabel H. de Pozas, *Los Indios en las Clases Sociales de México* (Mexico City: Siglo Veintiuno Editores, 1971) and Bonfil Batalla, *México Profundo*. What we are calling the dual-economy thesis is related to a debate that took place among Mexican researchers in the 1970s. One side, the *campesinistas*, argued that not only did a peasant subsistence economy that was substantially outside of the market exist in the Mexican countryside, but it was also reproducing and growing because it conformed to cultural needs of Indian and other rural communities. The other side, the *descampesinistas*,

argued that capitalist development was inexorably undercutting and would eventually eliminate the peasant self-subsistence economy.

15. Gonzalo Aguirre Beltrán, *Regiones de Refugio*, 2nd ed. (Mexico City: Instituto Nacional Indigenista, 1973, originally published in 1967), p. xvi.

16. The Declaration of Independence stated that King George "has endeavored to bring on the inhabitants of our frontiers, the merciless Indian Savages, whose known rule of warfare, is an undistinguished destruction of all ages, sexes and conditions."

17. Quoted in R. Douglas Francis, Richard Jones, and Donald B. Smith, *Origins: Canadian History to Confederation* (Toronto: Holt, Rinehart and Winston of Canada, 1988), p. 209.

18. Bruce Johansen and Roberto Maestas, *Wasi'Chu: The Continuing Indian Wars* (New York: Monthly Review Press, 1979), p. 27.

19. Francis, Jones, and Smith, *Origins: Canadian History to Confederation*, p. 218.

20. Carey McWilliams, *North from Mexico* (Westport, CT: Greenwood Press, 1968, originally published in 1949), p. 52.

21. For a description see Hall, *Social Change in the Southwest, 1350–1880*, pp. 217–230.

22. Officer, *Hispanic Arizona*, p. 306.

23. Johansen and Maestas, *Wasi'Chu*, p. 32.

24. U.S. Bureau of the Census, *Census of Population and Housing, 1990*, Summary Tape Files 1C—CD-ROM (Washington, DC: U.S. Government Printing Office, 1992).

25. U.S. Bureau of the Census, *1990 Census of Population and Housing: Summary Social, Economic, and Housing Characteristics* (Washington, DC: U.S. Government Printing Office, 1992), Table 8.

26. Ibid., Table 9.

27. George Brown and Ron Maguire, "Indian Treaties in Historical Perspective." In James S. Frideres, *Native People in Canada* (Scarborough, Ontario: Prentice Hall Canada, 1983), p. 78.

28. Ibid., p. 64.

29. Ibid., p. 72.

30. Seymour Martin Lipset, *Continental Divide: The Values and Institutions of the United States and Canada* (London: Routledge, 1990).

31. Frideres, *Native People in Canada*, pp. 140–145.

32. Statistics Canada, *Canada Year Book, 1989* (Ottawa: Minister of Industry, Science and Technology, 1989), pp. 2–25.

33. Statistics Canada, *Ethnic Origin,* 1991 Census (Ottawa: Minister of Industry, Science and Technology, 1993), Table 1A.

34. John Porter, *The Vertical Mosaic* (Toronto: University of Toronto Press, 1965), p. 86; Hugh Lautard and Neil Guppy, "The Vertical Mosaic Revisited: Occupational Differentials among Canadian Ethnic Groups." In Peter S. Li, ed., *Race and Ethnic Relations in Canada* (Toronto: Oxford University Press, 1990); Ryan J. McDonald, "Canada's Off-Reserve Aboriginal Population," *Canadian Social Trends*, no. 23 (Winter 1991), pp. 2–7.

35. James S. Frideres, "Institutional Structures and Economic Deprivation: Native People in Canada." In B. Singh Bolaria and Peter S. Li, *Racial Oppression in Canada* (Toronto: Garamond Press, 1988), p. 82.

36. Statistics Canada, *A Portrait of Children in Canada* (Ottawa: Minister of Industry, Science and Technology, 1990), p. 25.

CHAPTER 9. AFRO–NORTH AMERICANS

1. W. E. B. Du Bois, *Black Reconstruction in America* (New York: Russell & Russell, 1962, originally published in 1935).
2. Ibid.
3. For example, James S. Allen, *Reconstruction: The Battle for Democracy* (New York: International Publishers, 1937). Also, in 1944, Howard Fast published *Freedom Road*, (New York: Duell, Sloan and Pearce) a best-selling historical novel about blacks struggling for land, equality, and democracy during Reconstruction. Fast based himself on the Communist Party's interpretation, and the book contained a forward by Du Bois.
4. Eric Foner, *Reconstruction: America's Unfinished Revolution, 1863–1877* (New York: Harper & Row, 1988).
5. Ibid., p. 140.
6. Ibid., p. 581.
7. Richard T. Schaefer, *Racial and Ethnic Groups*, 4th ed. (Glenview, IL: Scott, Foresman, 1990), p. 226.
8. Frances Fox Piven and Richard A. Cloward, *Regulating the Poor* (New York: Vintage, 1971).
9. For exit poll data on black voters, see the *New York Times*, November 5, 1992, p. B9.
10. Gonzalo Aguirre Beltrán, *La Población Negra de México* (Mexico City: Secretaria de la Reforma Agraria, Centro de Estudios Históricos del Agrarismo en México reprint, 1981, originally published in 1946), p. 234.
11. Gonzalo Aguirre Beltrán, *Cuijla: Esbozo Etnográfico de un Pueblo Negro* (Mexico City: Fondo de Cultura Económica, 1958), p. 59.
12. Ibid.
13. Most of the information reported here on slave escapes to Mexico was obtained from Rosalie Schwartz's impressively researched but unfortunately obscurely published and therefore relatively unknown article on the subject, "Across the Rio to Freedom: U.S. Negroes in Mexico," *Southwestern Studies* monograph 44 (El Paso: Texas Western Press, 1975).
14. Ibid., p. 26.
15. Ibid., p. 40.
16. María Luisa Herrera Casasus, *Presencia y Esclavitud del Negro en la Huasteca* (Mexico City: Porrua, 1989), p. 25.
17. Schwartz, "Across the Rio to Freedom," p. 33.
18. Gabriel Moedano Navarro, "El Estudio de las Tradiciones Orales y Musicales de los Afromestizos de México," *Antropología e Historia*, ecoca III, no. 31 (Julio-Septiembre 1980).
19. Aguirre Beltrán, *Cuijla*, p. 7.
20. Gonzalo Aguirre Beltrán, "The Integration of the Negro into the National Society of Mexico." In Magnus Mörner, ed., *Race and Class in Latin America* (New York: Columbia University Press, 1970).

21. James W. Walker, *A History of Blacks in Canada* (Ottawa: Minister of State and Multiculturalism, 1980).
22. B. Singh Bolaria and Peter S. Li, *Racial Oppression in Canada*, 2nd ed. (Toronto: Garamond Press, 1988), p. 190.
23. Robin W. Winks, *The Blacks in Canada* (New Haven, CT: Yale University Press, 1971); Headley Tulloch, *Black Canadians* (Toronto: N.C. Press, 1975).
24. Walker, *A History of Blacks in Canada*, p. 56.
25. Winks, *The Blacks in Canada*.
26. Agnes Calliste, "Canada's Immigration Policy and Domestics from the Caribbean: The Second Domestic Scheme." In Jesse Vorst, ed., *Race, Class, Gender: Bonds and Barriers* (Toronto: Between the Lines, 1989).
27. Hugh Lautard and Neil Guppy, "The Vertical Mosaic Revisited: Occupational Differentials among Canadian Ethnic Groups." In Peter S. Li, ed., *Race and Ethnic Relations in Canada* (Toronto: Oxford University Press, 1990).

CHAPTER 10. ORIGINAL AND NEW ASIAN COMMUNITIES

1. Victor G. Nee and Bret de Bary Nee, *Longtime Californ': A Documentary Study of an American Chinatown* (New York: Pantheon Books, 1973), p. 41.
2. Ibid.
3. Carey McWilliams, *Factories in the Field* (Santa Barbara, CA: Peregrine Smith, 1971, originally published in 1935), p. 69.
4. Ibid., p. 68.
5. Moises González Navarro, *La Colonización en México, 1877–1910* (Mexico City: Talleres de Impresión de Estampillas y Valores, 1960), p. 84.
6. José Jorge Gómez Izquierdo, *El Movimiento Anti-Chino en México, 1871–1934* (Mexico City: Universidad Nacional Autónoma de México Facultad de Ciencias Políticas y Sociales, 1988), p. 53.
7. Ibid.; Charles C. Cumberland, "The Sonora Chinese and the Mexican Revolution," *Hispanic American Historical Review*, vol. 40 (May 1960), pp. 191–223.
8. B. Singh Bolaria and Peter S. Li, *Racial Oppression in Canada*, 2nd ed. (Toronto: Garamond Press, 1988), p. 114.
9. Evelyn Hu-DeHart, "Immigrants to a Developing Society: The Chinese in Northern Mexico, 1875–1932," *Journal of Arizona History* (Autumn 1980), pp. 275–313.
10. Ibid.; Cumberland, "The Sonora Chinese and the Mexican Revolution"; Gómez Izquierdo, *El Movimiento Anti-Chino en México,* p. 85.
11. Hu-DeHart, "Immigrants to a Developing Society."
12. Gómez Izquierdo, *El Movimiento Anti-Chino en México,* p. 124.
13. Ibid., p. 138.
14. Hu-DeHart, "Immigrants to a Developing Society."
15. Gómez Izquierdo, *El Movimiento Anti-Chino en México,* p. 127.

16. K. Victor Ujimoto, "Racism, Discrimination and Internment: Japanese in Canada." In Bolaria and Li, *Racial Oppression in Canada*, p. 130.

17. Carey McWilliams, *Prejudice—Japanese Americans: Symbol of Racial Intolerance* (Boston: Little, Brown, 1944).

18. By 1916 the labor movement had reversed its position and disassociated itself from anti-Asian agitation, arguing the need instead to organize all immigrants.

19. McWilliams, *Prejudice—Japanese Americans*.

20. Ujimoto, "Racism, Discrimination and Internment," p. 130.

21. Edna Bonacich and John Modell, *The Economic Basis of Ethnic Solidarity: Small business in the Japanese American Community* (Berkeley: University of California Press, 1980).

22. McWilliams, *Prejudice—Japanese Americans*.

23. Richard T. Schaefer, *Racial and Ethnic Groups*, 4th ed. (Glenview, IL: Scott, Foresman, 1990), p. 396.

24. Ibid., p. 401.

25. Ujimoto, "Racism, Discrimination and Internment."

26. Blanca Torres, *Historia de la Revolución Mexicana, 1940–1952* (Mexico City: El Colegio de México, 1979), p. 80n.

27. María Elena Ota Mishima, *Siete Migraciones Japonesas en México, 1890–1978* (Mexico City: El Colegio de México, 1982), pp. 95–102.

28. See Gonzalo Aguirre Beltrán, *La Población Negra de México* (Mexico City: Secretaria de la Reforma Agraria, Centro de Estudios Históricos del Agrarismo en México reprint, 1981, originally published in 1946).

29. H. Brett Melendy, *Asians in America: Filipinos, Koreans, and East Indians* (Boston: Twayne, 1977).

30. Carey McWilliams, *Brothers under the Skin* (Boston: Little, Brown, 1964), p. 43.

31. Melendy, *Asians in America*.

32. Robert W. Gardner, Bryant Robey, and Peter C. Smith, "Asian Americans: Growth, Change, and Diversity," *The Population Bulletin*, vol. 40, no. 4 (October 1985); U.S. Bureau of the Census, *Census of Population and Housing 1990*, Summary Tape Files 1C—CD-ROM (Washington, DC: U.S. Government Printing Office, 1992).

33. Bolaria and Li, *Racial Oppression in Canada*, p. 133.

34. Statistics Canada, *Canada Year Book, 1989* (Ottawa: Minister of Industry, Science and Technology, 1989), pp. 2–29.

35. Statistics Canada, *Ethnic Origin,*—1991 Census (Ottawa: Minister of Industry, Science and Technology, 1993), Table 1A.

36. Because Canada and India were both British Commonwealth nations, there was some immigration in the early decades of the twentieth century. The early immigrants took jobs mostly as manual laborers in farming, mining, and lumber. As such, they suffered serious racial discrimination, including being denied the right to vote until 1947 and being a target of the 1907 Vancouver anti-Asian riot.

37. *New York Times,* November 5, 1992, p. B9.

38. McWilliams, *Factories in the Field*, p. 104.

CHAPTER 11. THE FIFTH RACE

1. Overall, the numbers of Eurasians in North America are slight. But in Hawaii, which contains significant numbers of Japanese-origin as well as white citizens, there are significant numbers. A third of Hawaiians identify themselves as white, 2 percent as black, and the remaining 65 percent as "other." This latter category contains Japanese and a large number of Eurasians. Hawaii, according to F. James Davis in *Who Is Black? One Nation's Definition* (University Park: Pennsylvania State University Press, 1991), p. 109, is the one area in North America where racially mixed persons enjoy complete social equality. It is the area in North America where there is the least correlation between race and class; there is no noticeable whitening of faces as the social ladder is climbed. The U.S. military presence in Asia continues to result in the births of a number of mixed-race children. During the Korean War, U.S. soldiers, both white and black, fathered thousands of mixed-race children. During the Vietnam War, the number fathered was 80,000. Most of these children, though, remained in Korea and Vietnam, where, according to Davis (ibid., p. 86), they have suffered considerable discrimination as outcasts. A much smaller number now reside in the United States. People in the United States generally refer to these individuals as Amerasians.

   Most of Mexico's population that is socially perceived to be black (see Chapter 9) is in reality a mixed population of African and indigenous descent. For that reason a number of contemporary researchers call it an *Afromestizo* population. In the United States a number of Indian tribes welcomed escaped slaves and other blacks into their ranks. Resulting marriages produced children with Indian and black descent. Overall, according to Thomas F. Pettigrew in *Racial Discrimination in the United States* (New York: Harper & Row, 1975), one-fourth of blacks in the United States have some Indian ancestry.

2. Quoted in Lilian Alvarez de Testa, *Mexicanidad y Libro de Texto Gratuito* (Mexico City: Universidad Nacional Autónoma de México, 1992), p. 14.

3. Magnus Mörner, *El Mestizaje en la Historia de Ibero-América* (Mexico City: Instituto Panamericano de Geografía e Historia, 1961), pp. 29–30.

4. Magnus Mörner, *Race Mixture in the History of Latin America* (Boston: Little, Brown, 1967), p. 30.

5. Moises González Navarro, "*Mestizaje* in Mexico during the National Period." In Magnus Mörner, ed., *Race and Class in Latin America* (New York: Columbia University Press, 1970).

6. Mörner, *Race Mixture in the History of Latin America*, pp. 59–60.

7. Ibid., p. 40.

8. Quoted in Agustín Basave Benítez, *México Mestizo: Análisis del Nacionalismo Mexicano en torno a la Mestizofilia de Andrés Molina Enríquez* (Mexico City: Fondo de Cultura Económica, 1992), p. 27.

9. González Navarro, "*Mestizaje* in Mexico during the National Period."

10. Vasconcelos is most remembered as a philosopher, man of letters, and one of Mexico's most controversial postrevolutionary politicians. He occupied such posts as minister of public instruction, secretary of public education, and rector of the National University. He saw his mission as overseeing the development of public education and a revolutionary nationalist culture for the nation as a whole. Vasconcelos infused his work with his own

commitment to revolutionary nationalist values. He was responsible for the Mexican government's financing the production of murals by Diego Rivera, David Siquieros, José Orozco, and other artists that portrayed Mexico's history on public walls so that it could be seen and learned by the masses. In 1929 he ran and lost as an oppositional candidate for the presidency. After finding himself on the losing side of this power struggle over postrevolutionary Mexican development, he became a bitter critic of the government.

11. José Vasconcelos, *La Raza Cósmica* (Mexico City: Espasa-Calpe Mexicana, Colección Austral, 1992, originally published in 1925), p. 27.

12. Cited in José Jorge Gómez Izquierdo, *El Movimiento Anti-Chino en México, 1871–1934* (Mexico City: Universidad Nacional Autónoma de México, Facultad de Ciencias Políticas y Sociales undergraduate thesis, 1988), p. 116.

13. Samuel Ramos, *El Perfil del Hombre y la Cultura en México* (Mexico City: Colección Austral, 1990, originally published in 1934).

14. Octavio Paz, *El Laberinto de la Soledad* (Mexico City: Fondo de Cultura Popular, 1950). Translated to English by Lysander Kemp as *The Labyrinth of Solitude* (New York: Grove Press, 1961), p. 87.

15. Roger Bartra, *La Jaula de la Melancolía: Indentidad y Metamórfosis del Mexicano* (Mexico City: Grijalbo, 1987).

16. Emile Durkheim, *The Division of Labor in Society*, translated by G. Simpson (New York: Free Press, 1964, originally published in 1893).

17. James S. Frideres, *Native People in Canada* (Scarborough, Ontario: Prentice Hall Canada, 1983), p. 267.

18. Statistics Canada, *Ethnic Origin,* 1991 Census (Ottawa: Minister of Industry, Science and Technology, 1993), Table 1A.

19. Statistics Canada, *Canada Year Book, 1989* (Ottawa: Minister of Industry, Science and Technology, 1989), pp. 2–28.

20. Paul W. Bennett and Cornelius J. Jaenen, *Emerging Identities: Selected Problems and Interpretations in Canadian History* (Scarborough, Ontario: Prentice Hall Canada, 1986), p. 268.

21. Ibid., p. 275.

22. Jean H. Lagassé, *The People of Indian Ancestry in Manitoba* (Winnipeg: Department of Agriculture and Immigration, 1959). Cited in Nicole St-Onge, "Race, Class and Marginality in a Manitoba Interlake Settlement, 1850–1950." In Jesse Vorst, ed., *Race, Class, Gender: Bonds and Barriers* (Toronto: Between the Lines, 1989).

23. Davis, *Who Is Black?* p. 84.

24. Ibid., p. 21.

25. Joel Williamson, *New People: Miscegenation and Mulattoes in the United States* (New York: Free Press, 1980), p. 7.

26. Ibid., p. 42.

27. See John G. Mencke, *Mulattoes and Race Mixture* (Ann Arbor, MI: UMI Research Press, 1979).

28. One of the most prominent cases of unacknowledged mulattoes emerging out of relations between slave owners and slaves involved Thomas Jefferson, the third president of the United States. Jefferson's household, Monticello, had a number of slaves attached to it. He is widely believed to have sired mulatto children with one of them, Sally Hemings; and

there are blacks who claim descent from him. Historians, though, are divided as to whether it was Jefferson or some other male in his family who was the actual father of Sally Hemings' mulatto children—for accounts, see Fawn M. Brodie, *Thomas Jefferson: An Intimate History* (New York: Norton, 1974); Williamson, *New People*; and Davis, *Who Is Black?*

29. Calculated from U.S. Bureau of the Census, *Negro Population of the United States, 1790–1915* (Washington, DC: U.S. Government Printing Office, 1918).

30. Davis, *Who Is Black?* p. 36.

31. Mencke, *Mulattoes and Race Mixture*, p. 13.

32. Cited in Williamson, *New People*, p. 18.

33. Ibid.

34. Ibid., p. 81.

35. See Mencke, *Mulattoes and Race Mixture*, p. 26.

36. Williamson, *New People*, p. 3.

37. Davis, *Who Is Black?*, pp. 104–105.

38. Ibid., p. 121.

39. Ibid., p. 118. For a unique description of East Coast mestizo communities in the 1950s, see Brewton Berry, *Almost White* (New York: Macmillan, 1963).

40. *New York Times,* November 5, 1992, p. B9.

41. Special tabulations from the 1981 census of Canada (Statistics Canada) reported in U.S. Bureau of the Census, *Migration between the United States and Canada* (Washington, DC: U.S. Government Printing Office, 1990), Table A-23.

42. Mexicans, like Puerto Ricans and other Caribbeans and unlike people in the United States, distinguish blacks and mulattoes. See, for example, María Elena Cortés Jacome, "La Mulata Leonor de Ontiveros: Su Historia Familiar." In *Jornadas de Homenaje a Gonzalo Aguirre Beltrán* (Veracruz: Instituto Veracruzano de Cultura, 1988).

CHAPTER 12. THE NEW NORTH AMERICAN DIVISION OF LABOR

1. Michael Meyer and William L. Sherman, *The Course of Mexican History* (New York: Oxford University Press, 1979).

2. Richard Michel, "An Overview Report on the In-Bond Program: Border Plants and Interior Plants." Talk at the conference "The Maquiladora Industry in Mexico: Current Status and Prospects," sponsored by the American Chamber of Commerce in Mexico, April 26, Club Campestre, Chihuahua. Recording no. 371, 1978. On file at the Institute of Oral History, University of Texas at El Paso.

3. Jorge Carillo, oral report at the conference "Trabajadores y la Frontera Norte," Ciudad Juárez, Chihuahua, May 7, 1982.

4. Monica C. Gambrill, "The New Role of Maquiladoras in the Development of Mexico," paper presented at the 1993 Annual Meeting of the American Sociological Association in Miami, FL.

5. None of the U.S. border's nationality/racial terms are without problems. "Anglo" assumes British descent when many have German, Irish, and other national backgrounds. What gives the term its value, besides its everyday use, is the English language and many of the

British values that molded institutions in the United States. The term "Chicano" arose with the late 1960s and early 1970s social movement of people of Mexican descent in the United States. It was derived from *xicano* of *Mexicano*, the *x* being pronounced as "chi." As originally used, it meant people of Mexican descent born and raised in the United States, as opposed to Mexicanos who were immigrants born and raised in Mexico. The distinction was and is important because the experience of growing up in one or the other culture produces a different sense of national self-identity. In a related sense, the contrasting pulls of Mexico and the United States defined the ambiguities of the Chicano nationality. On the other hand, in the context of the border communities where many families count members on both sides, there is a counteracting pressure toward merger of the separate Chicano and Mexicano national identities. But the term "Chicano" may be becoming rapidly obsolete with the historical decline of the movement with which it was identified. There is evidence that by the 1990s few people of Mexican descent in the United States identified themselves as Chicanos, preferring instead such other terms as Mexicano or Mexican-American. According to the results of a 1990 national survey of 1,500 people of Mexican descent living in the United States that was conducted by Rodolfo de la Garza of the University of Texas in 1990 (reported at a Mexico City conference at the Centro de Investigación y Docencia Económica on February 2, 1991) only 25 out of the 1,500 people interviewed identified themselves most as Chicanos. The greatest plurality (45 percent) identified themselves as Mexicanos, while 30 percent identified themselves as Mexican-Americans. Thus there is now no universally acceptable term for identifying people of Mexican descent who live in the United States, despite the fact that the term "Chicano" continues to be almost universally employed in Mexico.

6. See, for example, Mario T. García, "Racial Dualism in the El Paso Labor Market, 1880–1920," *Aztlán*, no. 6 (Summer 1975), pp. 197–217; Oscar J. Martinez, *Border Boom Town: Ciudad Juárez since 1848* (Austin: University of Texas Press, 1978); and Refugio I. Rochin and Nicole Bellenger, "Labor and Labor Markets." In Ellwyn R. Stoddard et al., *Borderlands Sourcebook* (Norman: University of Oklahoma Press, 1980).

7. Carey Gelernter and Paul Sweeney, "The Influentials: El Paso's Ruling Elite Shapes City's Destiny," series of articles in the *El Paso Times*, December 17–27, 1978.

8. Nancy Rivera, "Paychecks: Climbing the Corporate Ladder Can Mean Scaling Corporate Heights," *El Paso Times*, January 18, 1981, p. 1–G.

9. U.S. Bureau of the Census, *Survey of Minority-Owned Businesses* (Washington, DC: U.S. Government Printing Office, 1977).

10. U.S. Small Business Administration, *The State of Small Business* (Washington, DC: U.S. Government Printing Office, 1989), p. 397.

11. For more detailed information, see James W. Russell, "Class and Nationality Relations in a Texas Border City: The Case of El Paso," *Aztlán*, vol. 16, no. 1 (1987), pp. 217–239.

12. NAFTA was a part of the package of reforms that the Salinas de Gortari administration included under the concept of modernization. It is useful in this context to examine the concept of modernization because it played such a pivotal ideological role in the Salinas administration. As a concept, modernization has at least three interrelated meanings and uses. The first we can call its rhetorical meaning. That is, it is a seemingly noncontroversial term that is used in public speeches to describe the government's motives and project. As such, it is a platitude, like justice, that is universally embraced, at least on the rhetorical level. The second we can call its intellectual meaning. In this sense the concept of modernization arose with Enlightenment thought and was associated with the general belief that so-

cieties could absolutely progress through mastery of science, domination of nature, and perfection of rational forms of social organization (for a good account, see David Harvey, *The Condition of Postmodernity* (Oxford, England: Basil Blackwell, 1989). The third is its sociological meaning, which is closest to what was ideologically behind the Salinista project. In the 1950s the modernization school, based largely on the turn-of-the-century theories of the French sociologist Emile Durkheim, arose within the Western sociology of development. It argued that third world societies were underdeveloped because large parts of their economies were not linked to the dynamic and modern first world economies by the international division of labor. This school advocated, it followed, that third world societies, if they wished to develop, needed to integrate themselves more thoroughly into the first world–led international economy by increasing export oriented production and allowing foreign investment. The relationship between this sociology of development modernization theory and the Salinas de Gortari administration's enthusiasm for NAFTA, which will result in increased North American economic integration through increased Mexican trading and investment relations with the United States and Canada, is obvious. The highly visible Solidaridad program, which promoted public works and other projects for the poorer strata, was the other side of the ideological coin of the Salinista "modernization" project. In the words of the president, "*Nosotros [el gobierno] trabajarémos mas para los que tienen menos*" ("We [the government] will work most for those who have the least.") In other words, at precisely the time that the Salinas administration was pursuing policies that would result in increased concentration of capital ownership and income inequality, it was rhetorically countering public perceptions that inequality was growing by pledging a commitment to the poor. The problem confronting the Salinas administration—how to pursue policies that would result in greater social-class inequality but at the same time not engender class conflict and political instability—was also taken up earlier by Durkheim as an adjunct to what later came to be modernization theory. Writing in the aftermath of the 1871 Paris Commune, a period of class conflict that shook the foundations of French society, Durkheim in *The Division of Labor in Society* concluded that social-class stratification contributed to societal development, but only if the state managed it properly to avoid engendering dysfunctional class conflict. Durkheim advocated that the state develop a unitary national spirit—what he called a sense of "solidarity"—as a partial antidote to class conflict.

13. For information on the public relations campaign, see Charles Lewis and Margaret Ebrahim, "Big $$$ Lobbying in Washington: Can Mexico and Big Business USA Buy NAFTA?" *The Nation*, vol. 256, no. 23 (June 14, 1993). In spring 1992, Guadalupe Jones, Miss Mexico, was crowned Miss Universe. The standing joke in Mexico was to call her Miss Fast Track and speculate that she was really a fictional creation of a public relations firm to make Mexico look good. She speaks fluent English as well as Spanish. She supported the United States' Persian Gulf War, when domestic political considerations obliged the Mexican government to be officially neutral, and went to Los Angeles to welcome U.S. troops home. Her very name symbolized the new relationship, being made up of the quintessential female Mexican first name, Guadalupe, from the Virgin of Guadalupe, and the quintessential United States last name Jones.

14. In 1991, a potential political scandal was averted, which could have undermined the positive image of the Mexican government in the eyes of the United States during the campaign for NAFTA. In September a drug-laden plane landed at a remote seldom-used Army airstrip in Veracruz. Minutes later a Judicial Police plane, in pursuit of the drug traffickers, touched down. Army troops at the field then opened fire and killed seven Judicial

Police agents in what was initially described in the press as a "tragic nighttime confusion." But there was considerable speculation in and out of Mexico that the Army may have been abetting the drug traffickers, all of whom escaped. Among the allegations were that peasants in the area reported that the Army troops had come to the airstrip the day before the drug-plane landed, that they had brought with them refueling tanks, and that the gun battle actually took place during daylight hours. It was further reported that a United States Drug Enforcement Agency plane had been following both of the planes and had videotaped the whole incident from the air. President Salinas de Gortari responded to the potential scandal by having the country's official Human Rights Commission carry out an investigation. The commission found that the killings were the result of a "tragic confusion," but one that army officers should have been able to avoid. It made no mention of collaboration between the Army and drug trafficking. Several officers were sent to jail, and the issue disappeared from the Mexican press. Though the United States press intially reported the incident, it did not follow the story. The potential scandal neither damaged the Mexican government's reputation in the United States nor interfered with the NAFTA negotiations. For more information, see the September and October 1991 issues of *Proceso,* published in Mexico.

15. Public perception of undocumented, mainly Mexican, workers in the United States also shifts according to the business cycle. When the economy is in an expansionary phase, little is heard in the press or from politicians regarding them as a problem. But when the economy falls into recession, politicians and editorialists almost immediately make the undocumented workers scapegoats for the country's economic difficulties, blaming them for stealing jobs.

16. None of this analysis is meant to imply that NAFTA will necessarily initiate the elimination of *all* Mexican small businesses. It implies only that the *tendency* will be for large numbers of small businesses to be outcompeted by large businesses and therefore to disappear from the market. Among the small businesses that will most likely survive will be those that serve nooks and crannies of the market that will be as unprofitable for foreign corporations to serve as they have been for Mexican large businesses, and those that offer specialized products or services of unusual quality, such as gourmet restaurants or highly skilled beauticians, which cannot be easily duplicated by corporations on a large scale. Also to be considered is the fact that there is a cultural preference among large numbers of Mexicans to continue patronizing small businesses and traditional markets that could act as a brake on the tendency for commercial capital to concentrate with free trade.

Bibliography

1. BOOKS AND ARTICLES

AGUIRRE BELTRÁN, GONZALO, *La Población Negra de México*. Mexico City: Secretaria de la Reforma Agraria, Centro de Estudios Históricos del Agrarismo en México reprint, 1981, originally published in 1946.

———, *Cuijla: Esbozo Etnográfico de un Pueblo Negro*. Mexico City: Fondo de Cultura Económica, 1958.

———, *Regiones de Refugio,* 2nd ed. Mexico City: Instituto Nacional Indigenista, 1973, originally published in 1967.

———, "The Integration of the Negro into the National Society of Mexico." In *Race and Class in Latin America*, ed. Magnus Mörner. New York: Columbia University Press, 1970.

ALLEN, JAMES S., *Reconstruction: The Battle for Democracy*. New York: International Publishers, 1937.

ÁLVAREZ DE TESTA, LILIAN, *Mexicanidad y Libro de Texto Gratuito*. Mexico City: Universidad Nacional Autónoma de México, 1992.

ASPE, PEDRO, AND JAVIER BERISTAIN, "Toward a First Estimate of the Evolution of Inequality in Mexico." In *The Political Economy of Income Distribution in Mexico*, ed. Pedro Aspe and Paul E. Sigmund. New York: Holmes & Meier, 1984.

BÁRCENA, ANDREA, "El INEGI en el Cemedin," *La Jornada* (Mexico City), April 30, 1992.

BARTRA, ROGER, "Tributo y Tenencia en la Tierra en la Sociedad Azteca." In *El Modo de Producción Asiático*, ed. Roger Bartra. Mexico City: Ediciones Era, 1969.

———, *Estructura Agraria y Clases Sociales en México*. Mexico City: Ediciones Era, 1974.

———, *La Jaula de la Melancolía: Indentidad y Metamórfosis del Mexicano*. Mexico City: Grijalbo, 1987.

BASAVE BENÍTEZ, AGUSTÍN, *México Mestizo: Análisis del Nacionalismo Mexicano en torno a la Mestizofilia de Andrés Molina Enríquez*. Mexico City: Fondo de Cultura Económica, 1992.

BELL, DANIEL, *The Coming of Post-industrial Society*. New York: Basic Books, 1973.

BELL, SPURGEON, "Productivity, Wages and National Income." In *The Capitalist System,* 2nd ed., edited by Richard Edwards, Michael Reich, and Thomas Weisskoff. Englewood Cliffs, NJ: Prentice Hall, 1977.

BENNETT, PAUL W., AND CORNELIUS J. JAENEN, *Emerging Identities: Selected Problems and Interpretations in Canadian History*. Scarborough, Ontario: Prentice Hall Canada, 1986.

BERRY, BREWTON, *Almost White*. New York: Macmillan, 1963.

BLAIR, JOHN, *Economic Concentration*. New York: Harcourt Brace Jovanovich, 1972.

BLOCH, MARC, "Feudalism, European." In *Encyclopedia of the Social Sciences*. New York: Macmillan, 1933.

———, *Feudal Society*, 2 vols. Chicago: University of Chicago Press, 1961, originally published in 1940.

BOLARIA, B. SINGH, AND PETER S. LI, *Racial Oppression in Canada*, 2nd ed. Toronto: Garamond Press, 1988.

BONACICH, EDNA, AND JOHN MODELL, *The Economic Basis of Ethnic Solidarity: Small Business in the Japanese American Community*. Berkeley: University of California Press, 1980.

BONFIL BATALLA, GUILLERMO, *México Profundo*. Mexico City: Grijalbo, 1990.

BRODIE, FAWN M., *Thomas Jefferson: An Intimate History*. New York: Norton, 1974.

BROWN, GEORGE, AND RON MAGUIRE, "Indian Treaties in Historical Perspective," in *Native People in Canada*, ed. James S. Frideres. Scarborough, Ontario: Prentice Hall Canada, 1983.

BUHMANN, BRIGITTE, LEE RAINWATER, GUENTHER SCHMAUS, AND TIMOTHY M. SMEETING, "Equivalence Scales, Well-being, Inequality, and Poverty: Sensitivity Estimates across Ten Countries Using the Luxembourg Income Study (LIS) Database," *Review of Income and Wealth*, series 34, no. 2 (June 1988), 115–142.

CALLISTE, AGNES, "Canada's Immigration Policy and Domestics from the Caribbean: The Second Domestic Scheme." In *Race, Class, Gender: Bonds and Barriers*, ed. Jesse Vorst. Toronto: Between the Lines, 1989.

CHAWLA, RAJ K., "The Distribution of Wealth in Canada and the United States." *Perspectives on Labour and Income*, vol. 2, no. 1 (Spring 1990).

CLARK, KENNETH B., AND MAMIE P. CLARK, "Racial Identification and Preferences in Negro Children." In *Readings in Social Psychology*, ed. Theodore M. Newcomb and Eugene L. Hartley. New York: Holt, Rinehart and Winston, 1947.

COLEMAN, RICHARD P., AND LEE RAINWATER, WITH KENT A. MCCLELLAND, *Social Standing in America: New Dimensions of Class*. New York: Basic Books, 1978.

CORNELIUS, WAYNE A., "The Politics and Economics of Reforming the *Ejido* Sector in Mexico," *LASA Forum*, vol. 23, no. 3 (Fall 1992), pp. 3–10.

CORTÉS JACOME, MARÍA ELENA, "La Mulata Leonor de Ontiveros: Su Historia Familiar." In *Jornadas de Homenaje a Gonzalo Aguirre Beltrán*. Veracruz: Instituto Veracruzano de Cultura, 1988.

CROSBY, ALFRED M., *The Columbian Exchange: Biological and Cultural Consequences of 1492*. Westport, CT: Greenwood Press, 1972.

CUMBERLAND, CHARLES C., "The Sonora Chinese and the Mexican Revolution," *Hispanic American Historical Review*, vol. 40 (May 1960), pp. 191–223.

DAVIDSON, DAVID M., "El Control de los Esclavos Negros y su Resistencia en el México Colonial, 1519–1650." In *Sociedades Cimarronas*, ed. Richard Price. Mexico City: Siglo Veintiuno Editores, 1981.

DAVIS, F. JAMES, *Who Is Black? One Nation's Definition*. University Park: Pennsylvania State University Press, 1991.

DOMHOFF, G. WILLIAM, *Who Rules America?* Englewood Cliffs, NJ: Prentice Hall, 1967.

———, *Who Rules America Now?* Englewood Cliffs, NJ: Prentice Hall, 1983.

DU BOIS, W. E. B., *Black Reconstruction in America*. New York: Russell & Russell, 1962, originally published in 1935.

DURKHEIM, EMILE, *The Division of Labor in Society*. New York: Free Press, 1964, originally published in 1893.

ENGELS, FRIEDRICH, Letter to Hermann Schuter, March 30, 1892, in Karl Marx and Friedrich Engels, *Letters to Americans*. New York: International Publishers, 1963.

————, Letter to Friedrich Sorge, September 12, 1888, in Karl Marx and Friedrich Engels, *Letters to Americans*. New York: International Publishers, 1963.

FELDSTEIN, STANLEY, AND LAWRENCE COSTELLO, eds., *The Ordeal of Assimilation: A Documentary History of the White Working Class*. Garden City, NY: Anchor Press, 1974.

FONER, ERIC, *Reconstruction: America's Unfinished Revolution, 1863–1877*. New York: Harper & Row, 1988.

FRANCIS, R. DOUGLAS, RICHARD JONES, AND DONALD B. SMITH, *Origins: Canadian History to Confederation*. Toronto: Holt, Rinehart and Winston of Canada, 1988.

FRANCO, JOSÉ L., "Rebeliones Cimmaronas y Esclavas en los Territorios Españoles," in *Sociedades Cimarronas*, ed. Richard Price. Mexico City: Siglo Veintiuno Editores, 1981.

FRIDERES, JAMES S., ed., *Native People in Canada*. Scarborough, Ontario: Prentice Hall Canada, 1983.

————, "Institutional Structures and Economic Deprivation: Native People in Canada." In *Racial Oppression in Canada*, ed. B. Singh Bolaria and Peter S. Li. Toronto: Garamond Press, 1988.

GAMBRILL, MONICA C. "The New Role of Maquiladoras in the Development of Mexico," paper presented at the 1993 American Sociological Association Annual Meeting in Miami, FL.

GARCÍA, MARIO T., "Racial Dualism in the El Paso Labor Market, 1880–1920," *Aztlán*, no. 6 (Summer 1975), pp. 197–217.

GARCÍA HERNÁNDEZ, ARTURO, "Racismo Latente y Peligroso en México," *La Jornada* (Mexico City), May 6, 1992, p. 39.

GARDNER, ROBERT W., BRYANT ROBEY, AND PETER C. SMITH, "Asian Americans: Growth, Change, and Diversity," *Population Bulletin*, vol. 40, no. 4 (October 1985).

GELERNTER, CAREY, AND PAUL SWEENEY, "The Influentials: El Paso's Ruling Elite Shapes City's Destiny," *El Paso Times*, December 17–27, 1978.

GILBERT, DENNIS, AND JOSEPH A. KAHL, *The American Class Structure,* 3rd ed. Chicago: Dorsey Press, 1987.

GÓMEZ IZQUIERDO, JOSÉ JORGE, *El Movimiento Anti-Chino en México, 1871–1934*. Mexico City: Universidad Nacional Autónoma de México, Facultad de Ciencias Políticas y Sociales undegraduate thesis, 1988.

GONZÁLEZ NAVARRO, MOISES, "*Mestizaje* in Mexico during the National Period." In *Race and Class in Latin America*, ed. Magnus Mörner. New York: Columbia University Press, 1970.

GUNDERSON, MORLEY, *Economics of Poverty and Income Distribution*. Toronto: Butterworths, 1983.

HALE, KENNETH, AND DAVID HARRIS, "Historical Linguistics and Archaelogy." In *Handbook of North American Indians*, vol. 9. Washington, DC: Smithsonian, 1979.

HALL, THOMAS D., *Social Change in the Southwest, 1350–1880*. Lawrence: University Press of Kansas, 1989.

HARVEY, DAVID, *The Condition of Postmodernity*. Oxford, England: Basil Blackwell, 1989.

HAYWOOD, HARRY, *Negro Liberation*. New York: International Publishers, 1948.

HERRERA CASASUS, MARÍA LUISA, *Presencia y Esclavitud del Negro en la Huasteca*. Mexico City: Porrua, 1989.

HOWE, CAROLYN, *Political Ideology and Class Formation: A Study of the Middle Class*. Westport, CT: Praeger, 1992.

HU-DEHART, EVELYN, "Immigrants to a Developing Society: The Chinese in Northern Mexico, 1875–1932," *Journal of Arizona History* (Autumn 1980), pp. 275–313.

HUERTA PRECIADO, MÁRIA TERESA, *Rebeliones Indígenas en el Noreste de México en la Epoca Colonial*. Mexico City: Instituto Nacional de Antropología e Historia, 1966.

JOHANSEN, BRUCE, AND ROBERTO MAESTAS, *Wasi'Chu: The Continuing Indian Wars*. New York: Monthly Review Press, 1979.

KLEIN, HERBERT S., *African Slavery in Latin American and the Caribbean*. New York: Oxford University Press, 1986.

LAUTARD, HUGH, AND NEIL GUPPY, "The Vertical Mosaic Revisited: Occupational Differentials among Canadian Ethnic Groups." In *Race and Ethnic Relations in Canada*, ed. Peter S. Li. Toronto: Oxford University Press, 1990.

LEMBCKE, JERRY, "Class Capacities and Labor Internationalism: The Case of the U.S. and Canada," *Critical Sociology*, Fall 1989, pp. 71–94.

LEWIS, CHARLES, AND MARGARET EBRAHIM, "Big $$$ Lobbying in Washington: Can Mexico and Big Business USA Buy NAFTA?" *The Nation*, vol. 256, no. 23 (June 14, 1993), pp. 826–839.

LI, PETER S., ed., *Race and Ethnic Relations in Canada*. Toronto: Oxford University Press, 1990.

LIPSET, SEYMOUR MARTIN, *Continental Divide: The Values and Institutions of the United States and Canada*. London: Routledge, 1990.

MANZER, RONALD, *Public Policies and Political Development in Canada*. Toronto: University of Toronto Press, 1985.

MARTINEZ, OSCAR J., *Border Boom Town: Ciudad Juárez since 1848*. Austin: University of Texas Press, 1978.

MCDONALD, RYAN J., "Canada's Off-Reserve Aboriginal Population," *Canadian Social Trends*, no. 23 (Winter 1991), pp. 2–7.

MCWILLIAMS, CAREY, *Factories in the Field*. Santa Barbara, CA: Peregrine Smith, 1971, originally published in 1935.

———, *Prejudice—Japanese Americans: Symbol of Racial Intolerance*. Boston: Little, Brown, 1944.

———, *North from Mexico*. Westport, CT: Greenwood Press edition, 1968, originally published in 1949.

———, *Brothers under the Skin*. Boston: Little, Brown, 1964.

MELENDY, H. BRETT, *Asians in America: Filipinos, Koreans, and East Indians*. Boston: Twayne, 1977.

MELLAFE, ROLANDO, *Negro Slavery in Latin America*. Berkeley: University of California Press, 1975.

MENCKE, JOHN G., *Mulattoes and Race Mixture*. Ann Arbor, MI: UMI Research Press, 1979.

MEYER, MICHAEL, AND WILLIAM L. SHERMAN, *The Course of Mexican History*. New York: Oxford University Press, 1979.

MILES, ROBERT, *Racism*. London: Routledge, 1989.

MILIBAND, RALPH, *The State in Capitalist Society*. New York: Basic Books, 1969.

MILLER, ROBERT RYAL, *Shamrock and Sword: The Saint Patrick's Battalion in the U.S.-Mexican War*. Norman: University of Oklahoma Press, 1989.

MOEDANO NAVARRO, GABRIEL, "El Estudio de las Tradiciones Orales y Musicales de los Afromestizos de México," *Antropología e Historia*, ecoca III, no. 31 (Julio-Septiembre).

MONTEMAYOR, CARLOS, *Guerra en el Paraiso*. Mexico City: Editorial Diana, 1991.

MÖRNER, MAGNUS, *El Mestizaje en la Historia de Ibero-América*. Mexico City: Instituto Panamericano de Geografía e Historia, 1961.

———, *Race Mixture in the History of Latin America*. Boston: Little, Brown, 1967.

———, ed., *Race and Class in Latin America*. New York: Columbia University Press, 1970.

NAVARRO, MOISES GONZÁLEZ, *La Colonización en México, 1877–1910*. Mexico City: Talleres de Impresión de Estampillas y Valores, 1960.

NEE, VICTOR G., AND BRET DE BARY, *Longtime Californ': A Documentary Study of an American Chinatown*. New York: Pantheon, 1973.

O'CONNOR, JAMES, *The Fiscal Crisis of the State*. New York: St. Martin's Press, 1973.
OFFICER, JAMES E., *Hispanic Arizona, 1536–1856*. Tucson: University of Arizona Press, 1987.
OROPEZA BERUMEN, TOMÁS, "Entrevista con Salvador Castañeda," *La Jornada Semanal* (Mexico City), No. 139, February 9, 1992.
ORTIZ PINQUETI, JOSÉ AGUSTIN, "El Festin de los Criollos," *La Jornada* (Mexico City), March 29, 1992.
OTA MISHIMA, MARÍA ELENA, *Siete Migraciones Japonesas en México, 1890–1978*. Mexico City: El Colegio de México, 1982.
OTHON DE MENDIZABAL, MIGUEL, ET AL., eds., *Ensayos sobre las Clases Sociales en México*. Mexico City: Editorial Nuestro Tiempo, 1968.
PALERM VICH, ANGEL, "Factores Históricos de la Clase Media en México." In *Ensayos sobre las Clases Sociales en México*, ed. Miguel Othon de Mendizabal et al. Mexico City: Editorial Nuestro Tiempo, 1968.
PALMER, HOWARD, "Reluctant Hosts: Anglo-Canadian Views of Multiculturalism in the Twentieth Century." In *Readings in Canadian History: Post-Confederation*, 2nd ed., ed. R. Douglas Francis and Donald B. Smith. Toronto: Holt, Rinehart and Winston of Canada, 1986.
PAZ, OCTAVIO, *El Laberinto de la Soledad*. Mexico City: Fondo de Cultura Popular, 1950.
PETTIGREW, THOMAS F., *Racial Discrimination in the United States*. New York: Harper & Row, 1975.
PIVEN, FRANCES FOX, AND RICHARD A. CLOWARD, *Regulating the Poor*. New York: Vintage, 1971.
PORTER, JOHN, *The Vertical Mosaic*. Toronto: University of Toronto Press, 1965.
POULTANZAS, NICOS, "The Problem of the Capitalist State," *New Left Review*, November-December 1969.
POZAS, RICARDO, AND ISABEL H. DE POZAS, *Los Indios en las Clases Sociales de México*. Mexico City: Siglo Veintiuno Editores, 1971.
PROGRAMA NACIONAL DE SOLIDARIDAD (PRONASOL), *El Combate a La Pobreza*. Mexico City: El Nacional, 1990.
RAMOS, SAMUEL, *El Perfil del Hombre y la Cultura en México*. Mexico City: Colección Austral, 1990, originally published in 1934.
REINA, LETICIA, *Las Rebeliones Campesinas en México, 1819–1906*. Mexico City: Siglo Veintiuno Editores, 1980.
RIDING, ALAN, *Distant Neighbors: A Portrait of the Mexicans*. New York: Vintage, 1989, originally published, 1984.
RIVERA, NANCY, "Paychecks: Climbing the Corporate Ladder Can Mean Scaling Corporate Heights," *El Paso Times*, January 18, 1981, p. 1–G.
ROCHIN, REFUGIO I., AND NICOLE BELLENGER, "Labor and Labor Markets." In *Borderlands Sourcebook*, ed. Ellwyn R. Stoddard et al. Norman: University of Oklahoma Press, 1980.
RUIZ, RAMON EDUARDO, *The People of Sonora and Yankee Capitalists*. Tucson: University of Arizona Press, 1988.
RUSSELL, JAMES W., "Class and Nationality Relations in a Texas Border City: the Case of El Paso," *Aztlán*, vol. 16, no. 1 (1987), pp. 217–239.
———, *Modes of Production in World History*. London: Routledge, 1989.
———, *Introduction to Macrosociology*. Englewood Cliffs, NJ: Prentice Hall, 1992.
SCHAEFER, RICHARD T., *Racial and Ethnic Groups*, 4th ed. Glenview, IL: Scott, Foresman, 1990.
SCHWARTZ, ROSALIE, "Across the Rio to Freedom: U.S. Negroes in Mexico," *Southwestern Studies* monograph 44. El Paso: Texas Western Press.
ST-ONGE, NICOLE, "Race, Class and Marginality in a Manitoba Interlake Settlement,

1850–1950." In *Race, Class, Gender: Bonds and Barriers*, ed. Jesse Vorst. Toronto: Between the Lines, 1989.

STERN, CLAUDIO, "Notas para la Delimitación de las Clases Medias en México." In *Las Clases Medias en la Coyuntura Actual*, ed. Soledad Loaeza and Claudio Stern. Mexico City: El Colegio de México, 1990.

SULLIVAN, EDWARD J., "Un Fenómeno Visual de América," *Artes de México*, no. 8 (verano 1990), pp. 60–72.

SWEEZY, PAUL M., "Power Elite or Ruling Class?" (pamphlet). New York: Monthly Review Press, 1956.

SZYMANSKI, ALBERT, *Class Structure: A Critical Perspective*. New York: Praeger, 1983.

THOMAS, W. I., AND FLORIAN ZNANIECKI, *The Polish Peasant in Europe and America*, 4 vols. New York: Dover, 1958, originally published 1918–20.

TORRES, BLANCA, *Historia de la Revolución Mexicana, 1940–1952*. Mexico City: El Colegio de México, 1979.

TULLOCH, HEADLEY, *Black Canadians*. Toronto: N.C. Press, 1975.

UJIMOTO, K. VICTOR, "Racism, Discrimination and Internment: Japanese in Canada." In *Racial Oppression in Canada*, ed. B. Singh Bolaria and Peter S. Li. Toronto: Garamond Press, 1988.

VALDÉS, LUZ MARÍA, *El Perfil Demográfico de los Indios Mexicanos,* 2nd ed. Mexico City: Siglo Veintiuno Editores, 1989.

VALDÉS, LUZ MARÍA, AND MARÍA TERESA MENÉNDEZ, *Dinámica de la Población de Habla Indígena (1900–1980)*. Mexico City: Instituto Nacional de Antropología e Historia, 1987.

VASCONCELOS, JOSÉ, *La Raza Cósmica*. Mexico City: Espasa-Calpe Mexicana, 1992, originally published in 1925.

WALKER, JAMES W., *A History of Blacks in Canada*. Ottawa: Minister of State and Multiculturalism, 1980.

WARNER, W. LLOYD, AND PAUL S. LUNT, *The Social Life of a Modern Community*. New Haven, CT: Yale University Press, 1941.

WEBER, DAVID J., *Myth and the History of the Hispanic Southwest*. Albuquerque: University of New Mexico Press, 1988.

WEBER, MAX, *The Protestant Ethic and the Spirit of Capitalism*. New York: Scribner's, 1948, originally published in 1905.

———, "Structures of Power." In *From Max Weber: Essays in Sociology*, trans. and ed. Hans H. Gerth and C. Wright Mills. New York: Oxford University Press, 1958, originally published in 1921.

———, *Economy and Society*, 2 vols. New York: Bedminster Press, 1968, originally published in 1922.

———, *General Economic History*, trans. Frank H. Knight. New York: Collier Books, 1961, originally published in 1923.

WEISSKOFF, RICHARD, AND ADOLFO FIGUEROA, "Traversing the Social Pyramid: A Comparative Review of Income Distribution in Latin America," *Latin American Research Review*, vol. 11, no. 2 (1976).

WILKIE, JAMES W., AND PAUL D. WILKINS, "Quantifying the Class Structure of Mexico, 1895–1970." In *Statistical Abstract of Latin America*, vol. 21, ed. James W. Wilkie and Stephen Haber. Los Angeles: University of California Press, 1981.

WILLIAMSON, JOEL, *New People: Miscegenation and Mulattoes in the United States*. New York: Free Press, 1980.

WILSON, WILLIAM JULIUS, *The Declining Significance of Race: Blacks and Changing American Institutions*. Chicago: University of Chicago Press, 1980.

WINKS, ROBIN W., *The Blacks in Canada*. New Haven, CT: Yale University Press, 1971.

WORLD BANK, *World Development Report*. New York: Oxford University Press, 1990.

WRIGHT, ERIK OLIN, CYNTHIA COSTELLO, DAVID HACHEN, AND JOEY SPRAGUE, "The American Class Structure," *American Sociological Review*, vol. 47 (1982), pp. 709–726.

2. GOVERNMENT PUBLICATIONS

CONSEJO NACIONAL DE POBLACIÓN (CONAPO), *Población y Desarrollo en México y el Mundo*, vol. 4, Anexo Estadístico. Mexico City: CONAPO, 1988.

INSTITUTO NACIONAL DE ESTADÍSTICA, GEOGRAFÍA E INFORMÁTICA (INEGI), *VI Censos Agrícola-Granjero y Ejidal, 1981*. Aguascalientes: INEGI, 1988.

———, *Encuesta Nacional de Ingresos y Gastos de los Hogares, 1984*. Aguascalientes: INEGI, 1989.

———, *Estadística de la Industria Maquiladora de Exportación, 1978–1988*. Aguascalientes: INEGI, 1989.

———, *Resultados Oportunos*. Aguascalientes: INEGI, 1990.

———, *XI Censo General de Población y Vivienda, 1990*. Aguascalientes: INEGI, 1992.

———, *Encuesta Nacional de Ingresos de los Hogares, 1989*. Aguascalientes: INEGI, 1992.

———, *Estadística de la Industria Maquiladora de Exportación, 1991*. Aguascalientes: INEGI, 1992.

REVENUE CANADA, *Taxation Statistics*. Ottawa: Minister of Supply and Services Canada, 1992.

STATISTICS CANADA, *Canada Year Book, 1989*. Ottawa: Minister of Industry, Science and Technology, 1989.

———, *A Portrait of Children in Canada*. Ottawa: Minister of Industry, Science and Technology, 1990.

———, *Income after Tax, Distributions by Size in Canada, 1989*. Ottawa: Minister of Industry, Science and Technology, 1991.

———, *Income Distributions by Size in Canada, 1990*. Ottawa: Minister of Industry, Science and Technology, 1991.

———, *Industry and Class of Worker*, 1991 Census. Ottawa: Minister of Industry, Science and Technology, 1991.

———, *Employment Income by Occupation*, 1991 Census. Ottawa: Minister of Industry, Science and Technology, 1993.

———, *Ethnic Origin*, 1991 Census. (Ottawa: Minister of Industry, Science and Technology, 1993.

U.S. BUREAU OF THE CENSUS, *Negro Population of the United States, 1790–1915*. Washington, DC: U.S. Government Printing Office, 1918.

———, *Census of Population, 1970: Characteristics of the Population*, Vol. 1, Part 45, Section 2. Washington, DC: U.S. Government Printing Office, 1972.

———, *Historical Statistics of the United States*. Washington, DC: U.S. Government Printing Office, 1976.

———, *Survey of Minority-Owned Businesses*. Washington, DC: U.S. Government Printing Office, 1977.

———, *Census of Population, 1980: Characteristics of the Population*, Vol. 1, Chapter D, Part 45. Washington, DC: U.S. Government Printing Office, 1982.

———, *Statistical Abstract of the United States*. Washington, DC: U.S. Government Printing Office, 1989.

———, *Migration between the United States and Canada*. Washington, DC: U.S. Government Printing Office, 1990.

———, *Statistical Abstract of the United States*. Washington, DC: U.S. Government Printing Office, 1990.

————, *The Hispanic Population in the United States*. Washington, DC: U.S. Government Printing Office, 1991.

————, *Measuring the Effect of Benefits and Taxes on Income and Poverty, 1990* (Current Population Reports, Series P-60). Washington, DC: U.S. Government Printing Office, 1991.

————, *1990 Census of Population and Housing: Summary Social, Economic, and Housing Characteristics*. Washington, DC: U.S. Government Printing Office, 1992.

————, *Census of Population and Housing, 1990*, Summary Tape Files 1C (CD-ROM). Washington, DC: U.S. Government Printing Office, 1992.

————, *Poverty in the United States, 1991*. Washington, DC: U.S. Government Printing Office, 1992.

————, *Money Income of Households, Families, and Persons in the United States, 1991*. Current Population Reports, Series P-60, No. 180. Washington, DC: U.S. Government Printing Office, 1992.

U.S. DEPARTMENT OF LABOR, *Handbook of Labor Statistics*. Washington, DC: U.S. Government Printing Office, 1989.

————, *Employment and Earnings*, vol. 38, no. 3 (March). Washington, DC: U.S. Government Printing Office, 1991.

————, *Employment and Earnings*, vol. 38, no. 12 (December). Washington, DC: U.S. Government Printing Office, 1991.

U.S. INTERNAL REVENUE SERVICE, STATISTICS OF INCOME DIVISION, *Individual Income Tax Returns, 1987*. Washington, DC: U.S. Government Printing Office, 1990.

U.S. SMALL BUSINESS ADMINISTRATION, *The State of Small Business*. Washington, DC: U.S. Government Printing Office, 1989.

Name Index

Subject Index

Great Britain, 6, 99, 108, 131, 175
Great Lakes, 27, 174
Guadalajara, 86, 117, 162, 223
Guatemala and Guatemalans, 4, 20, 116
Guaymas, 123, 159
Guerrero, 35, 86, 122, 126, 148

Haiti, 89, 140, 183
Halifax, 40
Hawaii, 160, 163, 164, 166, 229
Herding, 123
Heritage Foundation, 82
Hermosilla, 123
Hidalgo, 25, 122, 123, 126, 132
Hispanic, 8, 9, 181, 214, 224, 225, 227
Holland, 23, 29
Horticultural societies, 17, 27
Horticulturalists, 17, 122
Hunting and Gathering, 17, 18, 21, 25, 27,
   37, 49, 53, 122, 133, 136
Huron, 27

Immigration 40, 92, 99, 108, 109, 112, 115,
   123, 124, 151, 152, 155, 156, 157–160,
   163–166, 171, 188, 220, 222, 227, 228,
   230
Immigration Act of 1923 (Canada), 159
Immigration Act of 1924 (U.S.), 164
Immigration Act of 1967 (Canada), 151
Immigration and Naturalization Service
   (U.S.), 188
Income, 4, 11, 33, 38, 57–59, 62, 63, 66–68,
   70, 71, 77–81, 85, 87, 88, 115, 117,
   129, 130, 136, 146, 147, 158, 187, 197,
   208, 215, 217, 218–220, 222, 233
Indentured servitude, 40, 41, 153, 155, 169,
   176
India, 3, 8, 228
Indians (Asian), 152, 166, 167
Indians (North American), 3, 8, 10–20,
   23–39, 41,42, 49–51, 53–55, 62, 63,
   75,90–99, 101–105, 111–113, 115, 116,
   118, 119, 121–137, 147–150, 152, 166,
   167, 169–176, 181–184, 190, 212, 216,
   219, 220, 224, 225, 228, 229, 230 (*see
   also* Native Americans, Amerindians)
Indian Removal Act (U.S.), 132
Individualism, 6, 45, 135
Industrialization, 5, 17, 40, 44, 48, 49,
   52–54, 56, 62–65, 108, 113, 179, 186,
   188–191, 192, 200, 206, 209, 216, 217
Industrial Workers of the World, 188
Inequality, 1, 11, 13, 15, 16, 58, 80, 81, 92,

94, 95, 97–99, 113, 138, 168, 208,
   218–220, 233
Infant mortality rate, 5, 136, 137, 211
Informal economy, 216
Infrastructure, 21, 45, 52, 155
Institutionalized racism, 94
Integrationalists, 134
Internment camps, 161, 162
Inuit, 17 (*see also* Eskimos)
Irish-Americans, 8, 12, 100–102, 108–110,
   112, 185, 221, 222, 231
Iroquois, 20, 27
Iroquois Confederation, 20
Italian-Americans, 12, 13, 100–102, 109,
   110, 115, 162, 222

Jamaica, 89, 151, 182
Jamestown colony, 26, 27
Japan, 101, 160, 162, 166, 190, 200, 204
Japanese-North Americans, 9, 100, 134,
   152, 158, 160–163, 166, 167, 221, 228,
   229
Jewish-North Americans, 110, 116, 117,
   161, 222, 223
Judicial police (Mexico), 233

Kansas, 52, 143, 212, 224
King Phillip's War, 26
Korea, 164, 166, 190
Korean War, 229
Korean-North Americans, 164, 228
Ku Klux Klan, 99, 114, 141, 142, 176

Labor Force, 5, 27, 31, 33, 37, 40, 44–46,
   48, 57, 59–74, 77, 80, 87, 99, 113, 121,
   126, 128–130, 136, 141, 151, 155, 160,
   163, 164, 179, 183, 187, 197, 207,
   215–217, 222
Land Concentration, 47, 57, 207
Landlords, 18, 23, 33, 35, 38, 55
Language, 16, 17, 37, 42, 100–102, 106,
   109, 110, 114, 115, 125, 126, 136, 150,
   223
Latin America, 7, 34, 88, 177, 178, 190,
   195, 213, 216, 218, 219, 221, 226, 229
Latino, 9, 94, 101, 111, 181, 183, 184
Ley Lerdo (Mexico), 56
Liberalism, 5, 81, 85, 95, 124, 146, 200,
   205
Liberal Party (Canada), 85
Liga Comunista 23 de Septiembre, 86, 192
Los Angeles, 60, 133, 144, 145, 187, 218,
   233